NICKELODEON™

SpongeBob SquarePants™

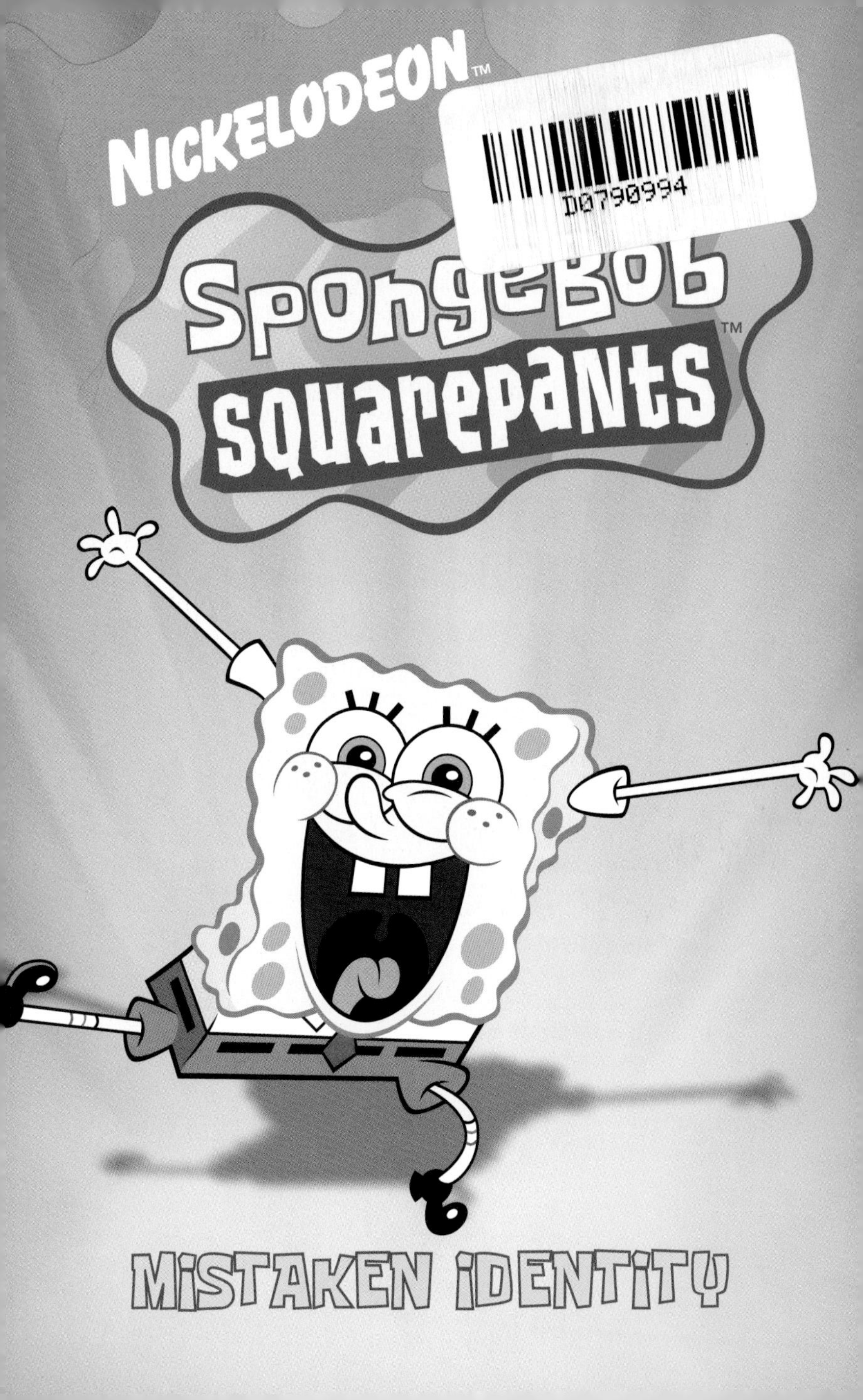

MISTAKEN IDENTITY

Contributing Editors - Marion Brown and Jeffrey Reeves
Cover Designer - Tomás Montalvo-Lagos
Graphic Designer, Letterer - Tomás Montalvo-Lagos

Digital Imaging Manager - Chris Buford
Production Managers - Elisabeth Brizzi
Senior Designer - Christian Lownds
Senior Editor - Julie Taylor
Managing Editor - Vy Nguyen
Editor in Chief - Rob Tokar
VP of Production - Ron Klamert
Publisher - Mike Kiley
President & C.O.O. - John Parker
C.E.O. & Chief Creative Officer - Stuart Levy

E-mail: info@TOKYOPOP.com
Come visit us online at www.TOKYOPOP.com

A **TOKYOPOP** Cine-Manga®
TOKYOPOP Inc.
5900 Wilshire Blvd., Suite 2000
Los Angeles, CA 90036

SpongeBob SquarePants: Mistaken Identity

ISBN: 978-1-4278-0778-6

First TOKYOPOP® printing: June 2007

10 9 8 7 6 5 4 3 2 1

Printed in the USA

NICKELODEON™

SpongeBob™ squarepants

Created by *Stephen Hillenburg*

MISTAKEN IDENTITY

TOKYOPOP®
HAMBURG · LOS ANGELES · LONDON · TOKYO

NICKELODEON™

SpongeBob SquarePants™

SPONGEBOB SQUAREPANTS: An optimistic and friendly sea sponge who lives in a pineapple with his snail, Gary, and works as a fry cook at The Krusty Krab. He loves his job and is always looking on the bright side of everything.

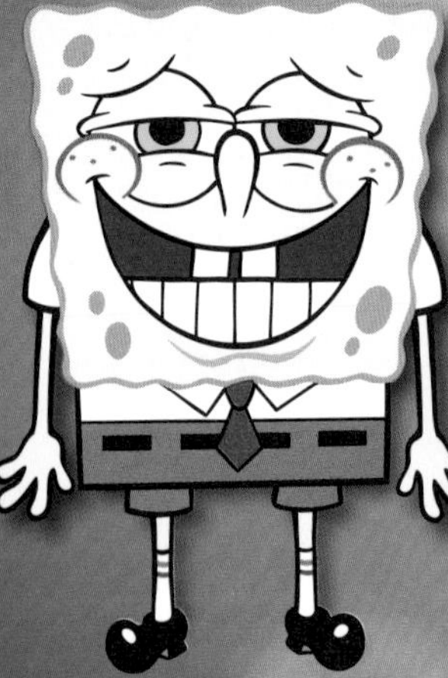

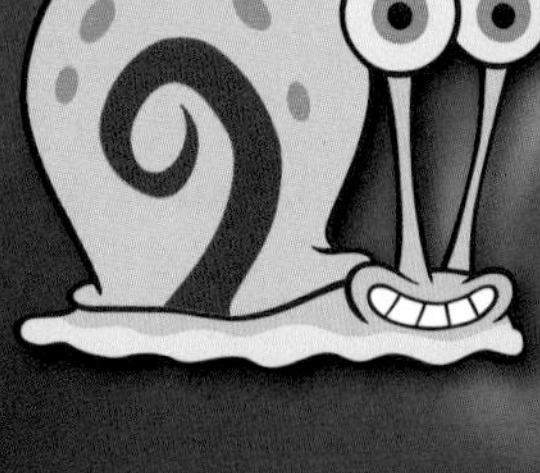

GARY: SpongeBob's pet snail. Meows like a cat.

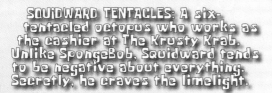

SQUIDWARD TENTACLES: A six-tentacled octopus who works as the cashier at The Krusty Krab. Unlike SpongeBob, Squidward tends to be negative about everything. Secretly, he craves the limelight.

PATRICK STAR: A starfish who is SpongeBob's best friend and neighbor.

MR. KRABS: A crab who owns and runs The Krusty Krab. Mr. Krabs loves money and will do anything to avoid losing it.

NICKELODEON™

SpongeBob™ SquarePants

MISTAKEN IDENTITY

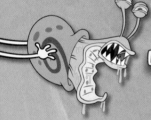

NICKELODEON

SpongeBob squarepants

Once Bitten

By Steve Fonti, Chris Mitchell and Mr. Lawrence

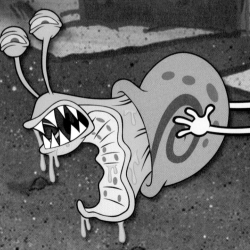

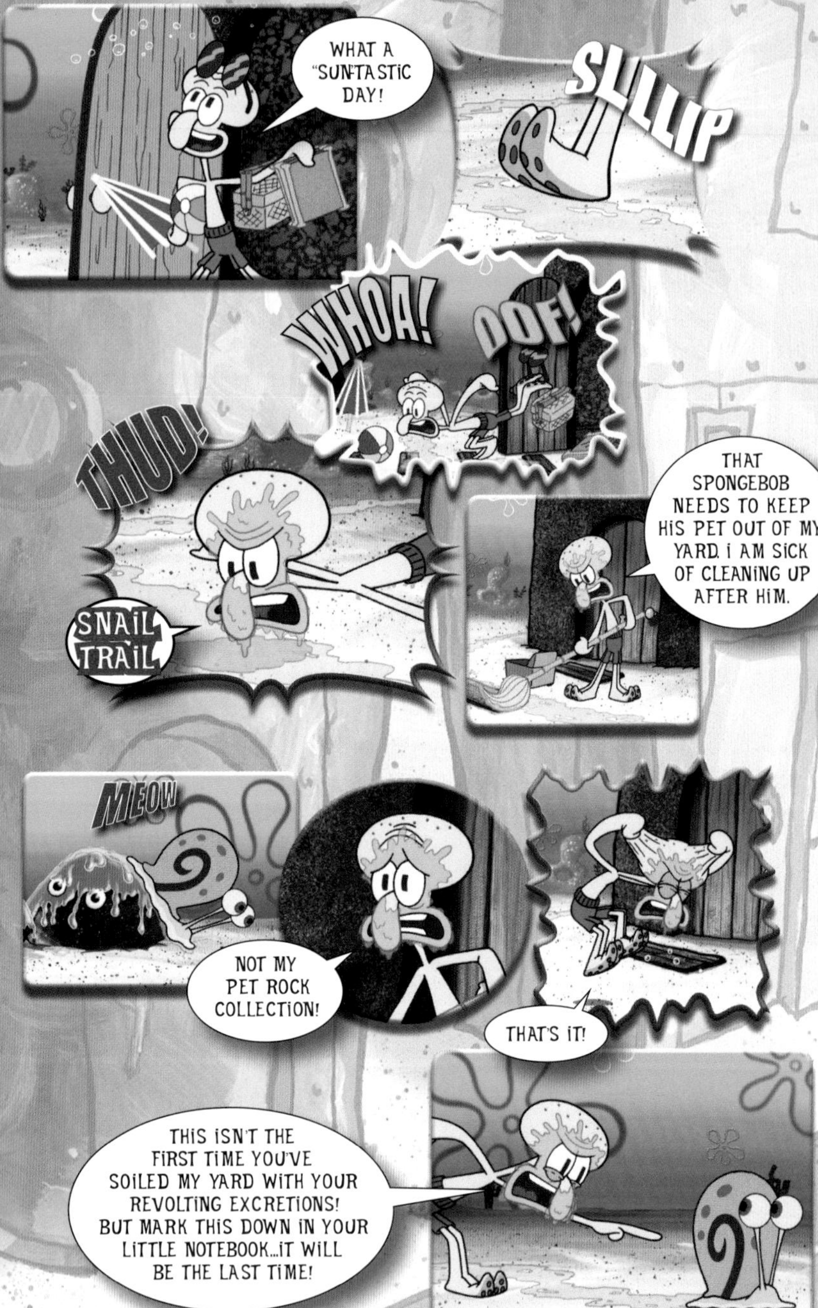
WHAT A "SUN-TASTIC DAY!
SLLLIP
WHOA!
OOF!
THUD!
SNAIL TRAIL
THAT SPONGEBOB NEEDS TO KEEP HIS PET OUT OF MY YARD. I AM SICK OF CLEANING UP AFTER HIM.
MEOW
NOT MY PET ROCK COLLECTION!
THAT'S IT!
THIS ISN'T THE FIRST TIME YOU'VE SOILED MY YARD WITH YOUR REVOLTING EXCRETIONS! BUT MARK THIS DOWN IN YOUR LITTLE NOTEBOOK...IT WILL BE THE LAST TIME!

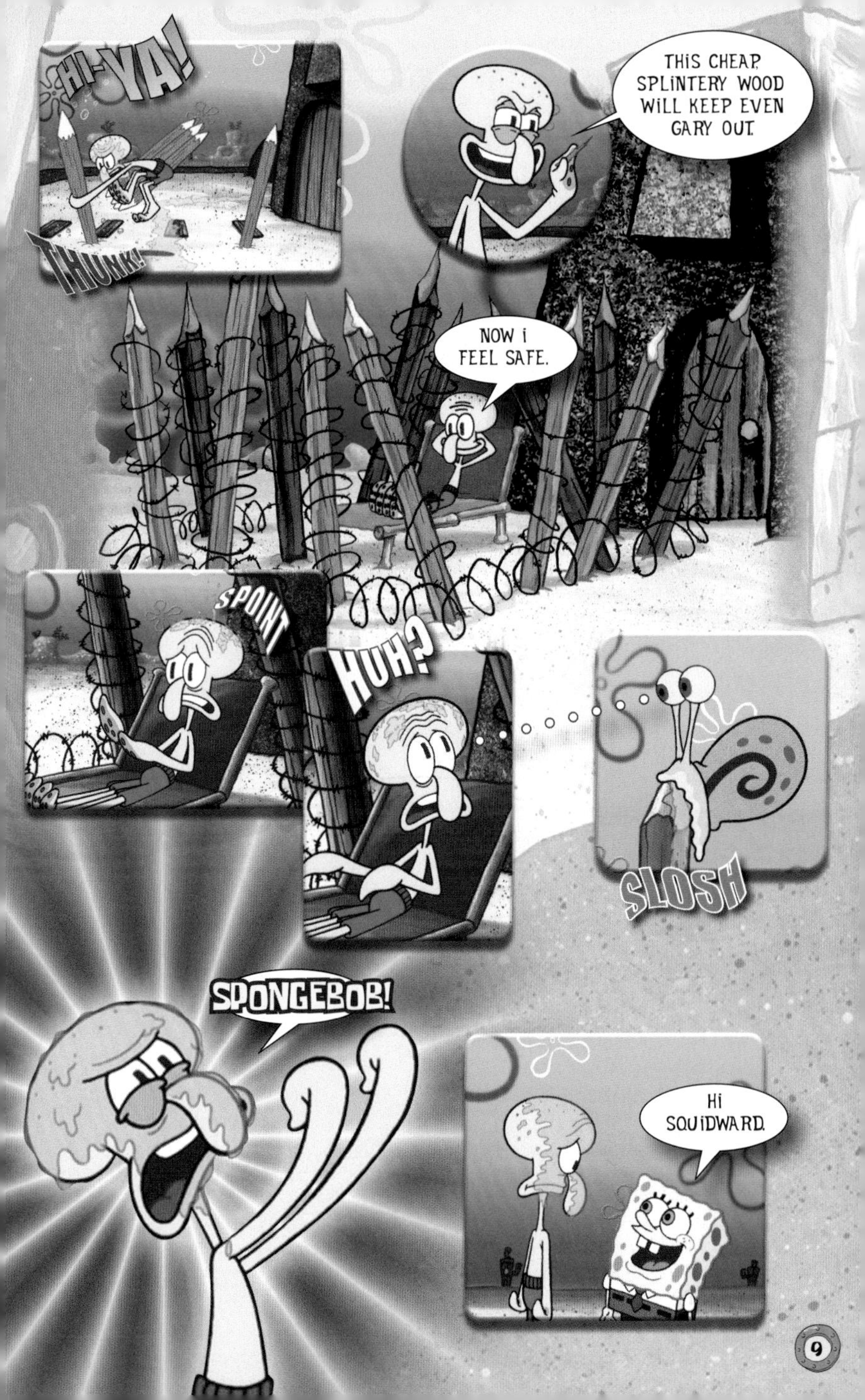
HI-YA!
THUNK!
THIS CHEAP, SPLINTERY WOOD WILL KEEP EVEN GARY OUT.
NOW I FEEL SAFE.
SPOINT
HUH?
SLOSH
SPONGEBOB!
HI SQUIDWARD.

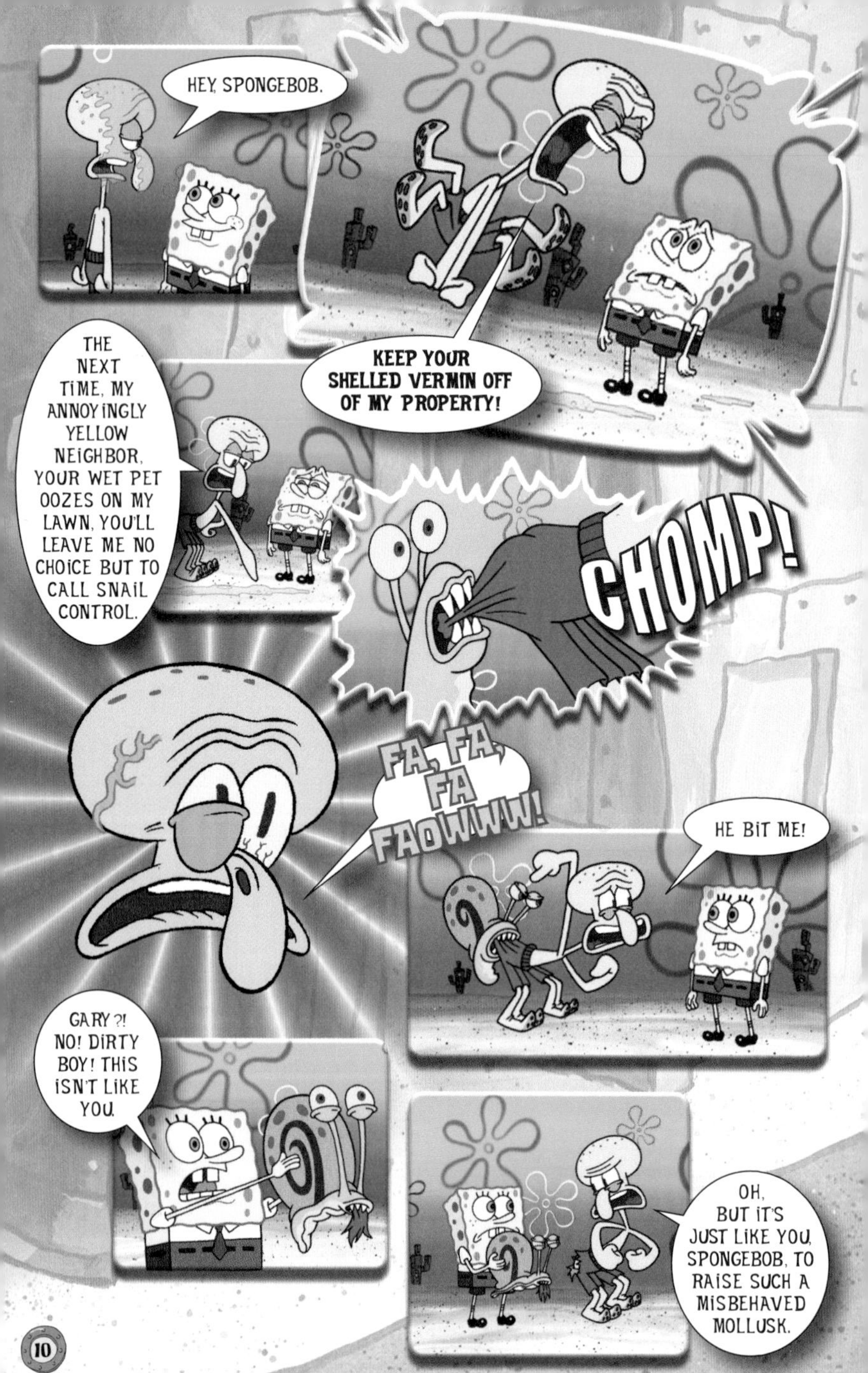
HEY, SPONGEBOB.
KEEP YOUR SHELLED VERMIN OFF OF MY PROPERTY!
THE NEXT TIME, MY ANNOYINGLY YELLOW NEIGHBOR, YOUR WET PET OOZES ON MY LAWN, YOU'LL LEAVE ME NO CHOICE BUT TO CALL SNAIL CONTROL.
CHOMP!
FA, FA, FA FAOWWWW!
HE BIT ME!
GARY?! NO! DIRTY BOY! THIS ISN'T LIKE YOU.
OH, BUT IT'S JUST LIKE YOU, SPONGEBOB, TO RAISE SUCH A MISBEHAVED MOLLUSK.

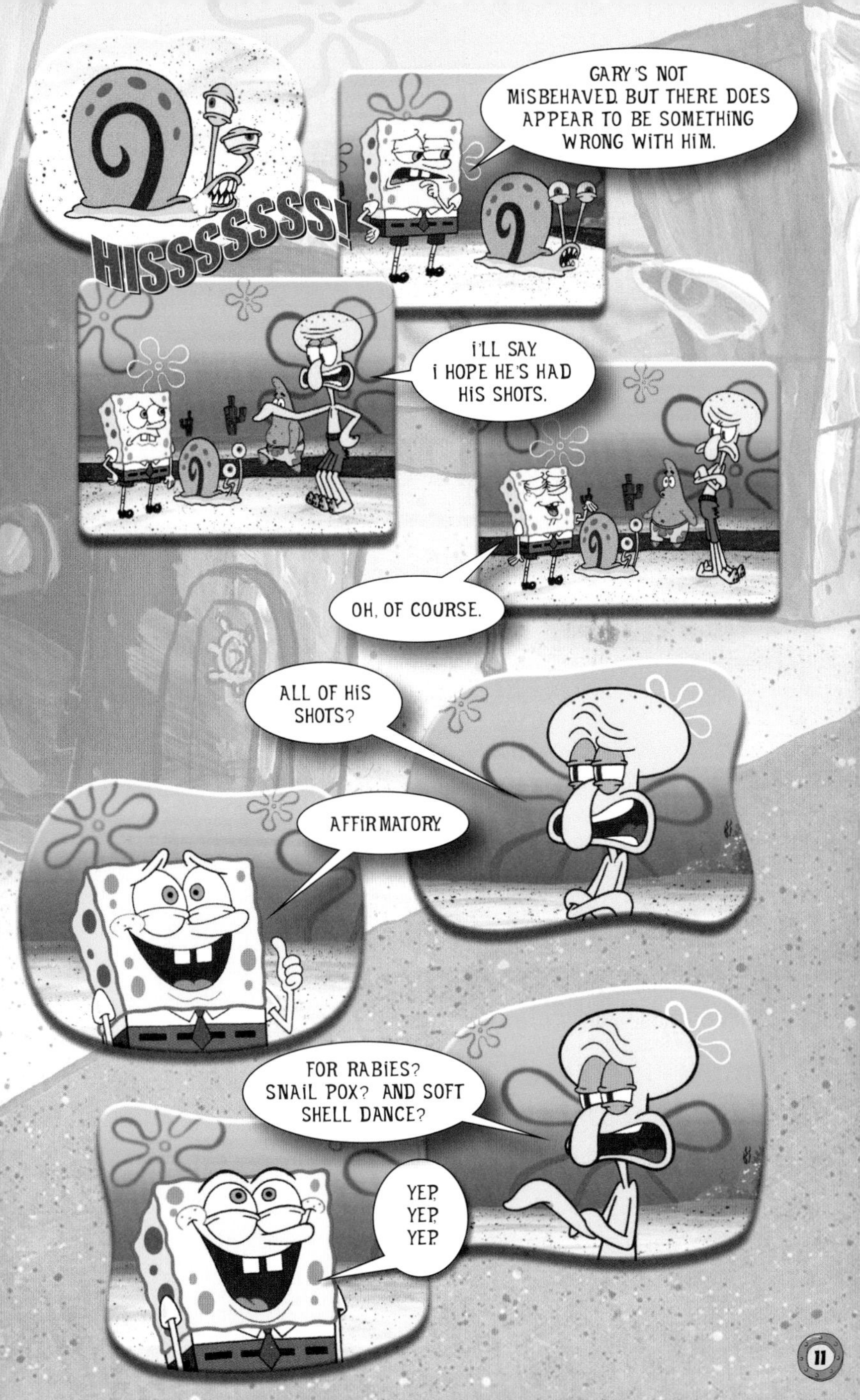
HISSSSSSS!
GARY'S NOT MISBEHAVED. BUT THERE DOES APPEAR TO BE SOMETHING WRONG WITH HIM.
I'LL SAY. I HOPE HE'S HAD HIS SHOTS.
OH, OF COURSE.
ALL OF HIS SHOTS?
AFFIRMATORY.
FOR RABIES? SNAIL POX? AND SOFT SHELL DANCE?
YEP, YEP, YEP.

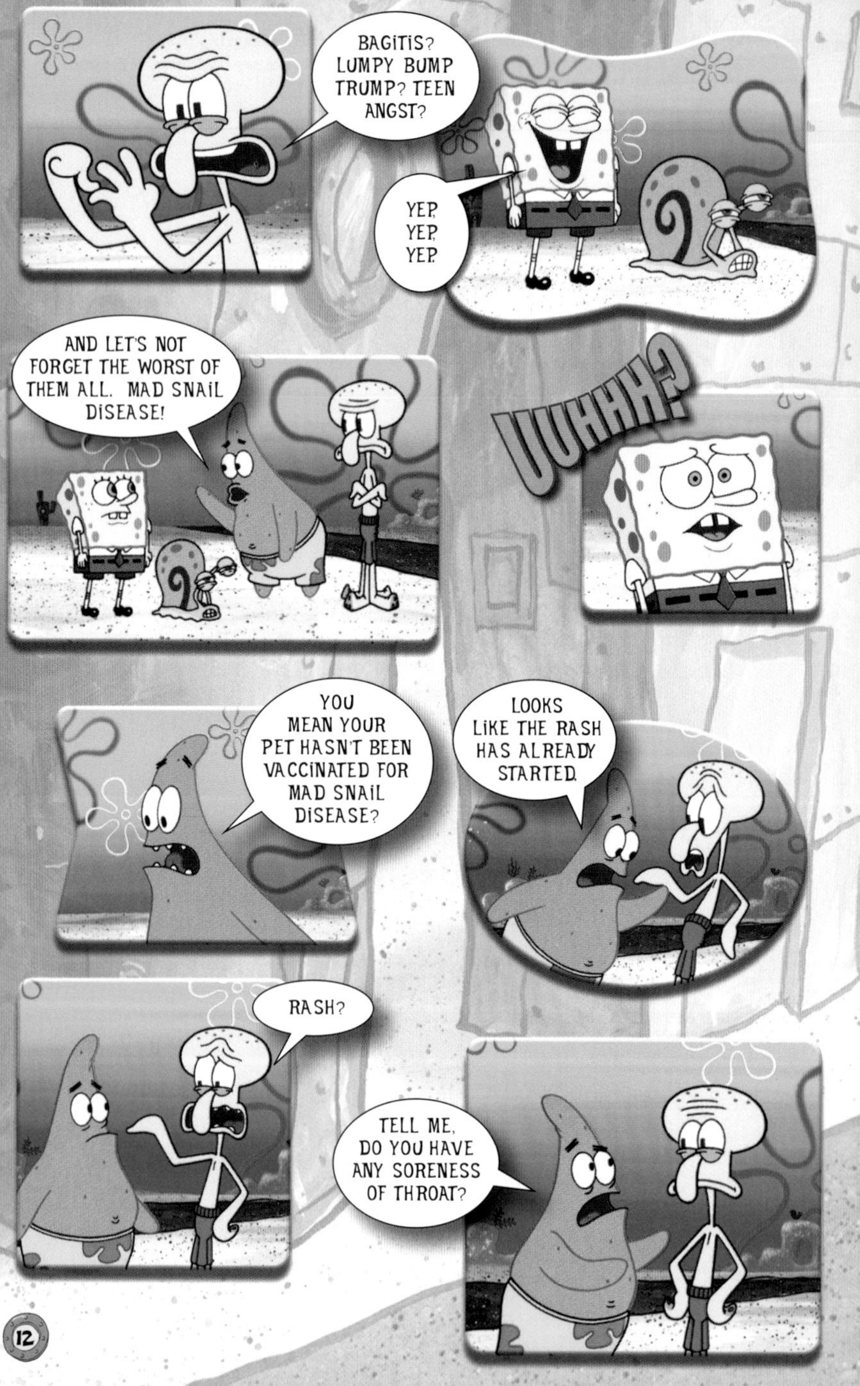

BAGITIS? LUMPY BUMP TRUMP? TEEN ANGST?
YEP, YEP, YEP.
AND LET'S NOT FORGET THE WORST OF THEM ALL. MAD SNAIL DISEASE!
UUHHHH?
YOU MEAN YOUR PET HASN'T BEEN VACCINATED FOR MAD SNAIL DISEASE?
LOOKS LIKE THE RASH HAS ALREADY STARTED.
RASH?
TELL ME, DO YOU HAVE ANY SORENESS OF THROAT?

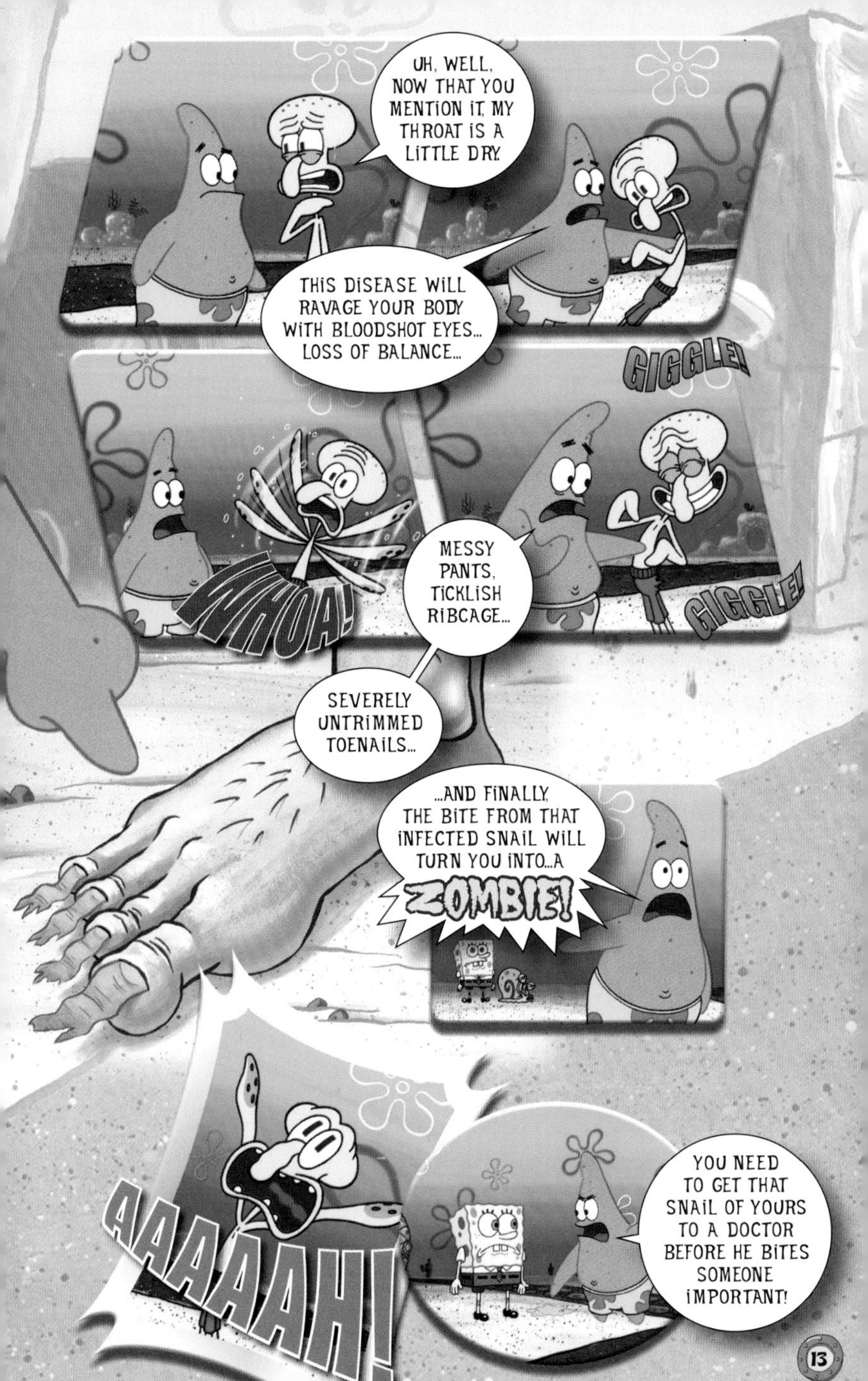
UH, WELL, NOW THAT YOU MENTION IT, MY THROAT IS A LITTLE DRY.
THIS DISEASE WILL RAVAGE YOUR BODY WITH BLOODSHOT EYES... LOSS OF BALANCE...
WHOA!
GIGGLE!
MESSY PANTS, TICKLISH RIBCAGE...
GIGGLE!
SEVERELY UNTRIMMED TOENAILS...
...AND FINALLY, THE BITE FROM THAT INFECTED SNAIL WILL TURN YOU INTO...A
ZOMBIE!
AAAAAH!
YOU NEED TO GET THAT SNAIL OF YOURS TO A DOCTOR BEFORE HE BITES SOMEONE IMPORTANT!

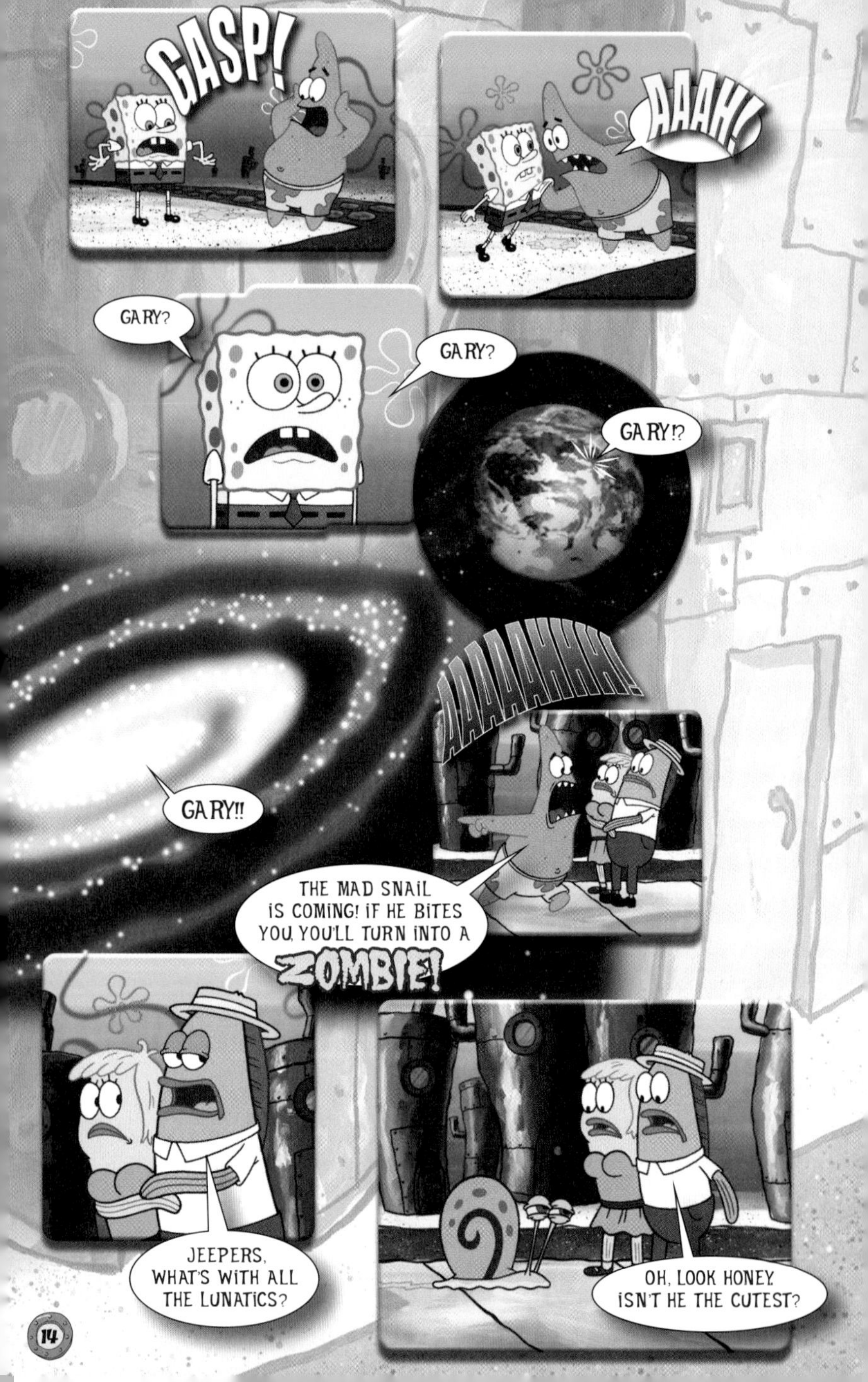
GASP!
AAAH!
GARY?
GARY?
GARY!?
GARY!!
AAAAAHHHH!
THE MAD SNAIL IS COMING! IF HE BITES YOU, YOU'LL TURN INTO A ZOMBIE!
JEEPERS, WHAT'S WITH ALL THE LUNATICS?
OH, LOOK HONEY. ISN'T HE THE CUTEST?

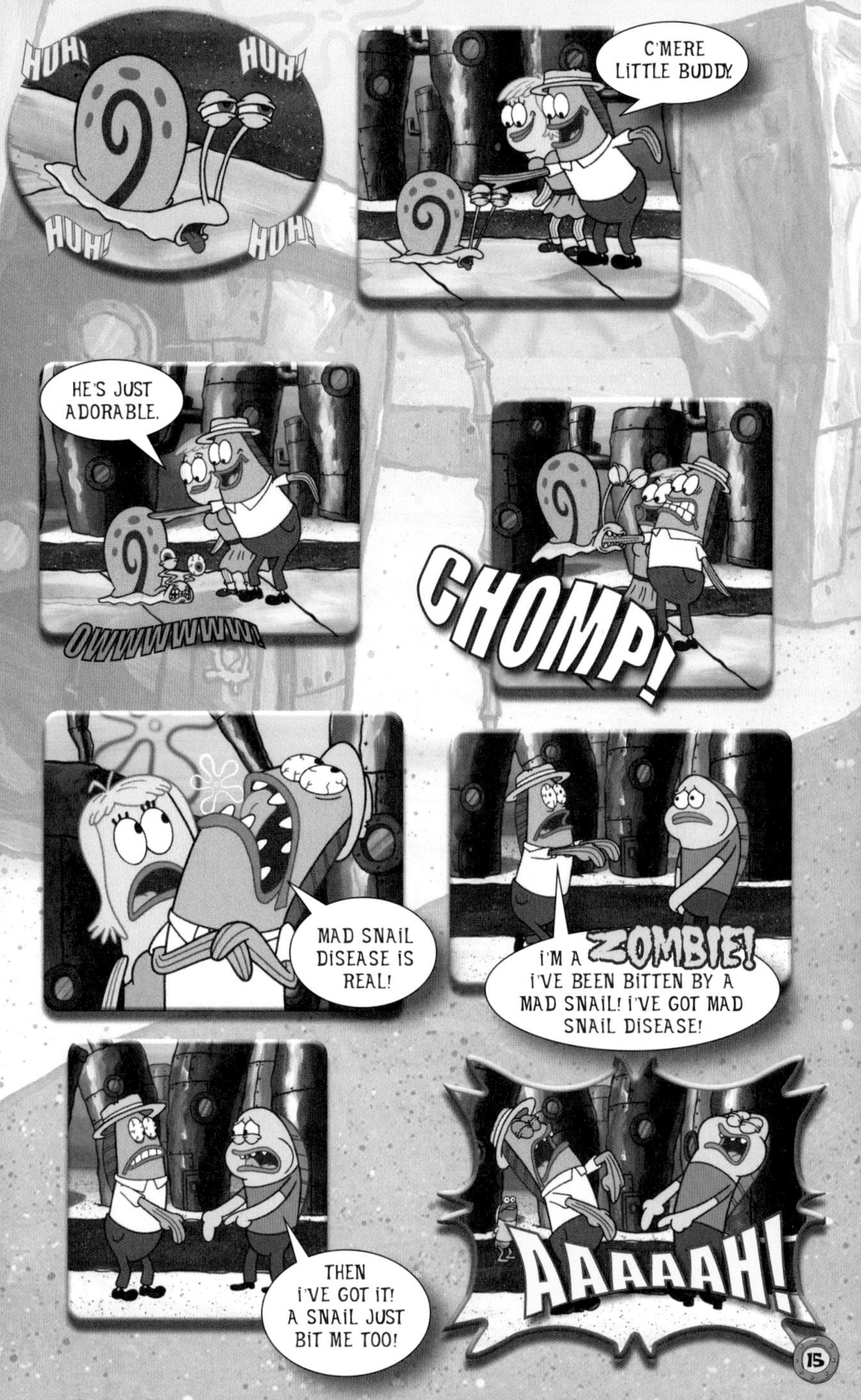
HUH!
HUH!
HUH!
HUH!
C'MERE LITTLE BUDDY.
HE'S JUST ADORABLE.
OWWWWWWW!
CHOMP!
MAD SNAIL DISEASE IS REAL!
I'M A ZOMBIE! I'VE BEEN BITTEN BY A MAD SNAIL! I'VE GOT MAD SNAIL DISEASE!
THEN I'VE GOT IT! A SNAIL JUST BIT ME TOO!
AAAAAH!

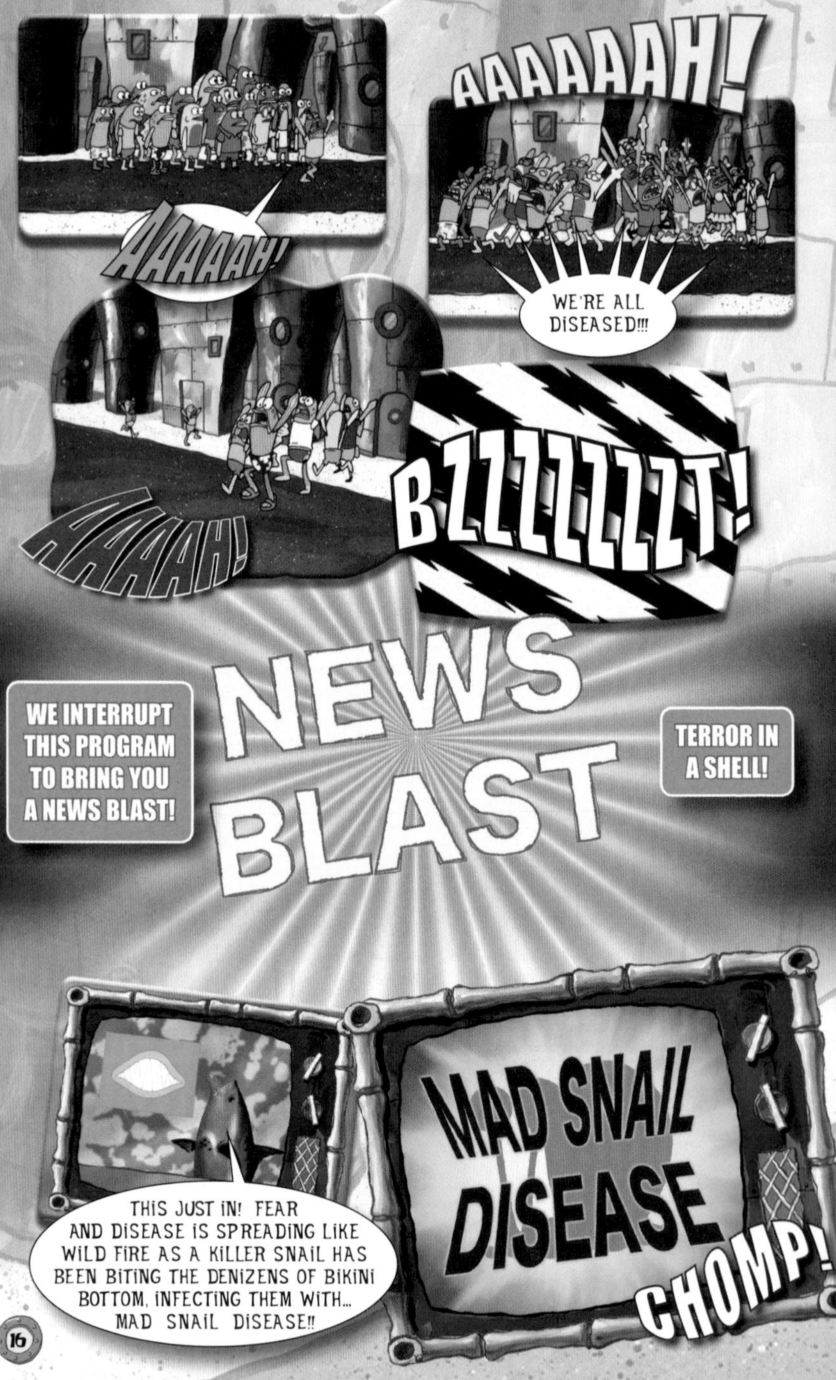

AAAAAH!
AAAAAAH!
WE'RE ALL DISEASED!!!
AAAAAH!
BZZZZZZZZT!
WE INTERRUPT THIS PROGRAM TO BRING YOU A NEWS BLAST!
NEWS BLAST
TERROR IN A SHELL!
THIS JUST IN! FEAR AND DISEASE IS SPREADING LIKE WILD FIRE AS A KILLER SNAIL HAS BEEN BITING THE DENIZENS OF BIKINI BOTTOM, INFECTING THEM WITH... MAD SNAIL DISEASE!!
MAD SNAIL DISEASE
CHOMP!

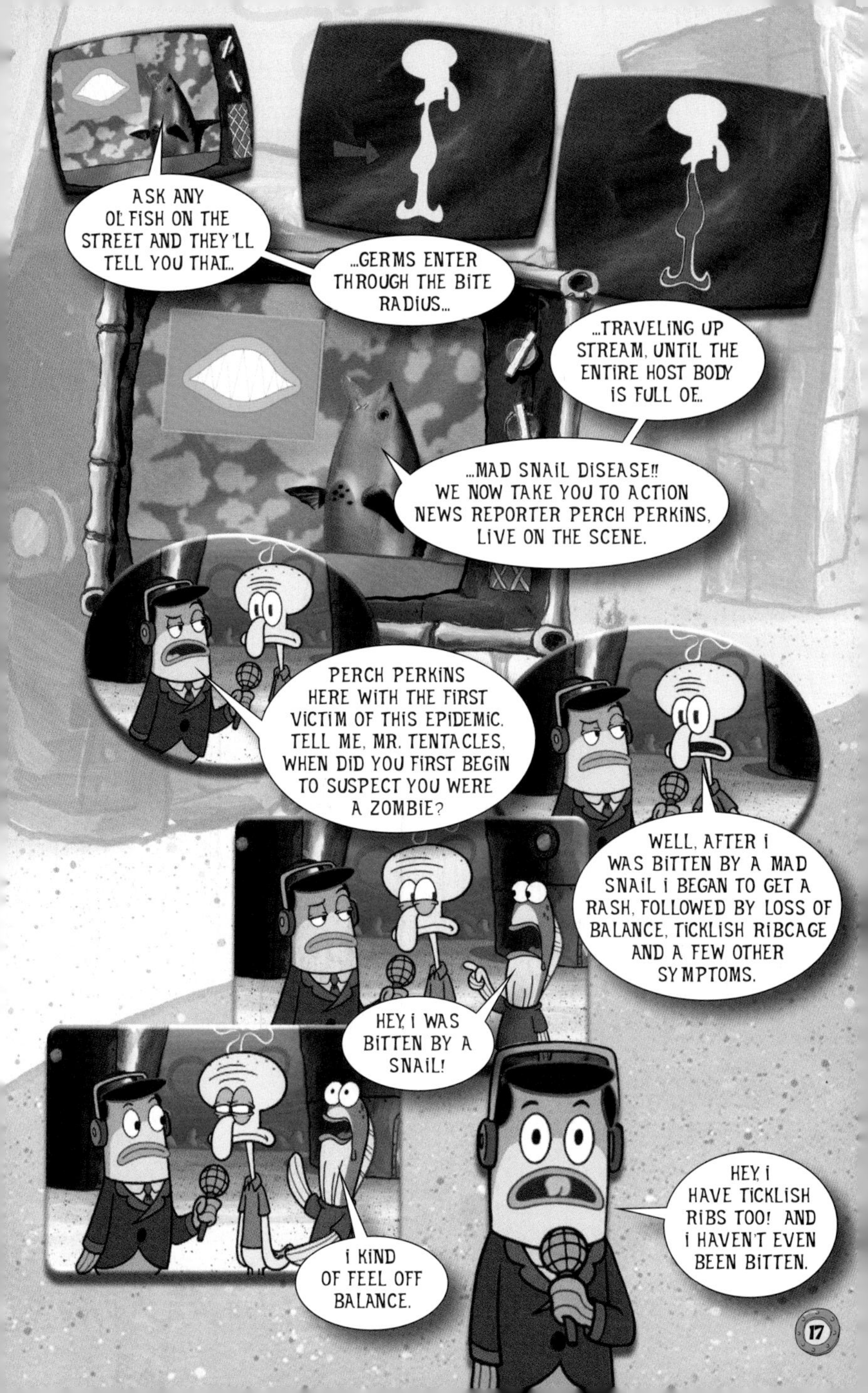
ASK ANY OL' FISH ON THE STREET AND THEY'LL TELL YOU THAT...
...GERMS ENTER THROUGH THE BITE RADIUS...
...TRAVELING UP STREAM, UNTIL THE ENTIRE HOST BODY IS FULL OF...
...MAD SNAIL DISEASE!! WE NOW TAKE YOU TO ACTION NEWS REPORTER PERCH PERKINS, LIVE ON THE SCENE.
PERCH PERKINS HERE WITH THE FIRST VICTIM OF THIS EPIDEMIC. TELL ME, MR. TENTACLES, WHEN DID YOU FIRST BEGIN TO SUSPECT YOU WERE A ZOMBIE?
WELL, AFTER I WAS BITTEN BY A MAD SNAIL I BEGAN TO GET A RASH, FOLLOWED BY LOSS OF BALANCE, TICKLISH RIBCAGE AND A FEW OTHER SYMPTOMS.
HEY, I WAS BITTEN BY A SNAIL!
I KIND OF FEEL OFF BALANCE.
HEY, I HAVE TICKLISH RIBS TOO! AND I HAVEN'T EVEN BEEN BITTEN.

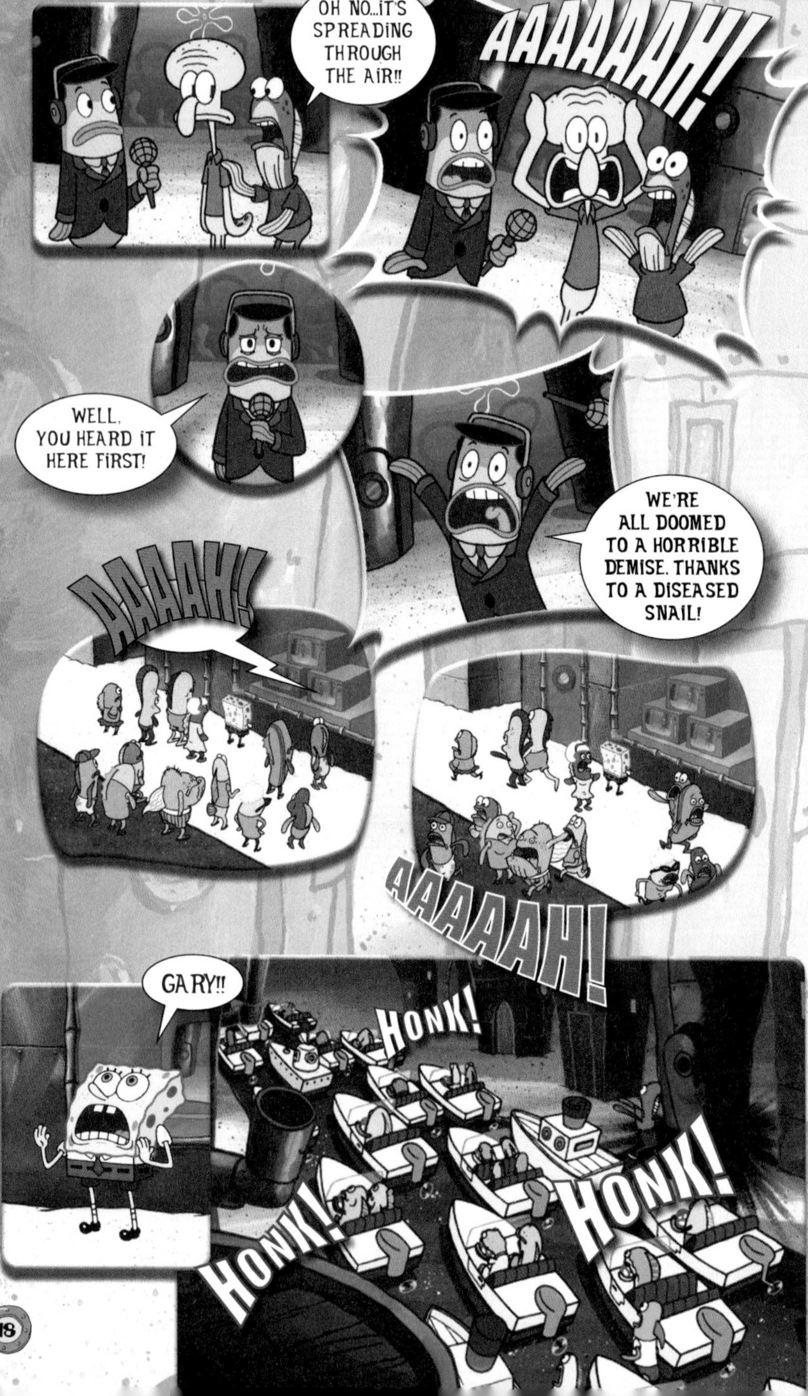
OH NO...IT'S SPREADING THROUGH THE AIR!!
AAAAAAH!
WELL, YOU HEARD IT HERE FIRST!
WE'RE ALL DOOMED TO A HORRIBLE DEMISE. THANKS TO A DISEASED SNAIL!
AAAAH!
AAAAAH!
GARY!!
HONK!
HONK!
HONK!

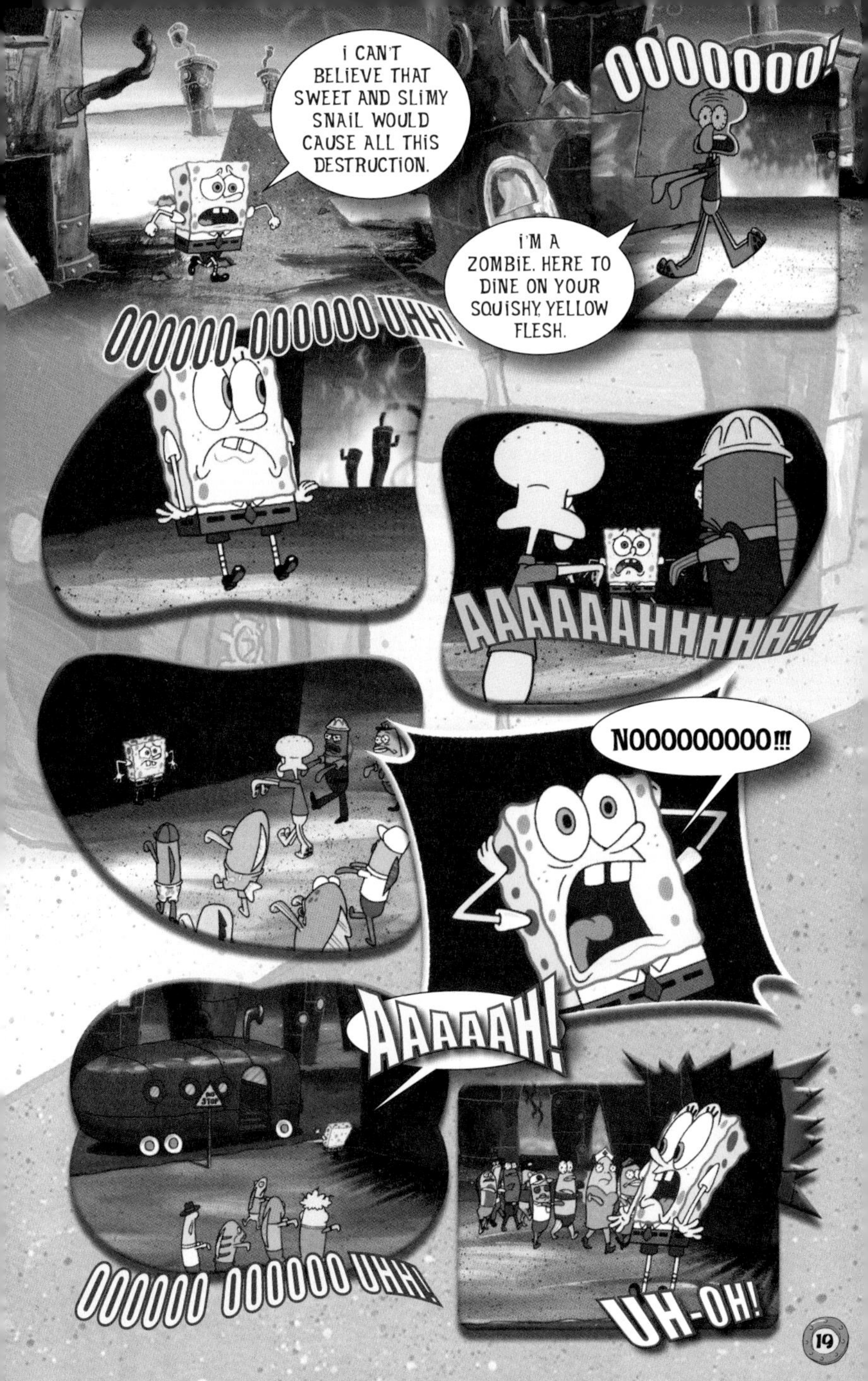
I CAN'T BELIEVE THAT SWEET AND SLIMY SNAIL WOULD CAUSE ALL THIS DESTRUCTION.
OOOOOOO!
I'M A ZOMBIE. HERE TO DINE ON YOUR SQUISHY, YELLOW FLESH.
OOOOOO OOOOOO UHH!
AAAAAAHHHHHH!!
NOOOOOOOOO!!!
AAAAAH!
OOOOOO OOOOOO UHH!
UH-OH!

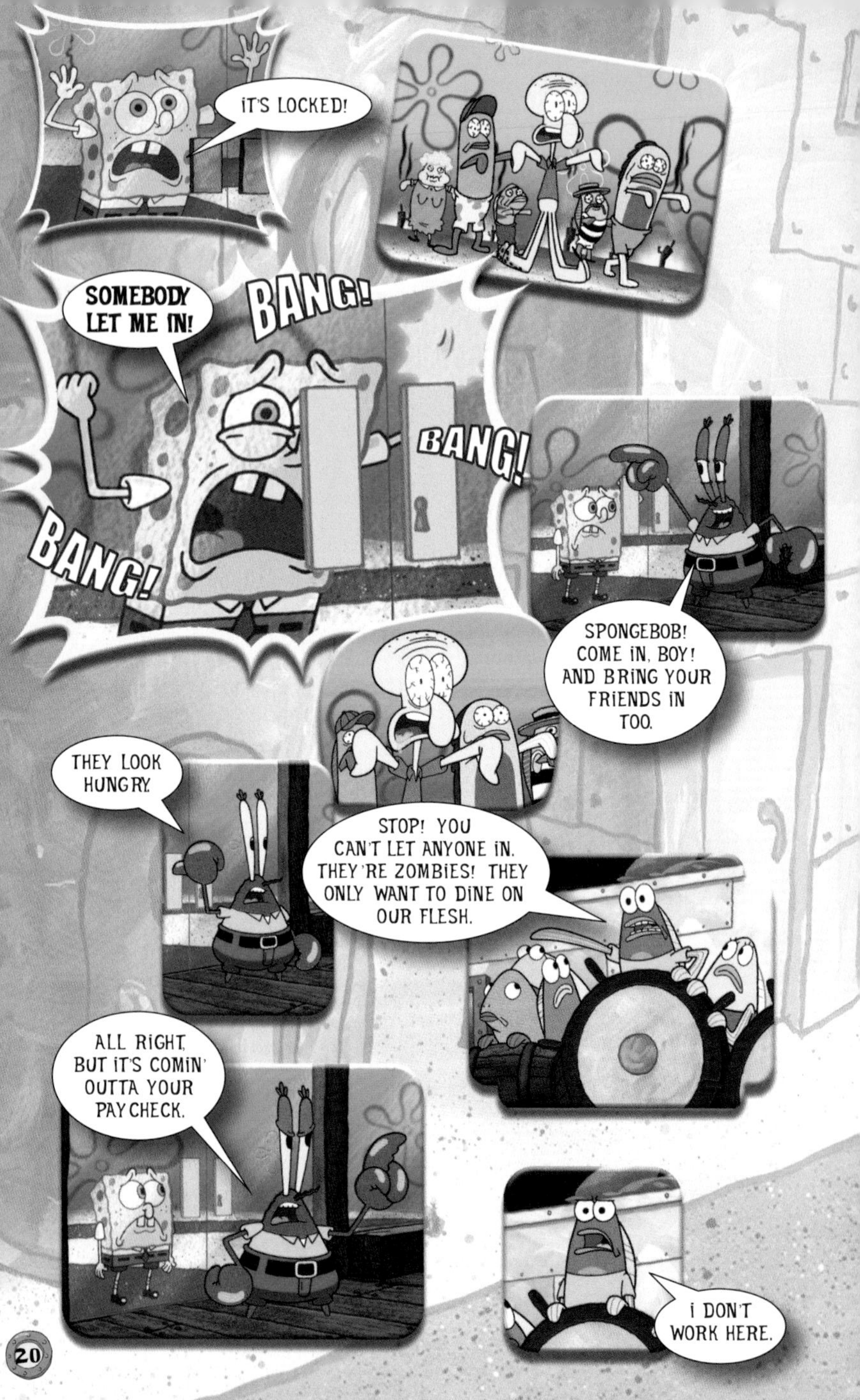
IT'S LOCKED!
SOMEBODY LET ME IN!
BANG!
BANG!
BANG!
SPONGEBOB! COME IN, BOY! AND BRING YOUR FRIENDS IN TOO.
THEY LOOK HUNGRY.
STOP! YOU CAN'T LET ANYONE IN. THEY'RE ZOMBIES! THEY ONLY WANT TO DINE ON OUR FLESH.
ALL RIGHT, BUT IT'S COMIN' OUTTA YOUR PAYCHECK.
I DON'T WORK HERE.

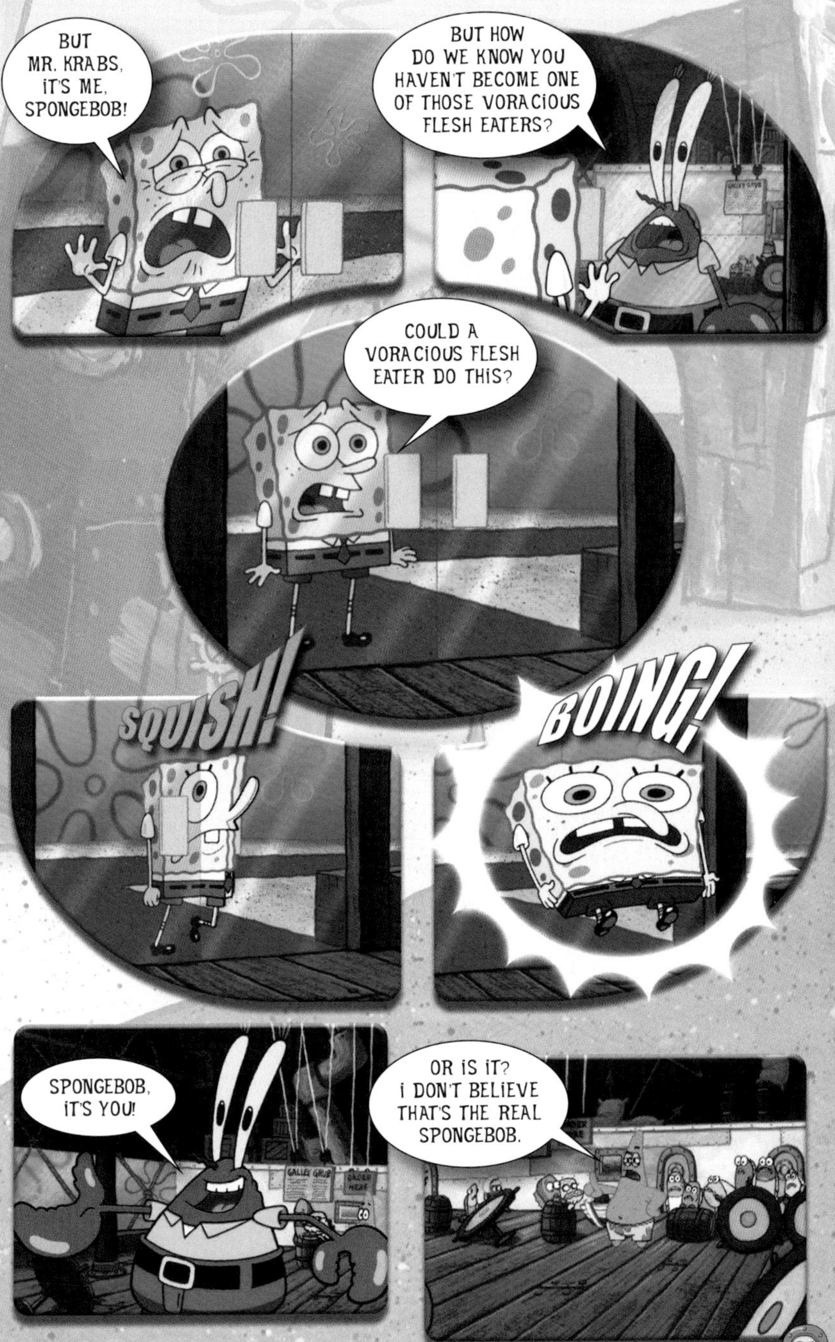
BUT MR. KRABS, IT'S ME, SPONGEBOB!
BUT HOW DO WE KNOW YOU HAVEN'T BECOME ONE OF THOSE VORACIOUS FLESH EATERS?
COULD A VORACIOUS FLESH EATER DO THIS?
SQUISH!
BOING!
SPONGEBOB, IT'S YOU!
OR IS IT? I DON'T BELIEVE THAT'S THE REAL SPONGEBOB.

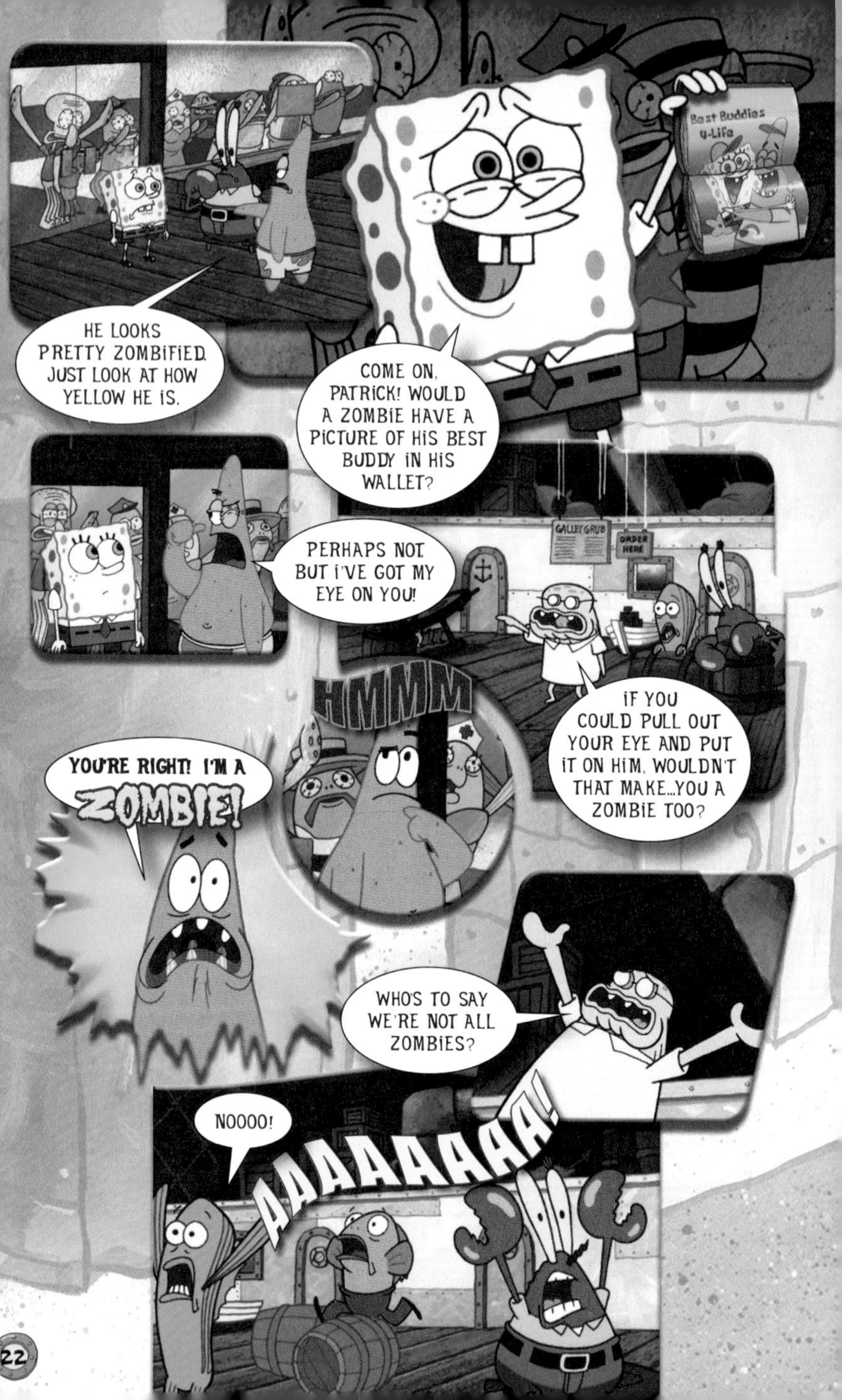
HE LOOKS PRETTY ZOMBIFIED. JUST LOOK AT HOW YELLOW HE IS.
COME ON, PATRICK! WOULD A ZOMBIE HAVE A PICTURE OF HIS BEST BUDDY IN HIS WALLET?
Best Buddies 4-Life
PERHAPS NOT. BUT I'VE GOT MY EYE ON YOU!
GALLEY GRUB
ORDER HERE
IF YOU COULD PULL OUT YOUR EYE AND PUT IT ON HIM, WOULDN'T THAT MAKE...YOU A ZOMBIE TOO?
HMMM
YOU'RE RIGHT! I'M A ZOMBIE!
WHO'S TO SAY WE'RE NOT ALL ZOMBIES?
NOOOO!
AAAAAAAA!

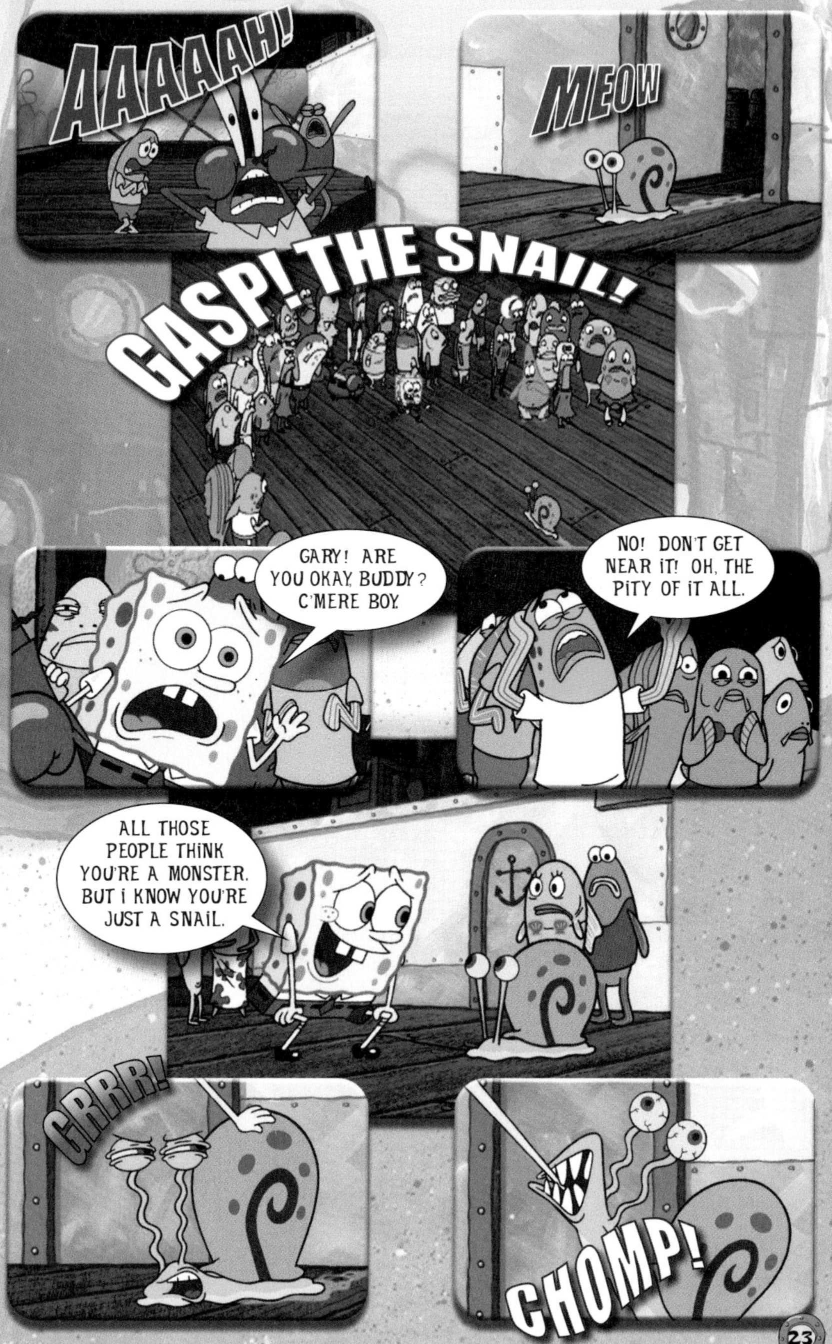
AAAAAH!
MEOW
GASP! THE SNAIL!
GARY! ARE YOU OKAY, BUDDY? C'MERE BOY.
NO! DON'T GET NEAR IT! OH, THE PITY OF IT ALL.
ALL THOSE PEOPLE THINK YOU'RE A MONSTER. BUT I KNOW YOU'RE JUST A SNAIL.
GRRR!
CHOMP!

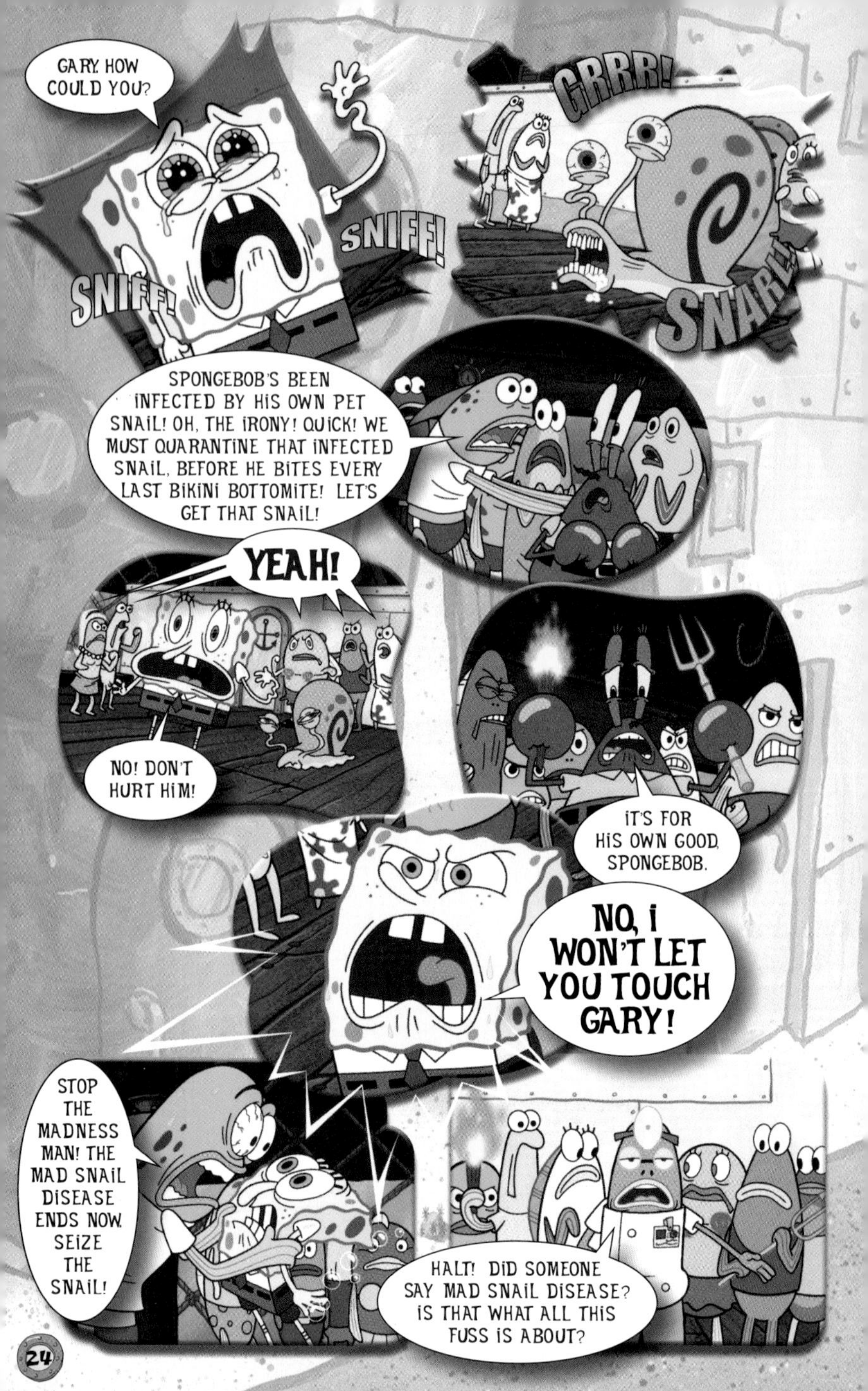
GARY. HOW COULD YOU?
SNIFF!
SNIFF!
GRRR!
SNARL!
SPONGEBOB'S BEEN INFECTED BY HIS OWN PET SNAIL! OH, THE IRONY! QUICK! WE MUST QUARANTINE THAT INFECTED SNAIL, BEFORE HE BITES EVERY LAST BIKINI BOTTOMITE! LET'S GET THAT SNAIL!
YEAH!
NO! DON'T HURT HIM!
IT'S FOR HIS OWN GOOD, SPONGEBOB.
NO, I WON'T LET YOU TOUCH GARY!
STOP THE MADNESS MAN! THE MAD SNAIL DISEASE ENDS NOW. SEIZE THE SNAIL!
HALT! DID SOMEONE SAY MAD SNAIL DISEASE? IS THAT WHAT ALL THIS FUSS IS ABOUT?

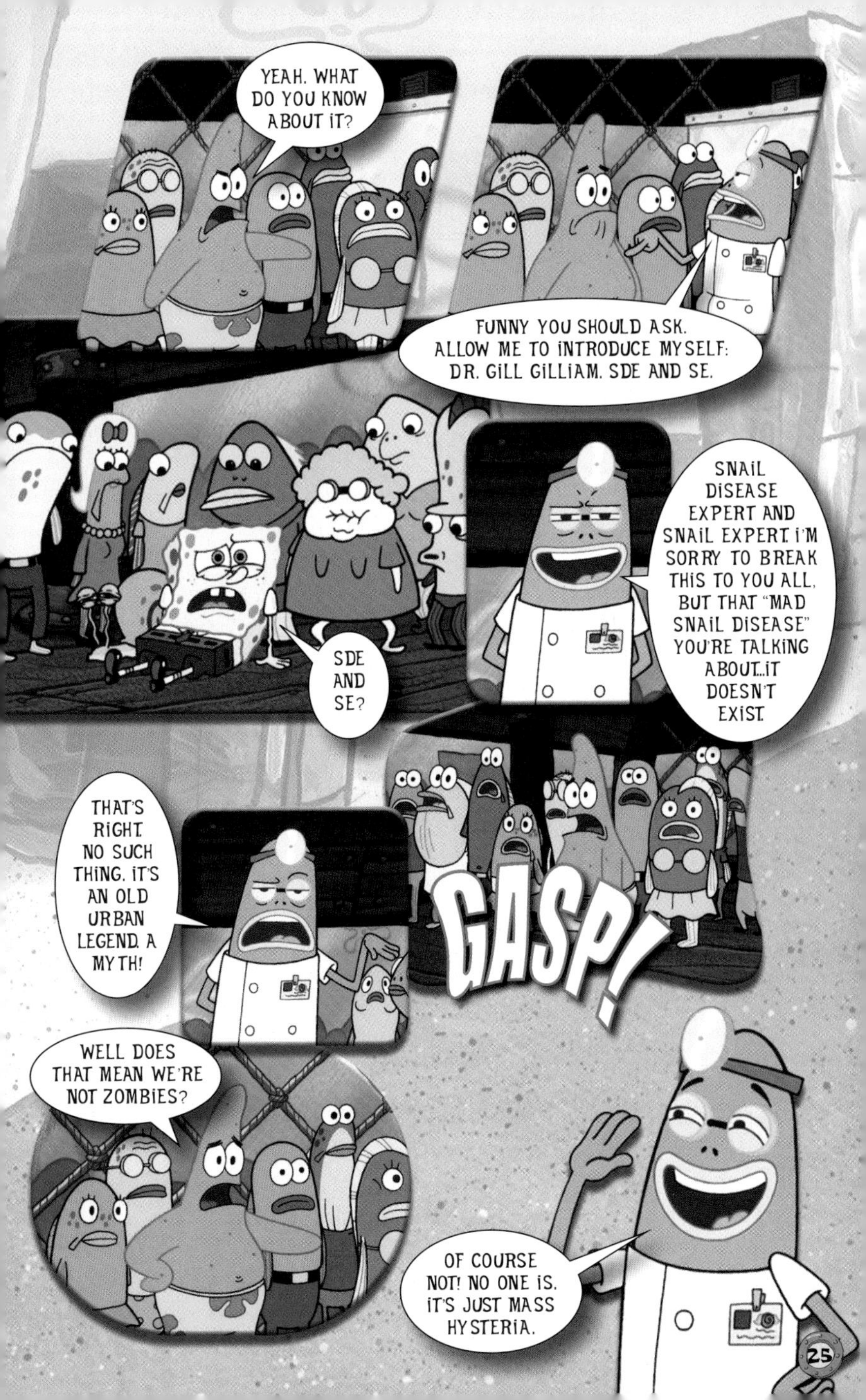
YEAH. WHAT DO YOU KNOW ABOUT IT?
FUNNY YOU SHOULD ASK. ALLOW ME TO INTRODUCE MYSELF: DR. GILL GILLIAM. SDE AND SE.
SDE AND SE?
SNAIL DISEASE EXPERT AND SNAIL EXPERT. I'M SORRY TO BREAK THIS TO YOU ALL, BUT THAT "MAD SNAIL DISEASE" YOU'RE TALKING ABOUT...IT DOESN'T EXIST.
THAT'S RIGHT. NO SUCH THING. IT'S AN OLD URBAN LEGEND. A MYTH!
GASP!
WELL DOES THAT MEAN WE'RE NOT ZOMBIES?
OF COURSE NOT! NO ONE IS. IT'S JUST MASS HYSTERIA.

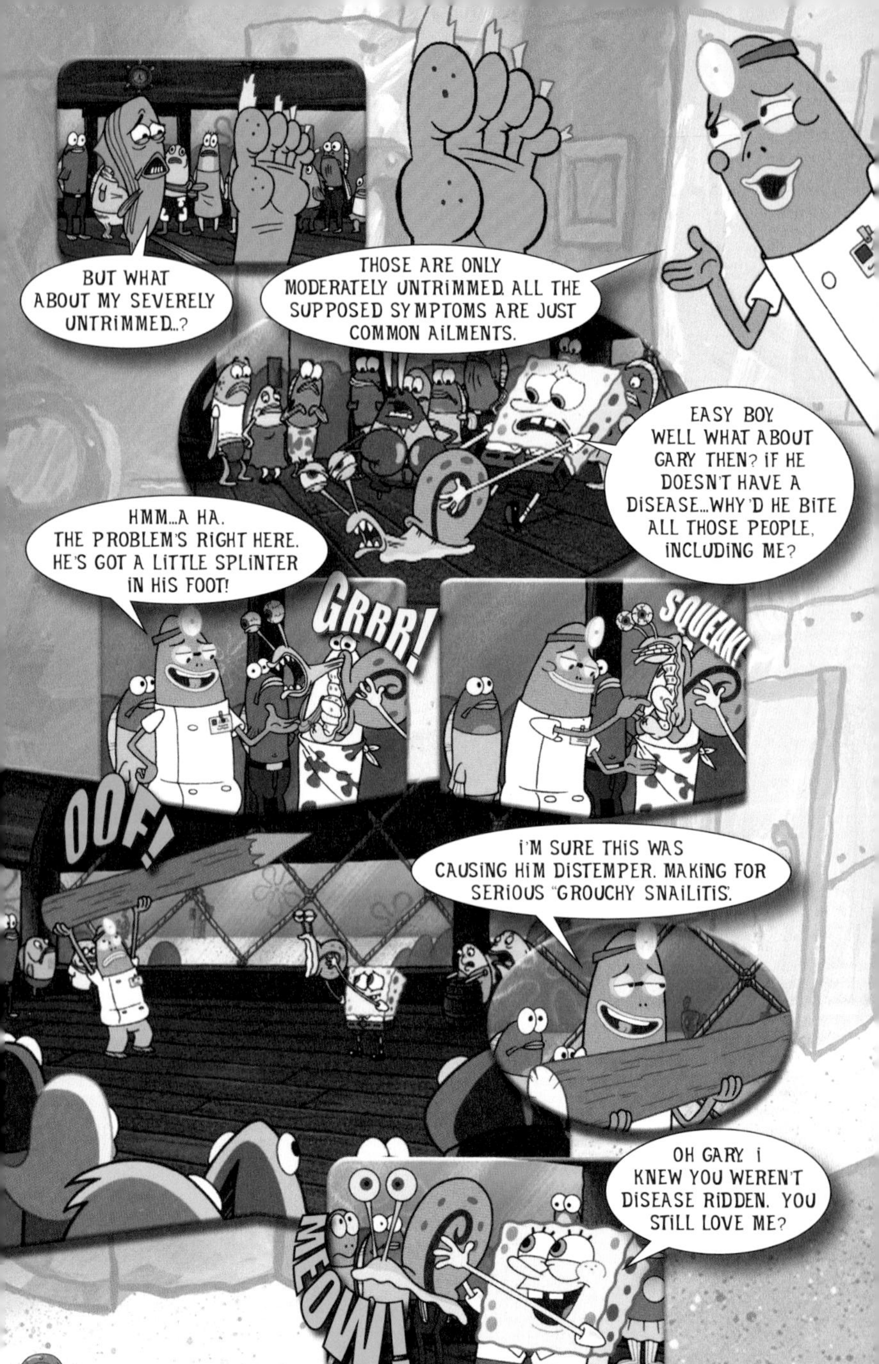
BUT WHAT ABOUT MY SEVERELY UNTRIMMED...?
THOSE ARE ONLY MODERATELY UNTRIMMED. ALL THE SUPPOSED SYMPTOMS ARE JUST COMMON AILMENTS.
EASY BOY. WELL WHAT ABOUT GARY THEN? IF HE DOESN'T HAVE A DISEASE...WHY'D HE BITE ALL THOSE PEOPLE, INCLUDING ME?
HMM...A HA. THE PROBLEM'S RIGHT HERE. HE'S GOT A LITTLE SPLINTER IN HIS FOOT!
GRRR!
SQUEAK!
OOF!
I'M SURE THIS WAS CAUSING HIM DISTEMPER. MAKING FOR SERIOUS "GROUCHY SNAILITIS".
MEOW!
OH GARY. I KNEW YOU WEREN'T DISEASE RIDDEN. YOU STILL LOVE ME?

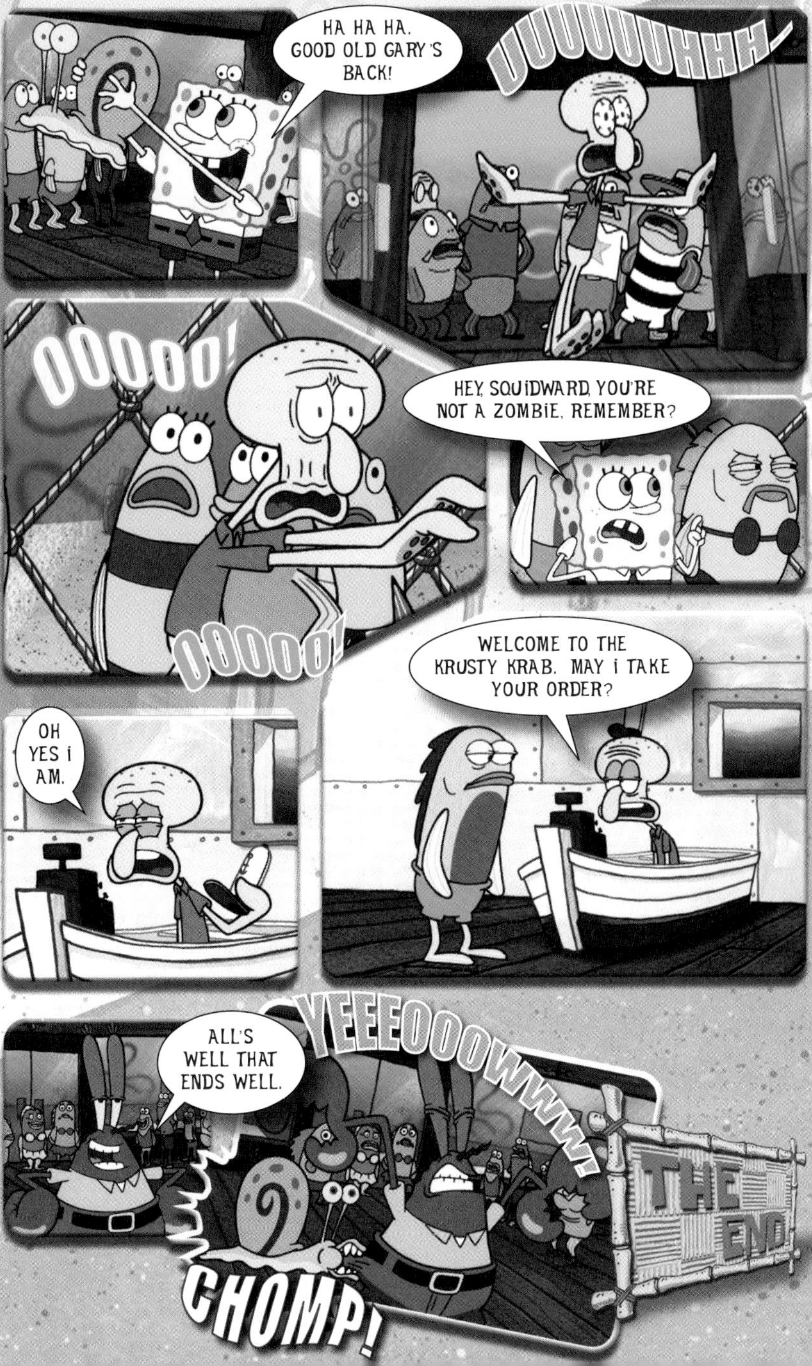
HA HA HA. GOOD OLD GARY'S BACK!
UUUUUUUHHH...
OOOOO!
OOOOO!
HEY, SQUIDWARD, YOU'RE NOT A ZOMBIE, REMEMBER?
OH YES I AM.
WELCOME TO THE KRUSTY KRAB. MAY I TAKE YOUR ORDER?
ALL'S WELL THAT ENDS WELL.
YEEEOOOWWW!
CHOMP!
THE END

Nickelodeon

SpongeBob SquarePants

That's No Lady

By Paul Tibbitt, Walt Dohrn and Merriwether Williams

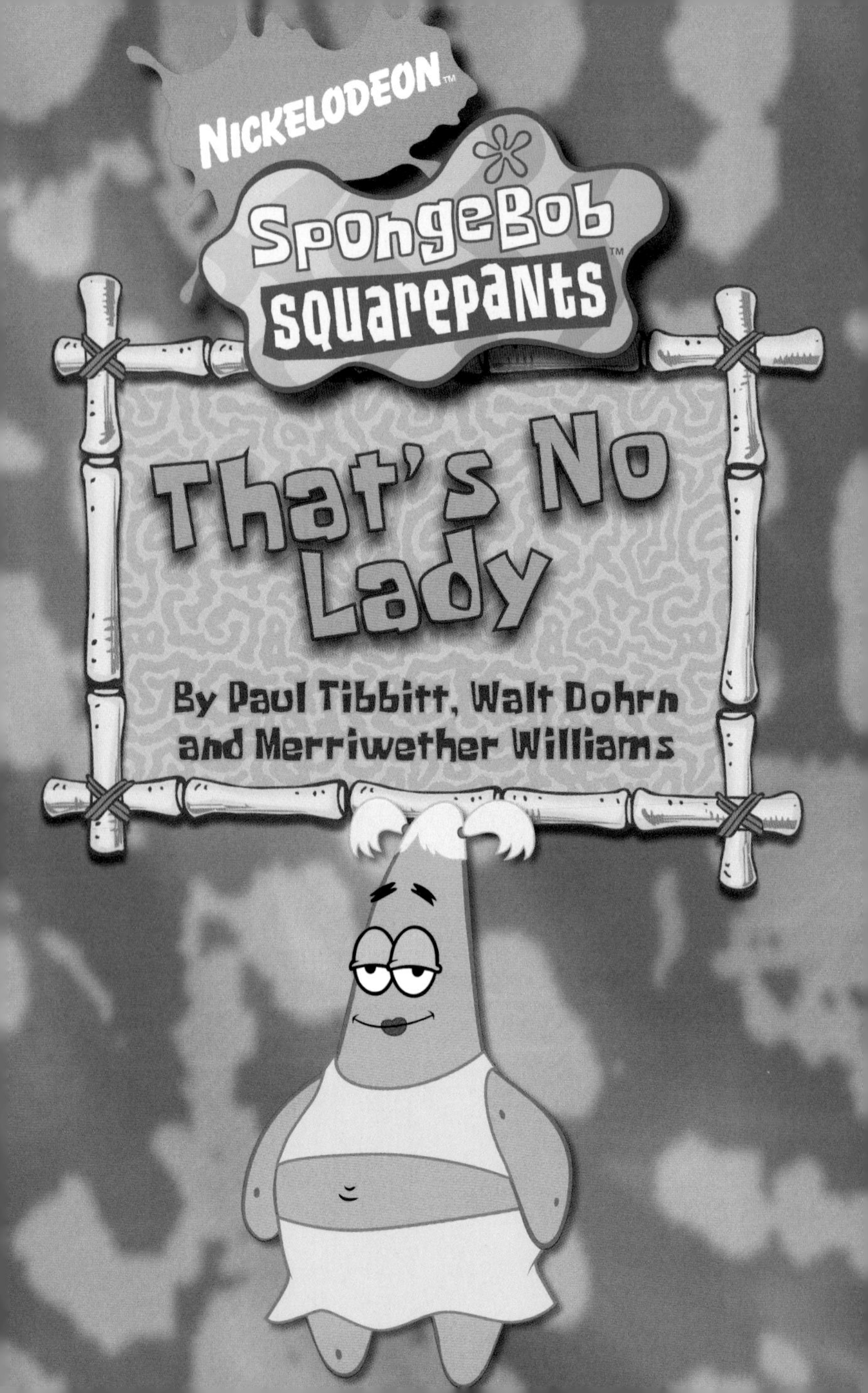

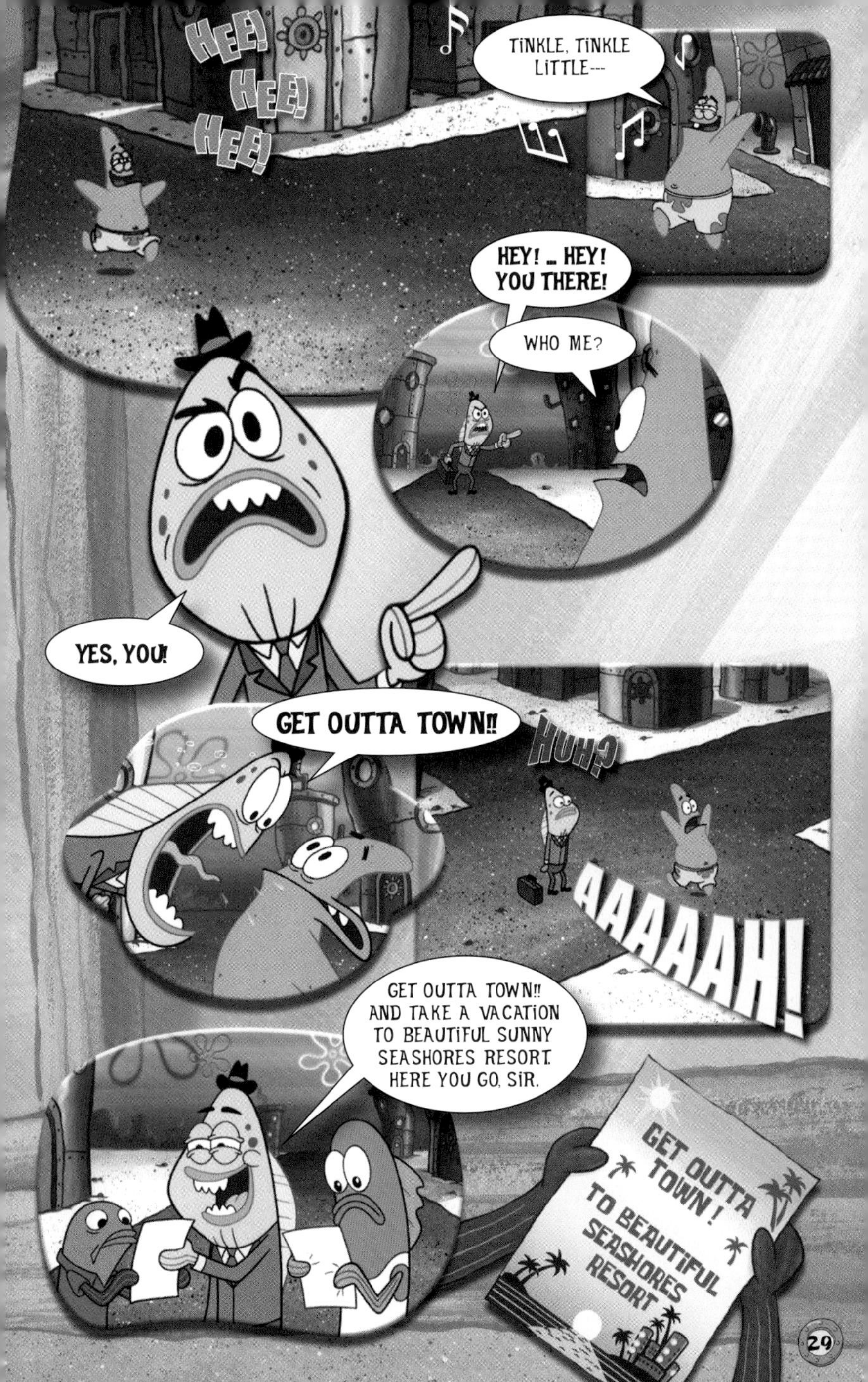
HEE!
HEE!
HEE!
TINKLE, TINKLE LITTLE---
HEY! ... HEY! YOU THERE!
WHO ME?
YES, YOU!
GET OUTTA TOWN!!
HUH?
AAAAAH!
GET OUTTA TOWN!! AND TAKE A VACATION TO BEAUTIFUL SUNNY SEASHORES RESORT. HERE YOU GO, SIR.
GET OUTTA TOWN! TO BEAUTIFUL SEASHORES RESORT

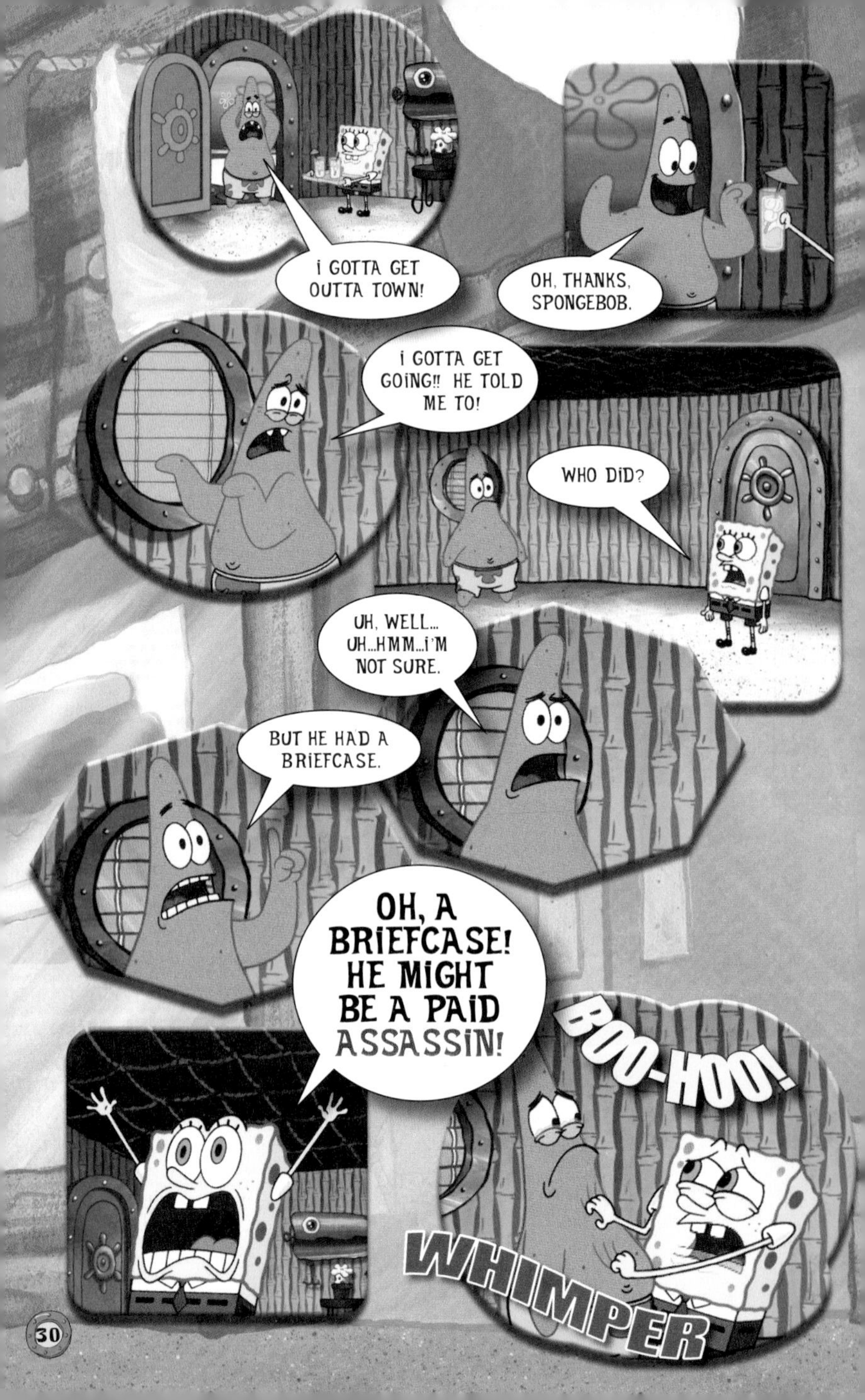
I GOTTA GET OUTTA TOWN!
OH, THANKS, SPONGEBOB.
I GOTTA GET GOING!! HE TOLD ME TO!
WHO DID?
UH, WELL... UH...HMM...I'M NOT SURE.
BUT HE HAD A BRIEFCASE.
OH, A BRIEFCASE! HE MIGHT BE A PAID ASSASSIN!
BOO-HOO!
WHIMPER

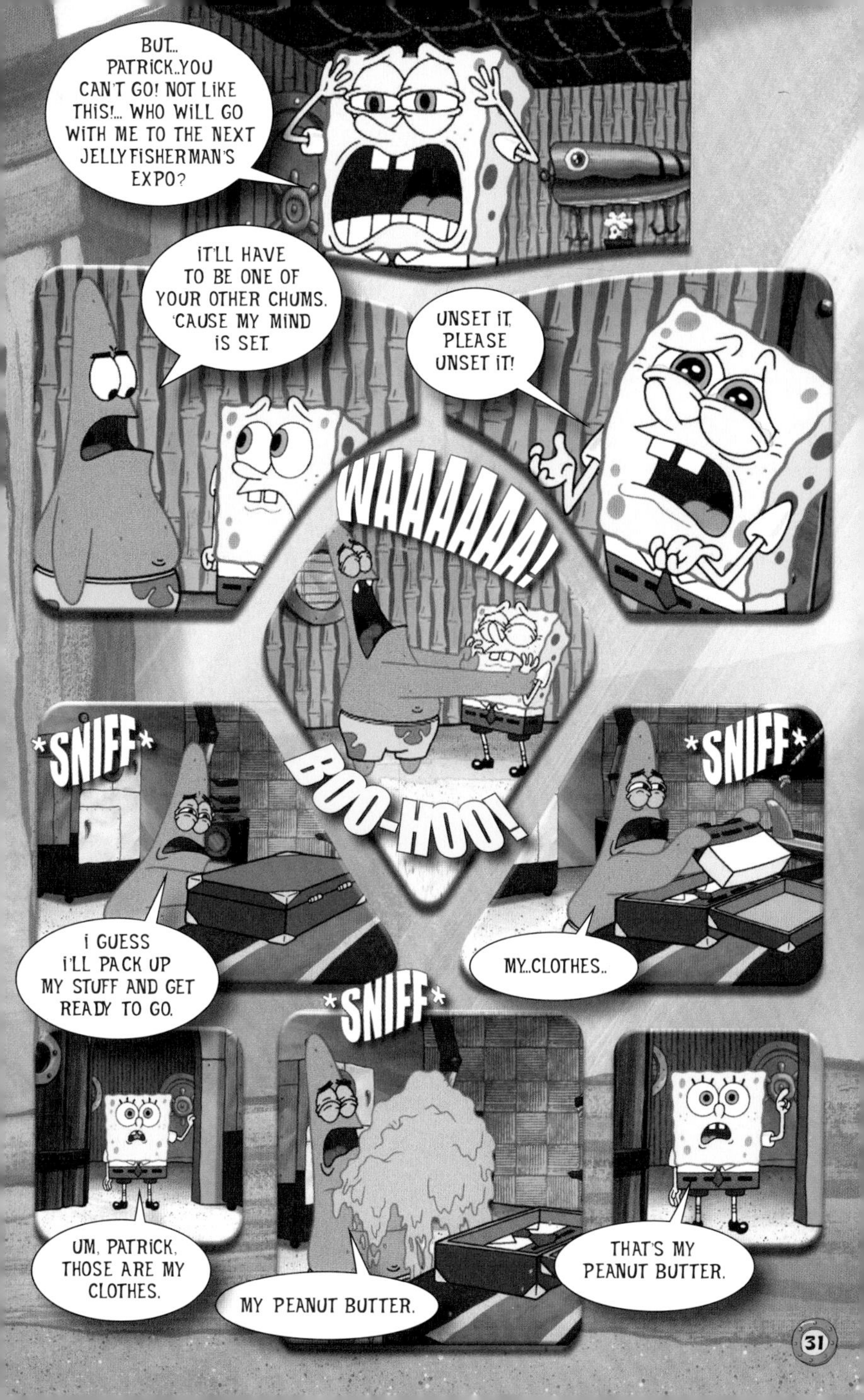
BUT... PATRICK...YOU CAN'T GO! NOT LIKE THIS!... WHO WILL GO WITH ME TO THE NEXT JELLYFISHERMAN'S EXPO?
IT'LL HAVE TO BE ONE OF YOUR OTHER CHUMS. 'CAUSE MY MIND IS SET.
UNSET IT, PLEASE UNSET IT!
WAAAAAA!
BOO-HOO!
SNIFF
I GUESS I'LL PACK UP MY STUFF AND GET READY TO GO.
SNIFF
MY...CLOTHES..
UM, PATRICK, THOSE ARE MY CLOTHES.
SNIFF
MY PEANUT BUTTER.
THAT'S MY PEANUT BUTTER.

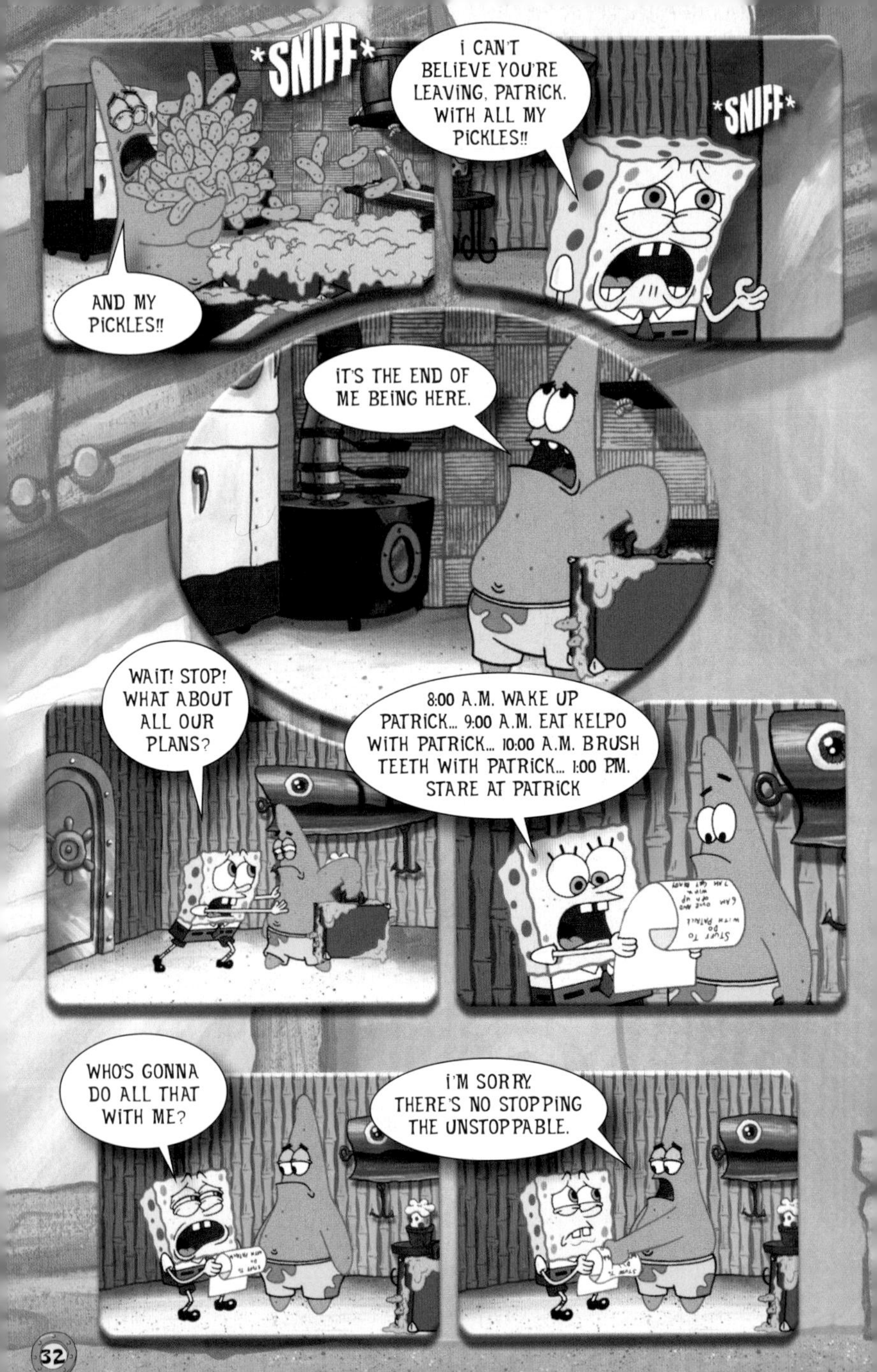
SNIFF
AND MY PICKLES!!
I CAN'T BELIEVE YOU'RE LEAVING, PATRICK. WITH ALL MY PICKLES!!
SNIFF
IT'S THE END OF ME BEING HERE.
WAIT! STOP! WHAT ABOUT ALL OUR PLANS?
8:00 A.M. WAKE UP PATRICK... 9:00 A.M. EAT KELPO WITH PATRICK... 10:00 A.M. BRUSH TEETH WITH PATRICK... 1:00 P.M. STARE AT PATRICK
WHO'S GONNA DO ALL THAT WITH ME?
I'M SORRY. THERE'S NO STOPPING THE UNSTOPPABLE.

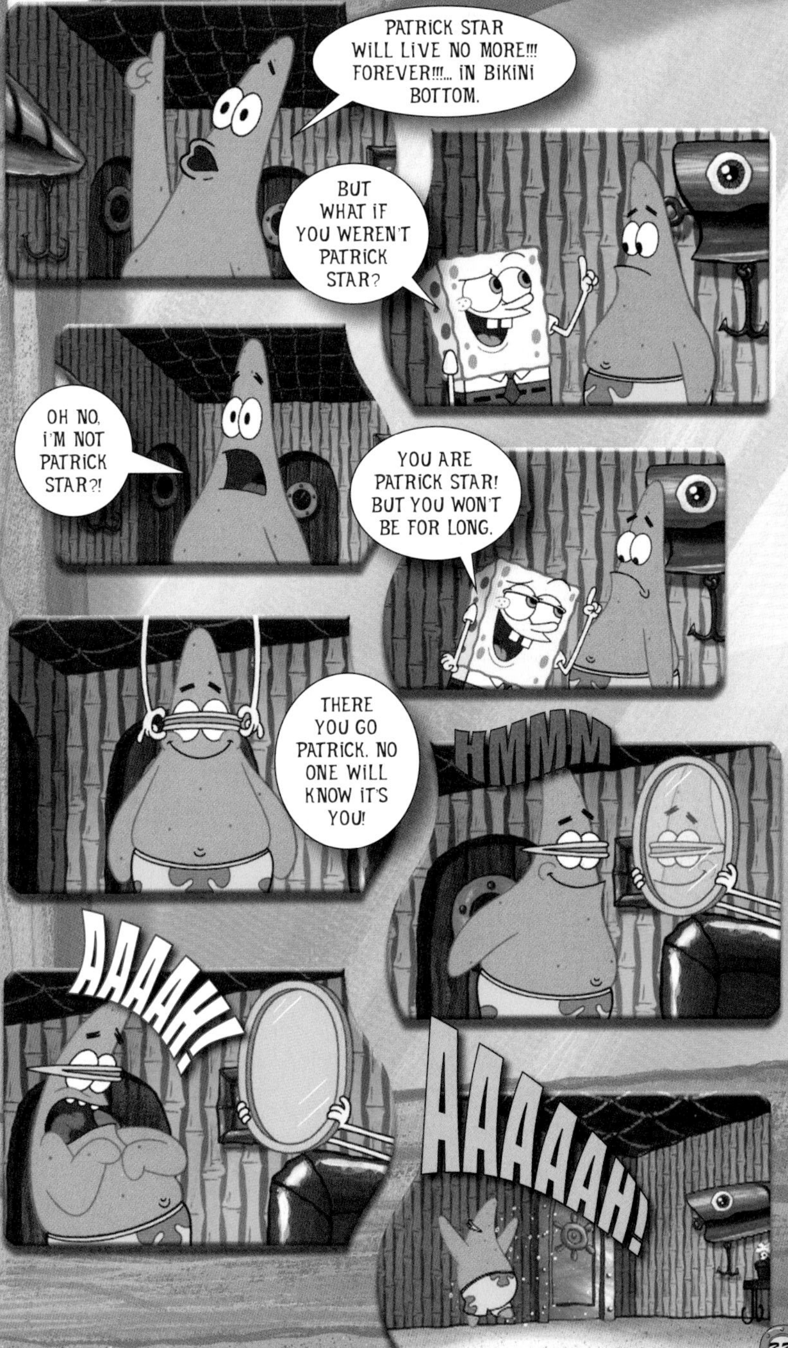
PATRICK STAR WILL LIVE NO MORE!!! FOREVER!!!... IN BIKINI BOTTOM.
BUT WHAT IF YOU WEREN'T PATRICK STAR?
OH NO, I'M NOT PATRICK STAR?!
YOU ARE PATRICK STAR! BUT YOU WON'T BE FOR LONG.
THERE YOU GO PATRICK. NO ONE WILL KNOW IT'S YOU!
HMMM
AAAAH!
AAAAAH!

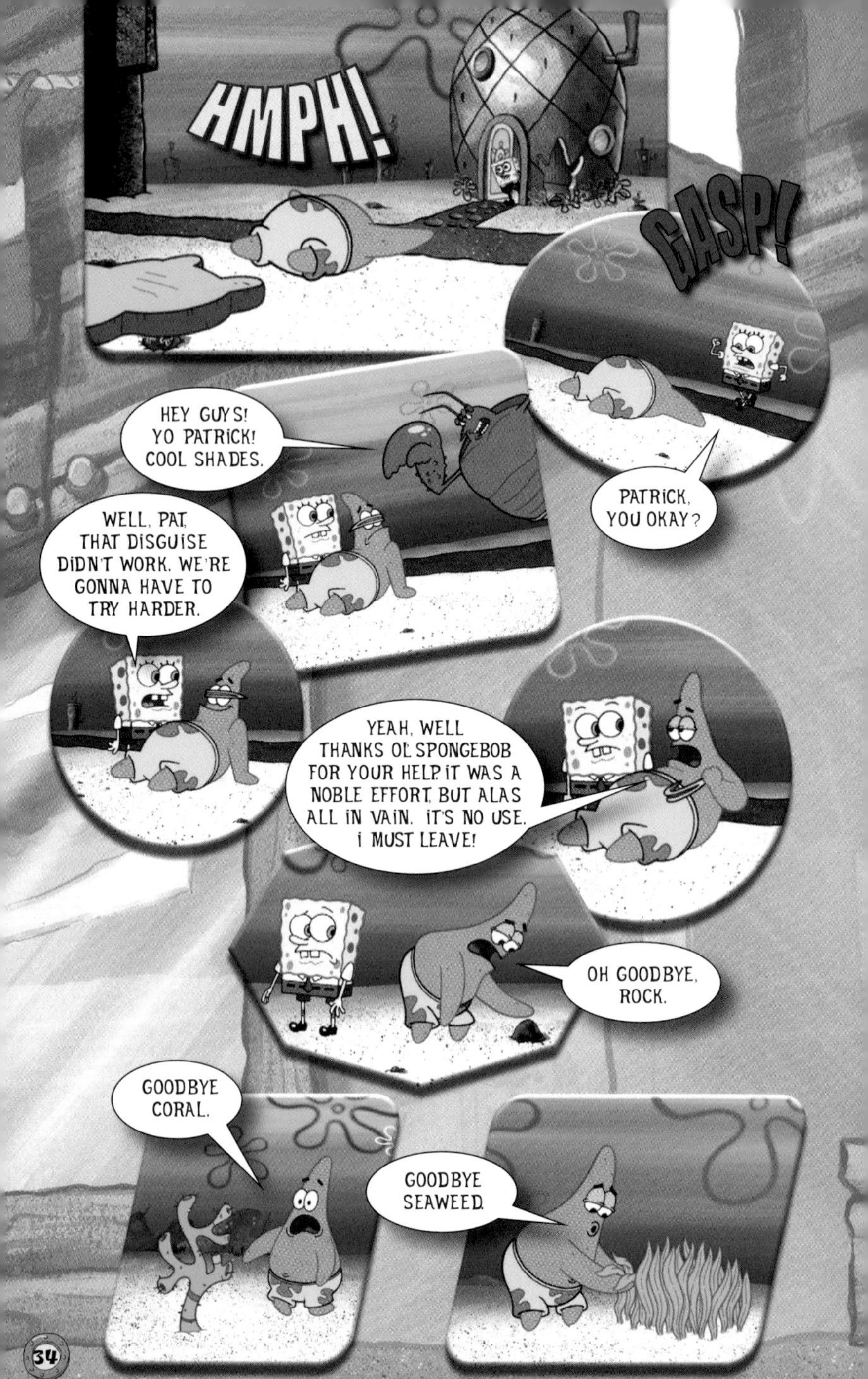

HMPH!
GASP!
PATRICK, YOU OKAY?
HEY GUYS! YO PATRICK! COOL SHADES.
WELL, PAT, THAT DISGUISE DIDN'T WORK. WE'RE GONNA HAVE TO TRY HARDER.
YEAH, WELL THANKS OL' SPONGEBOB FOR YOUR HELP. IT WAS A NOBLE EFFORT, BUT ALAS ALL IN VAIN. IT'S NO USE. I MUST LEAVE!
OH GOODBYE, ROCK.
GOODBYE CORAL.
GOODBYE SEAWEED.

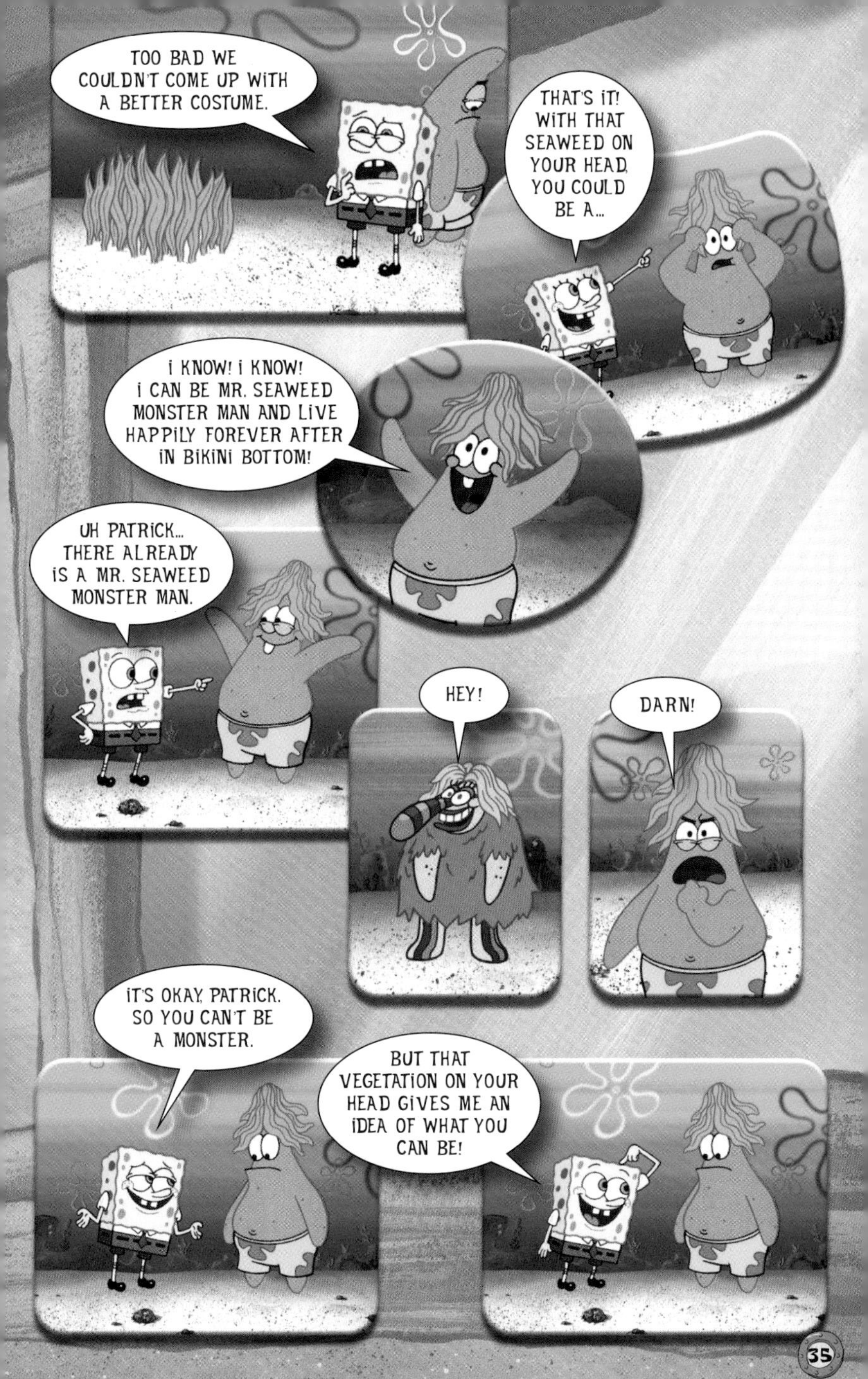
TOO BAD WE COULDN'T COME UP WITH A BETTER COSTUME.
THAT'S IT! WITH THAT SEAWEED ON YOUR HEAD, YOU COULD BE A...
I KNOW! I KNOW! I CAN BE MR. SEAWEED MONSTER MAN AND LIVE HAPPILY FOREVER AFTER IN BIKINI BOTTOM!
UH PATRICK... THERE ALREADY IS A MR. SEAWEED MONSTER MAN.
HEY!
DARN!
IT'S OKAY, PATRICK. SO YOU CAN'T BE A MONSTER.
BUT THAT VEGETATION ON YOUR HEAD GIVES ME AN IDEA OF WHAT YOU CAN BE!

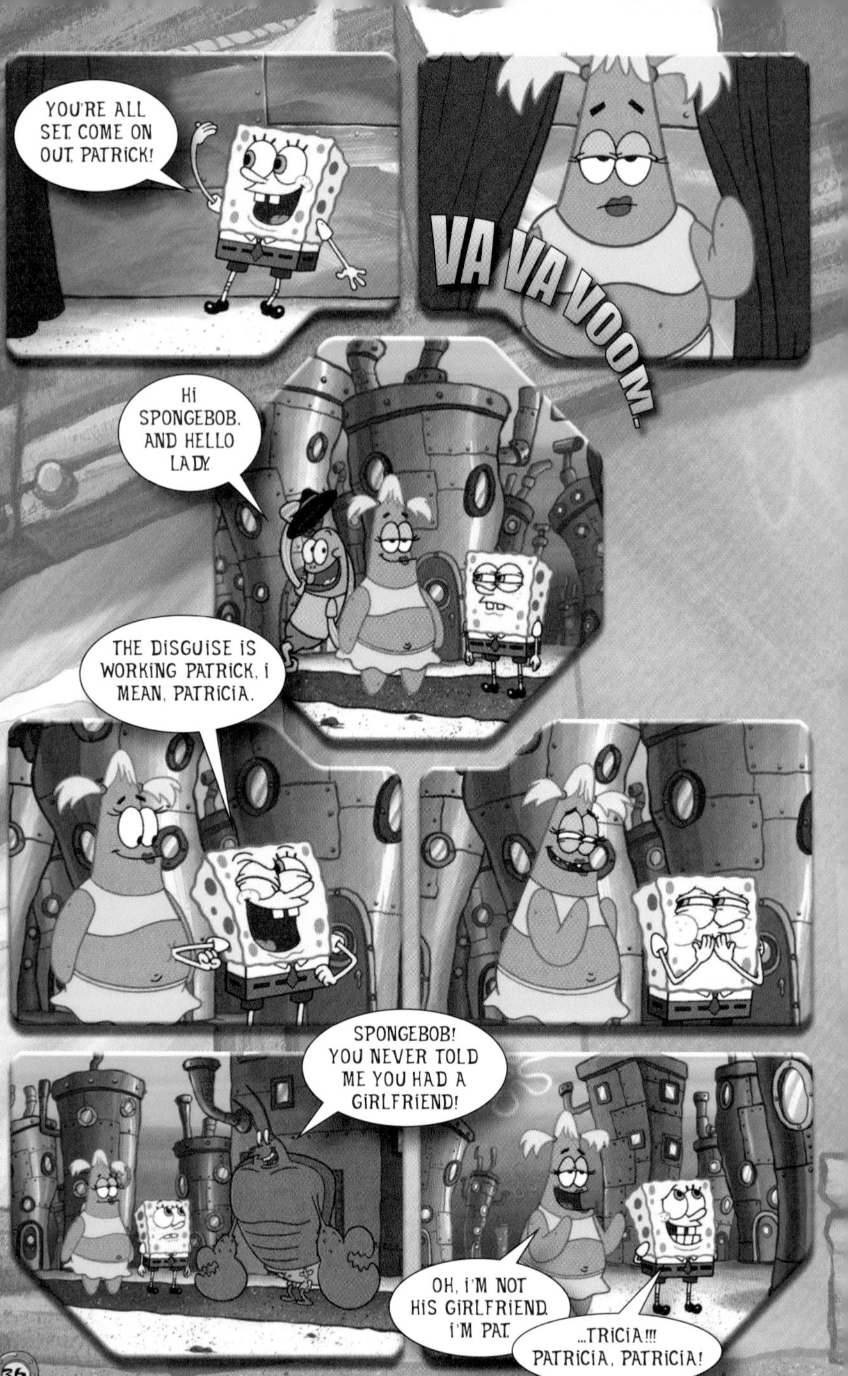
YOU'RE ALL SET. COME ON OUT, PATRICK!
VA VA VOOM.
HI SPONGEBOB. AND HELLO LADY.
THE DISGUISE IS WORKING PATRICK, I MEAN, PATRICIA.
SPONGEBOB! YOU NEVER TOLD ME YOU HAD A GIRLFRIEND!
OH, I'M NOT HIS GIRLFRIEND. I'M PAT.
...TRICIA!!! PATRICIA, PATRICIA!

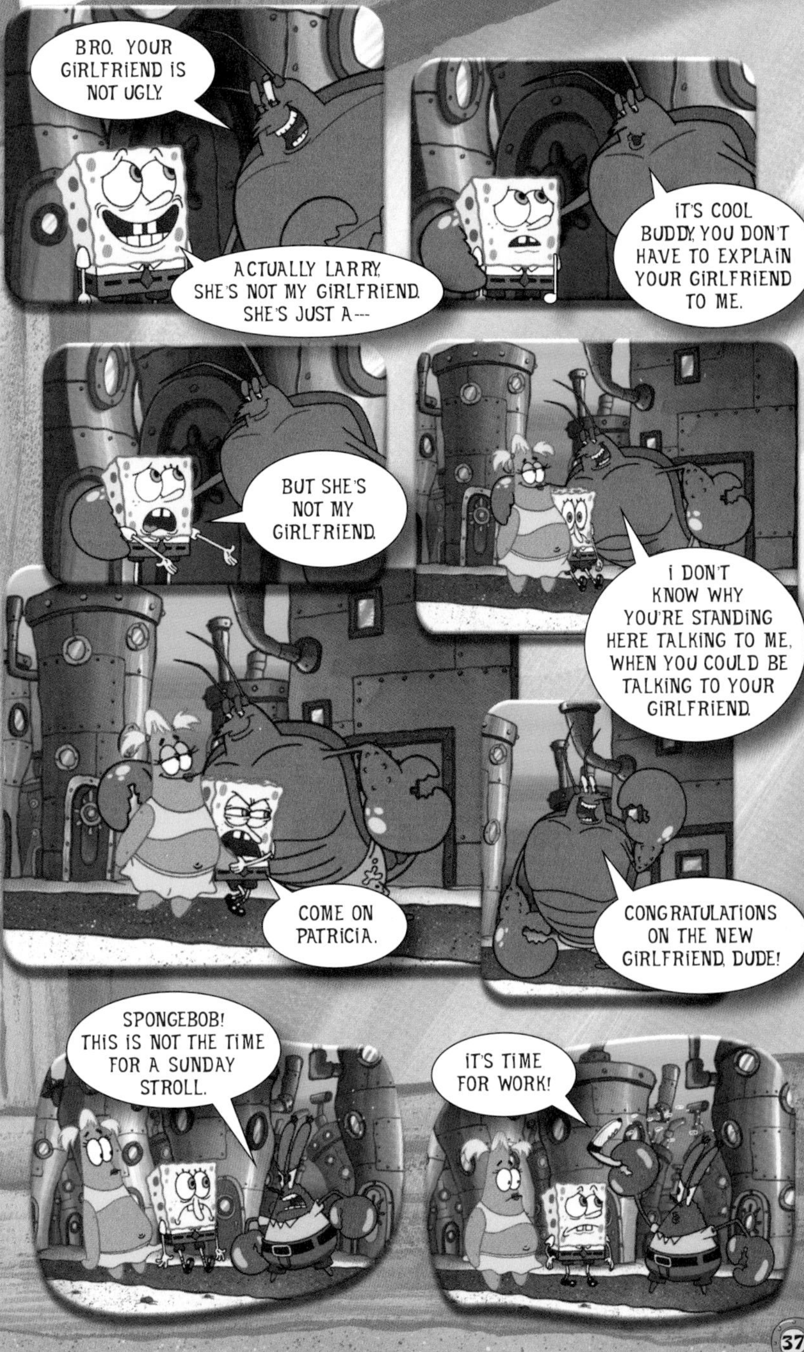
BRO. YOUR GIRLFRIEND IS NOT UGLY.
ACTUALLY LARRY, SHE'S NOT MY GIRLFRIEND. SHE'S JUST A---
IT'S COOL BUDDY, YOU DON'T HAVE TO EXPLAIN YOUR GIRLFRIEND TO ME.
BUT SHE'S NOT MY GIRLFRIEND.
I DON'T KNOW WHY YOU'RE STANDING HERE TALKING TO ME, WHEN YOU COULD BE TALKING TO YOUR GIRLFRIEND.
COME ON PATRICIA.
CONGRATULATIONS ON THE NEW GIRLFRIEND, DUDE!
SPONGEBOB! THIS IS NOT THE TIME FOR A SUNDAY STROLL.
IT'S TIME FOR WORK!

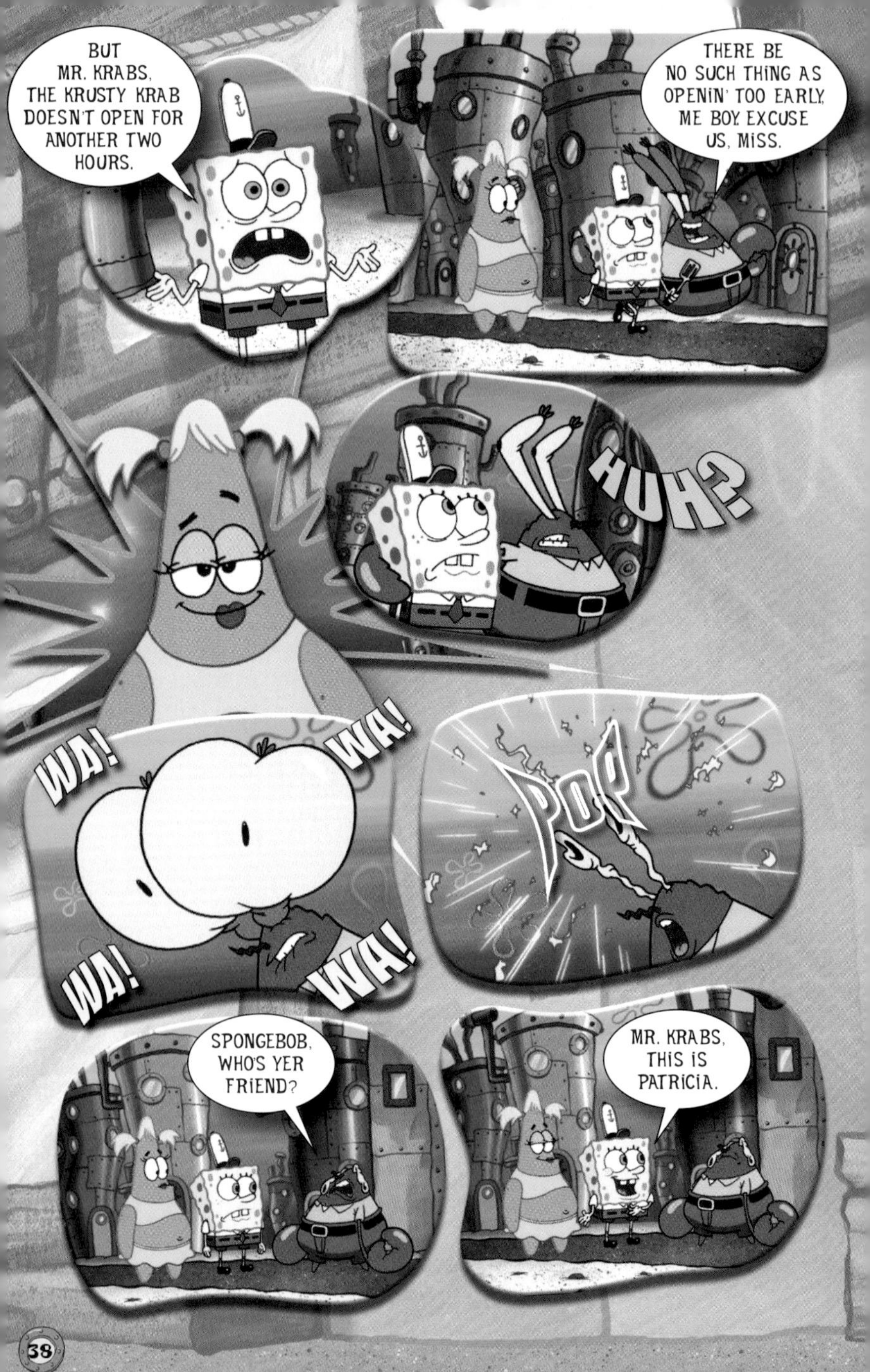

BUT MR. KRABS, THE KRUSTY KRAB DOESN'T OPEN FOR ANOTHER TWO HOURS.
THERE BE NO SUCH THING AS OPENIN' TOO EARLY, ME BOY. EXCUSE US, MISS.
HUH?
WA! WA! WA! WA!
POP
SPONGEBOB, WHO'S YER FRIEND?
MR. KRABS, THIS IS PATRICIA.

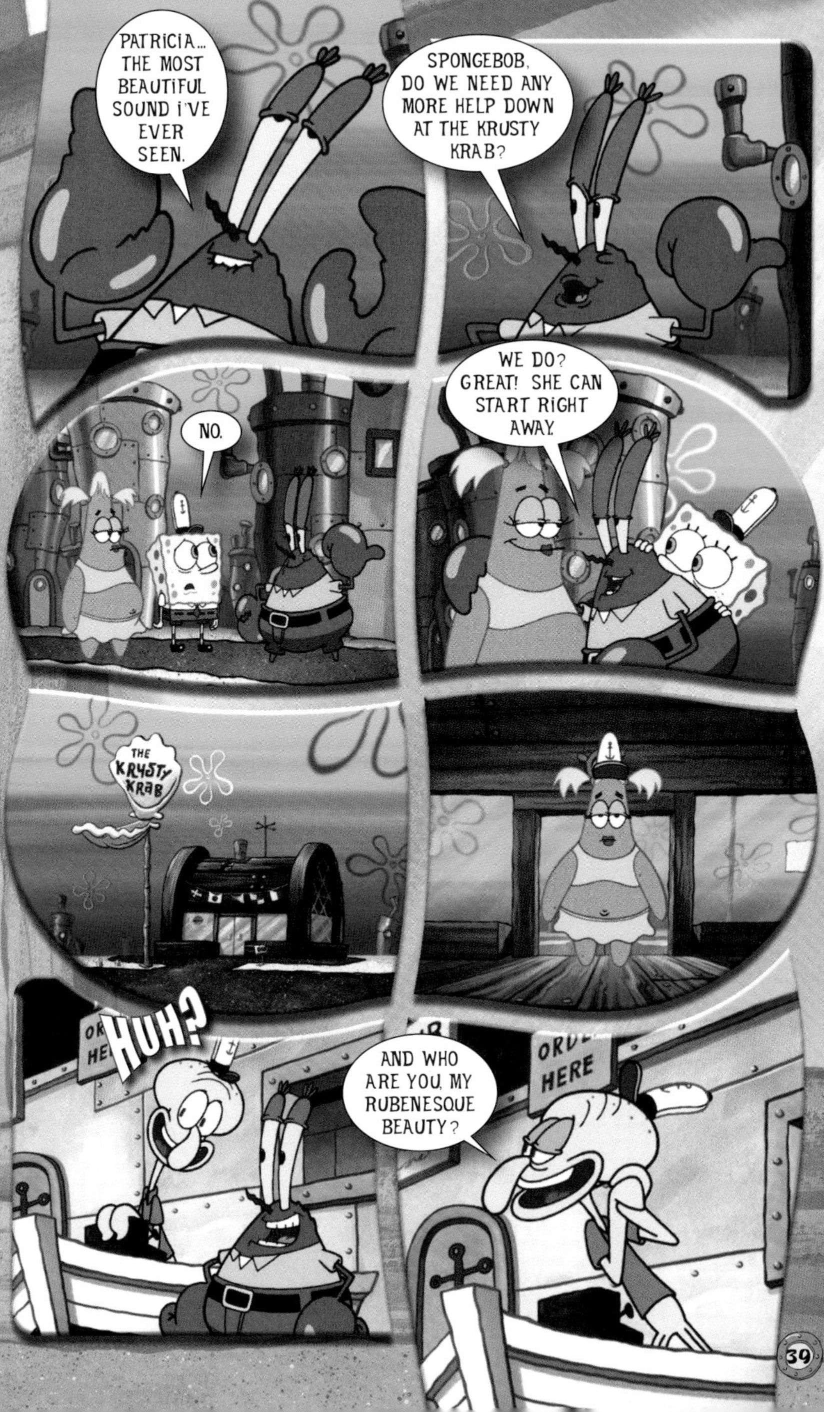
PATRICIA... THE MOST BEAUTIFUL SOUND I'VE EVER SEEN.
SPONGEBOB, DO WE NEED ANY MORE HELP DOWN AT THE KRUSTY KRAB?
NO.
WE DO? GREAT! SHE CAN START RIGHT AWAY.
THE KRUSTY KRAB
HUH?
AND WHO ARE YOU, MY RUBENESQUE BEAUTY?
ORDER HERE

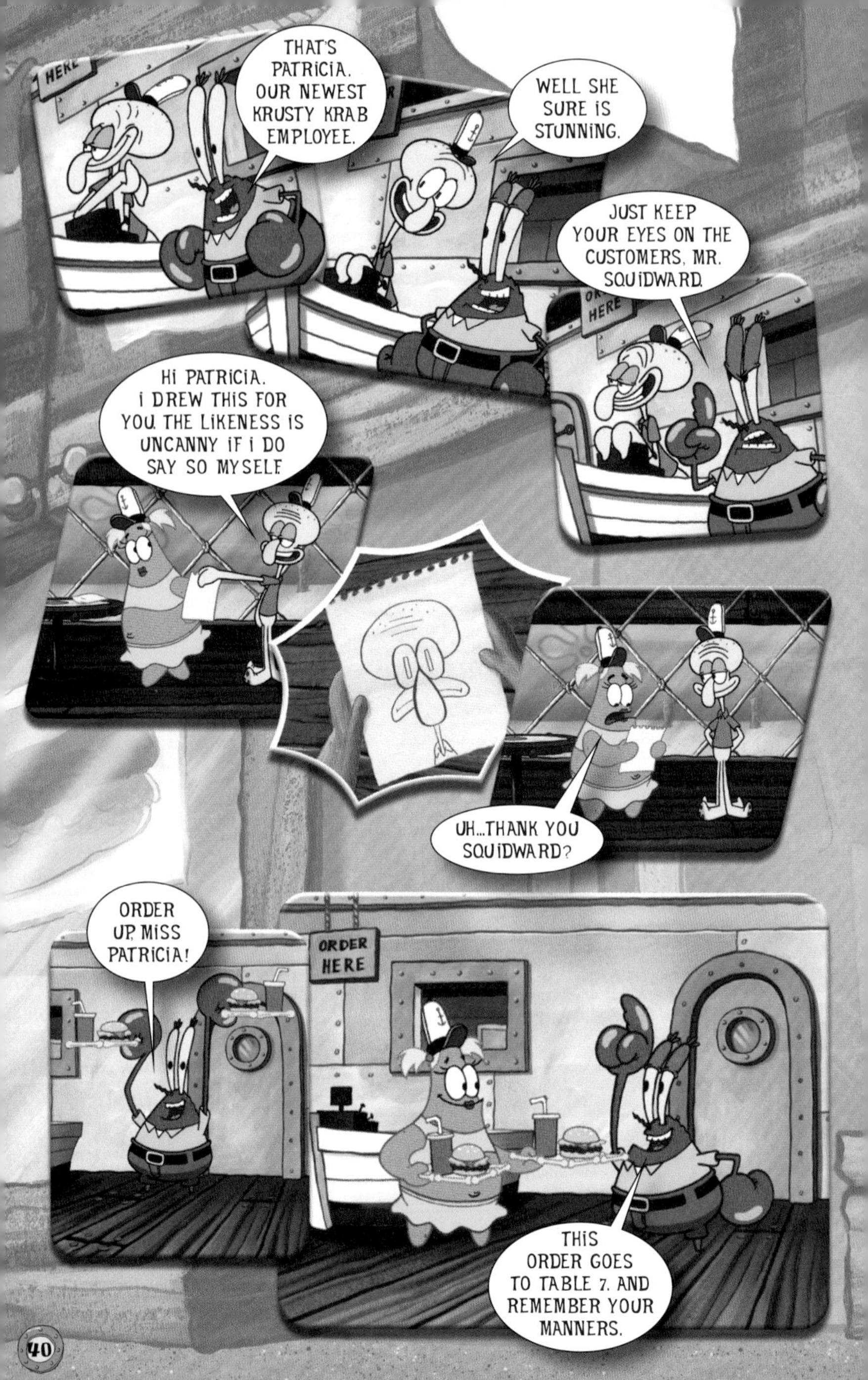

HERE
THAT'S PATRICIA. OUR NEWEST KRUSTY KRAB EMPLOYEE.
WELL SHE SURE IS STUNNING.
JUST KEEP YOUR EYES ON THE CUSTOMERS, MR. SQUIDWARD.
ORDER HERE
HI PATRICIA. I DREW THIS FOR YOU. THE LIKENESS IS UNCANNY IF I DO SAY SO MYSELF.
UH...THANK YOU SQUIDWARD?
ORDER UP, MISS PATRICIA!
ORDER HERE
THIS ORDER GOES TO TABLE 7. AND REMEMBER YOUR MANNERS.

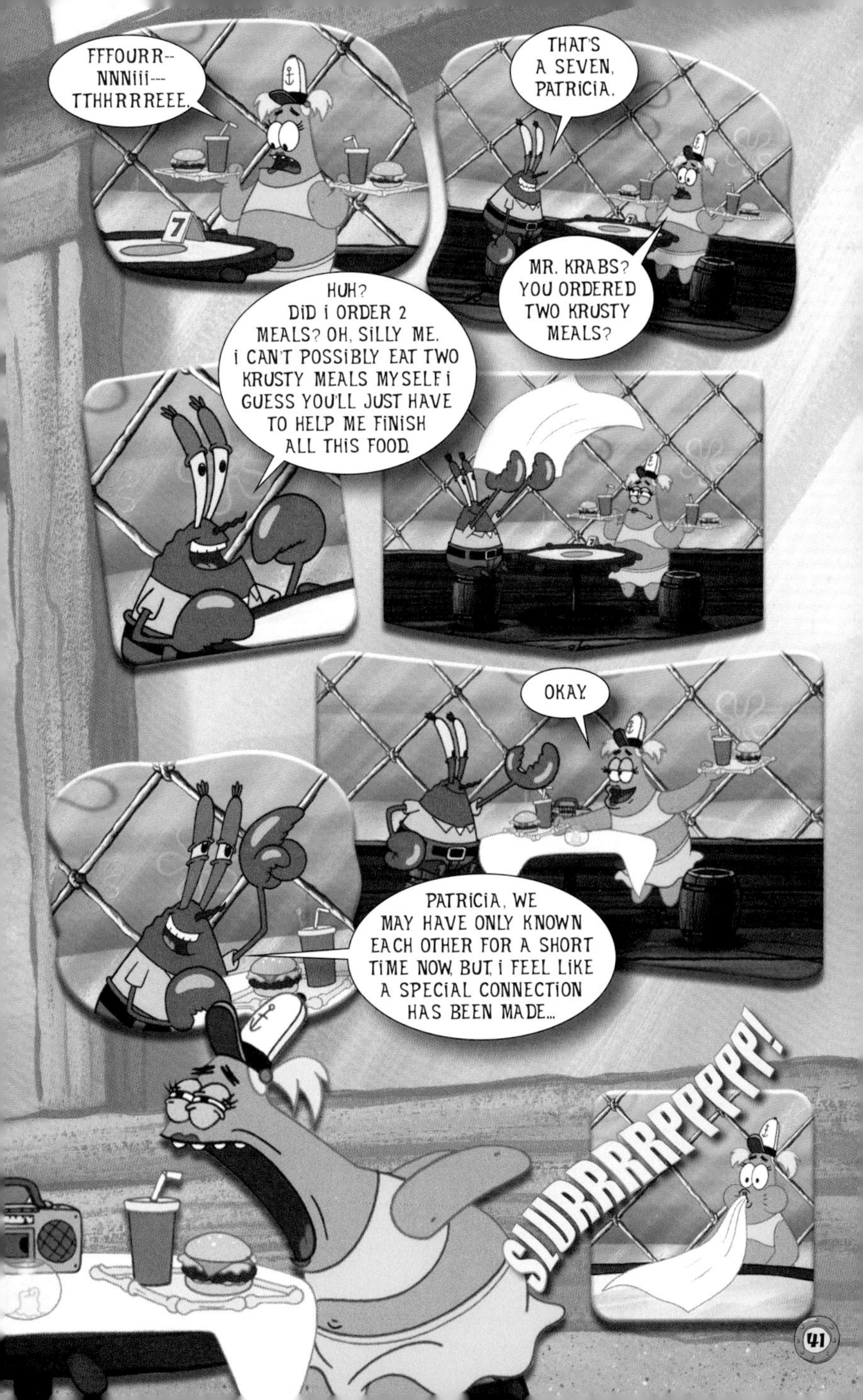
FFFOURR--
NNNiii---
TTHHRRRREEE.
7
THAT'S A SEVEN, PATRICIA.
MR. KRABS? YOU ORDERED TWO KRUSTY MEALS?
HUH? DID I ORDER 2 MEALS? OH, SILLY ME. I CAN'T POSSIBLY EAT TWO KRUSTY MEALS MYSELF. I GUESS YOU'LL JUST HAVE TO HELP ME FINISH ALL THIS FOOD.
OKAY.
PATRICIA, WE MAY HAVE ONLY KNOWN EACH OTHER FOR A SHORT TIME NOW, BUT, I FEEL LIKE A SPECIAL CONNECTION HAS BEEN MADE...
SLURRRRRPPPPP!

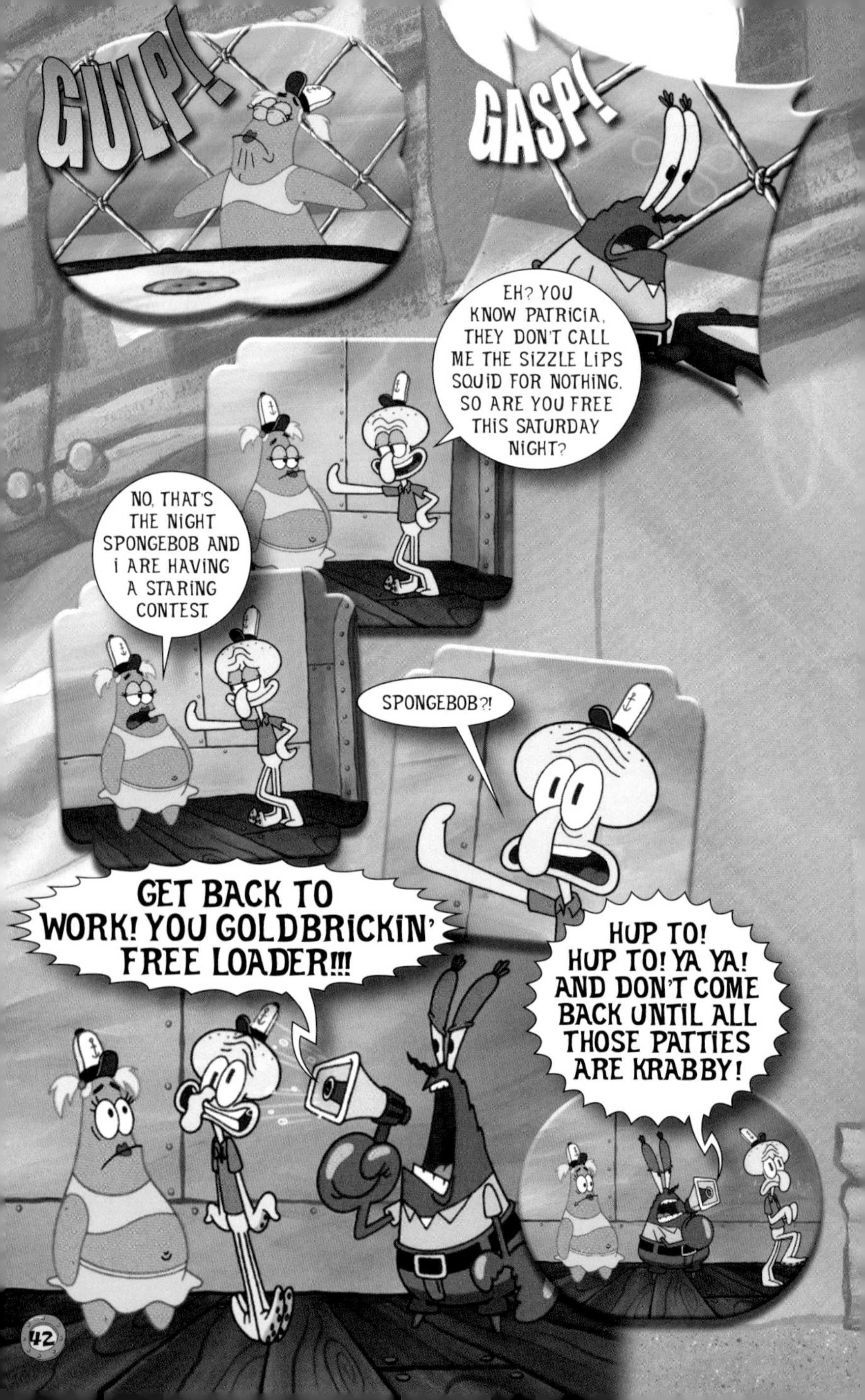
GULP!
GASP!
EH? YOU KNOW PATRICIA, THEY DON'T CALL ME THE SIZZLE LIPS SQUID FOR NOTHING. SO ARE YOU FREE THIS SATURDAY NIGHT?
NO, THAT'S THE NIGHT SPONGEBOB AND I ARE HAVING A STARING CONTEST.
SPONGEBOB?!
GET BACK TO WORK! YOU GOLDBRICKIN' FREE LOADER!!!
HUP TO! HUP TO! YA YA! AND DON'T COME BACK UNTIL ALL THOSE PATTIES ARE KRABBY!

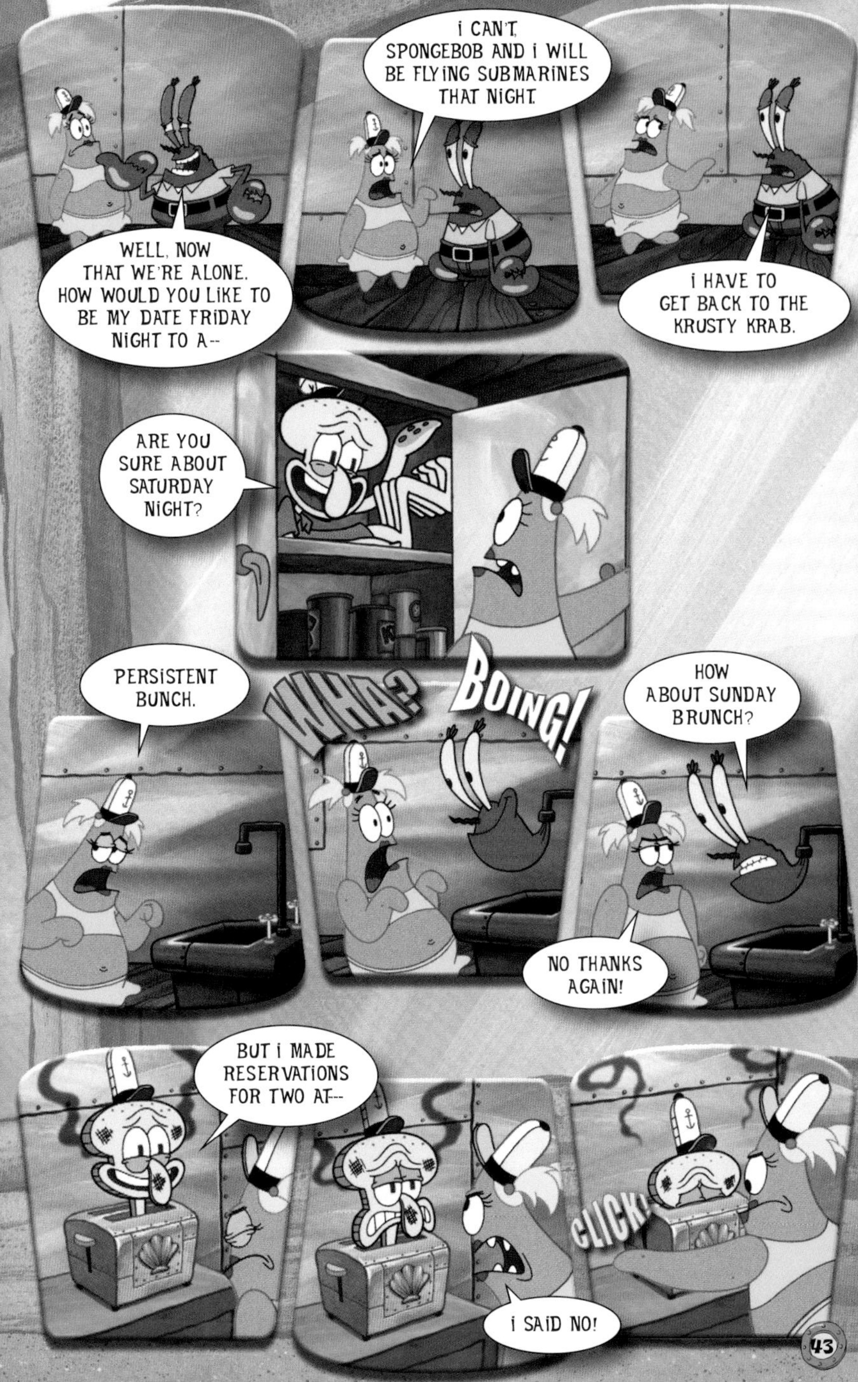
WELL, NOW THAT WE'RE ALONE. HOW WOULD YOU LIKE TO BE MY DATE FRIDAY NIGHT TO A--
I CAN'T. SPONGEBOB AND I WILL BE FLYING SUBMARINES THAT NIGHT.
I HAVE TO GET BACK TO THE KRUSTY KRAB.
ARE YOU SURE ABOUT SATURDAY NIGHT?
PERSISTENT BUNCH.
WHA?
BOING!
HOW ABOUT SUNDAY BRUNCH?
NO THANKS AGAIN!
BUT I MADE RESERVATIONS FOR TWO AT--
I SAID NO!
CLICK!

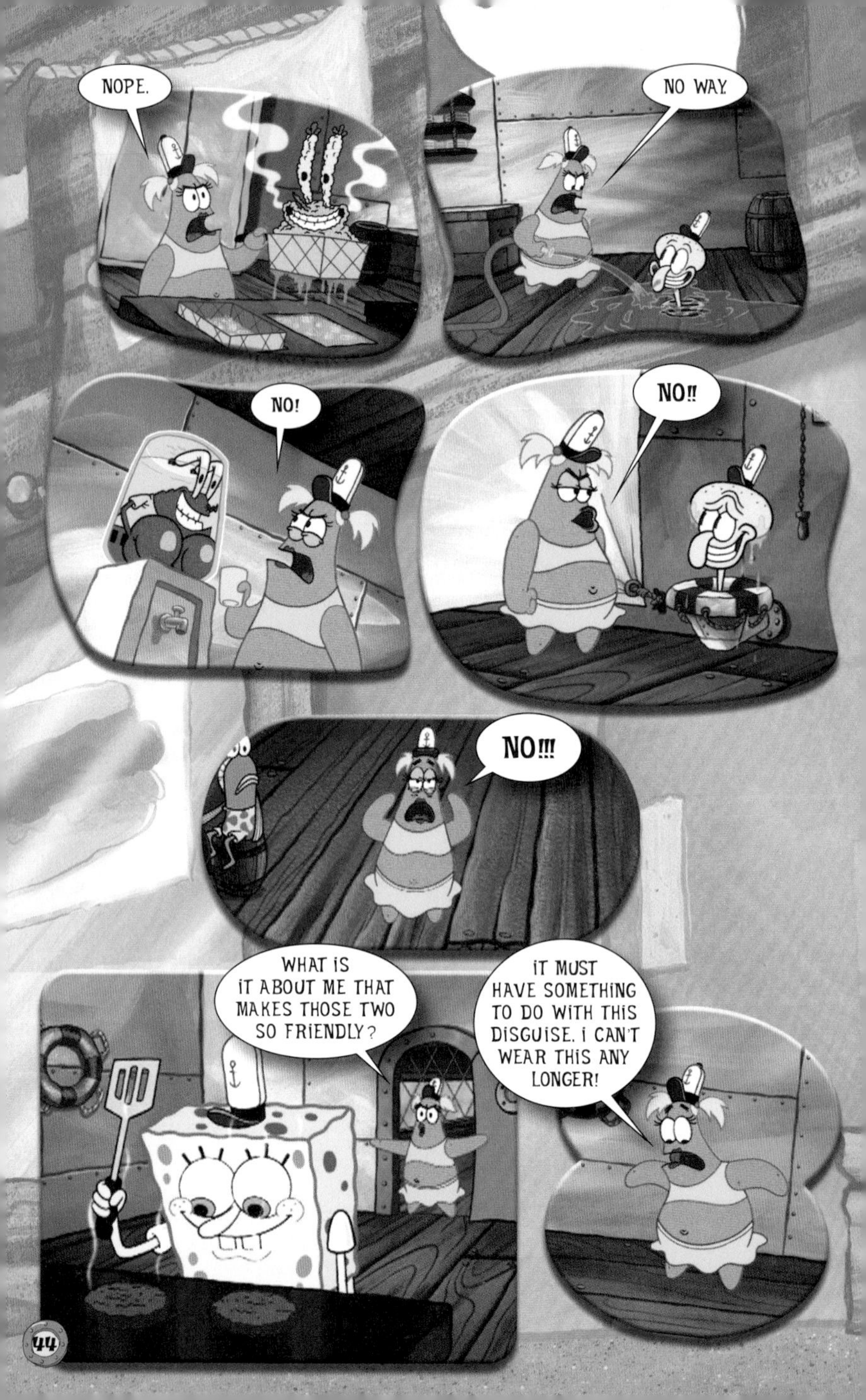
NOPE.
NO WAY.
NO!
NO!!
NO!!!
WHAT IS IT ABOUT ME THAT MAKES THOSE TWO SO FRIENDLY?
IT MUST HAVE SOMETHING TO DO WITH THIS DISGUISE. I CAN'T WEAR THIS ANY LONGER!

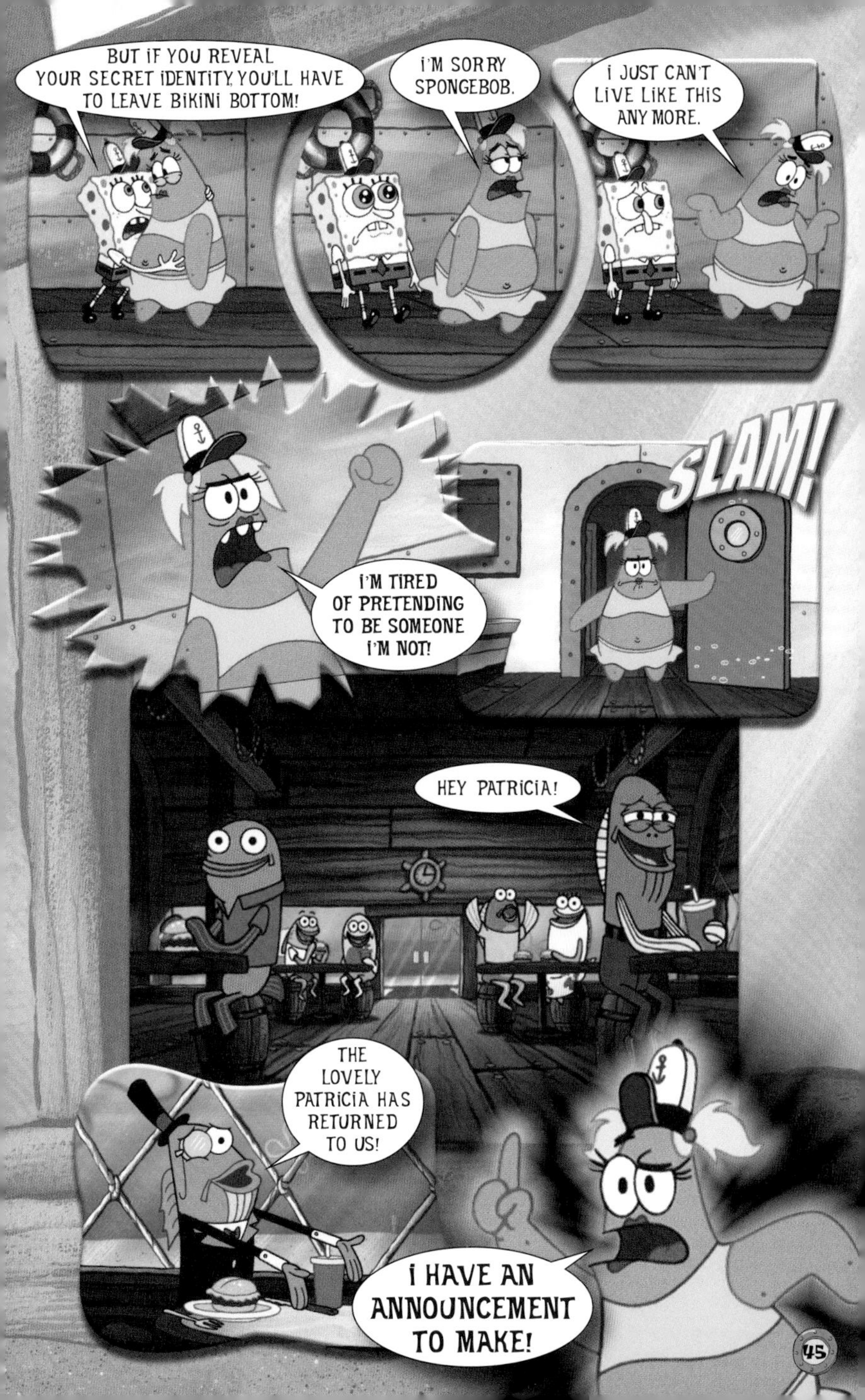
BUT IF YOU REVEAL YOUR SECRET IDENTITY, YOU'LL HAVE TO LEAVE BIKINI BOTTOM!
I'M SORRY SPONGEBOB.
I JUST CAN'T LIVE LIKE THIS ANY MORE.
I'M TIRED OF PRETENDING TO BE SOMEONE I'M NOT!
SLAM!
HEY PATRICIA!
THE LOVELY PATRICIA HAS RETURNED TO US!
I HAVE AN ANNOUNCEMENT TO MAKE!

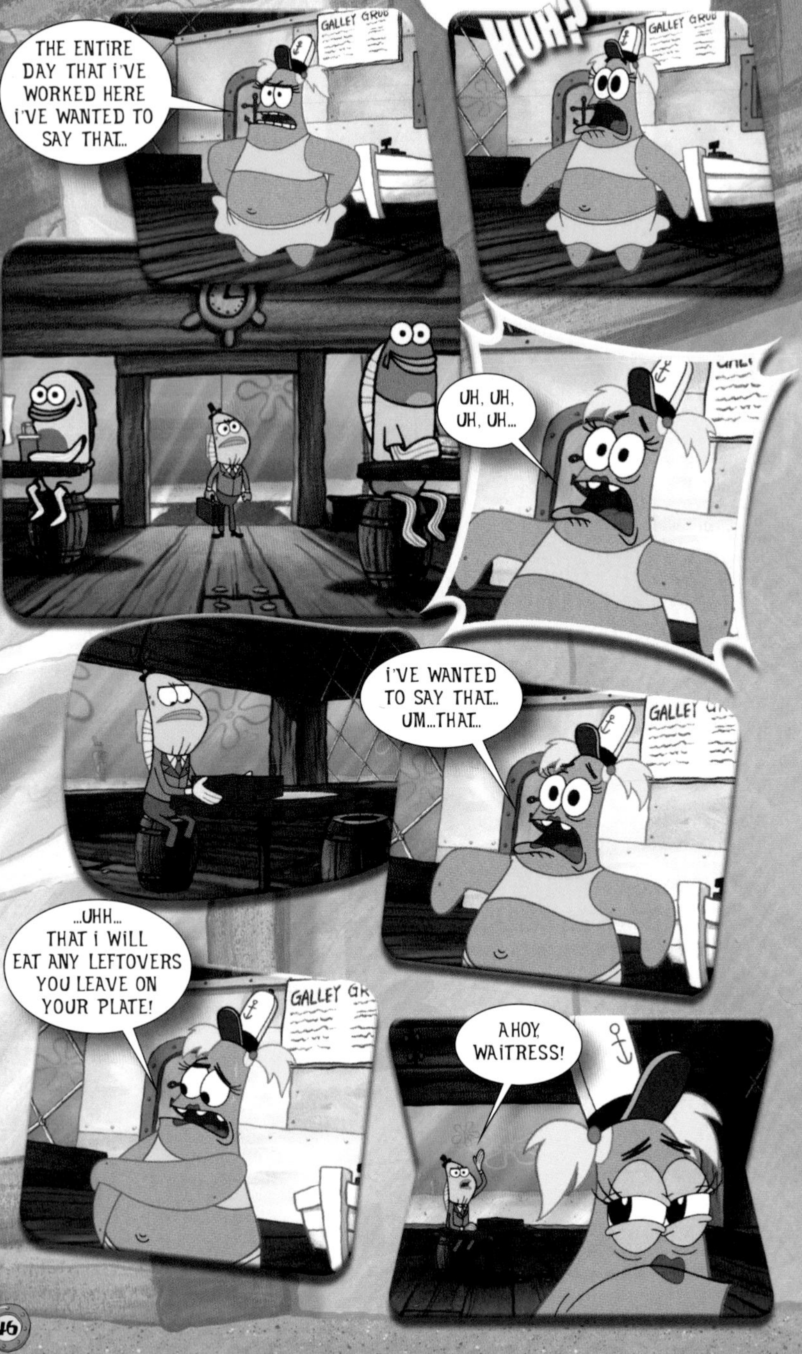
THE ENTIRE DAY THAT I'VE WORKED HERE I'VE WANTED TO SAY THAT...
GALLEY GRUB
HUH?
GALLEY GRUB
UH, UH, UH, UH...
I'VE WANTED TO SAY THAT... UM...THAT...
...UHH... THAT I WILL EAT ANY LEFTOVERS YOU LEAVE ON YOUR PLATE!
AHOY, WAITRESS!

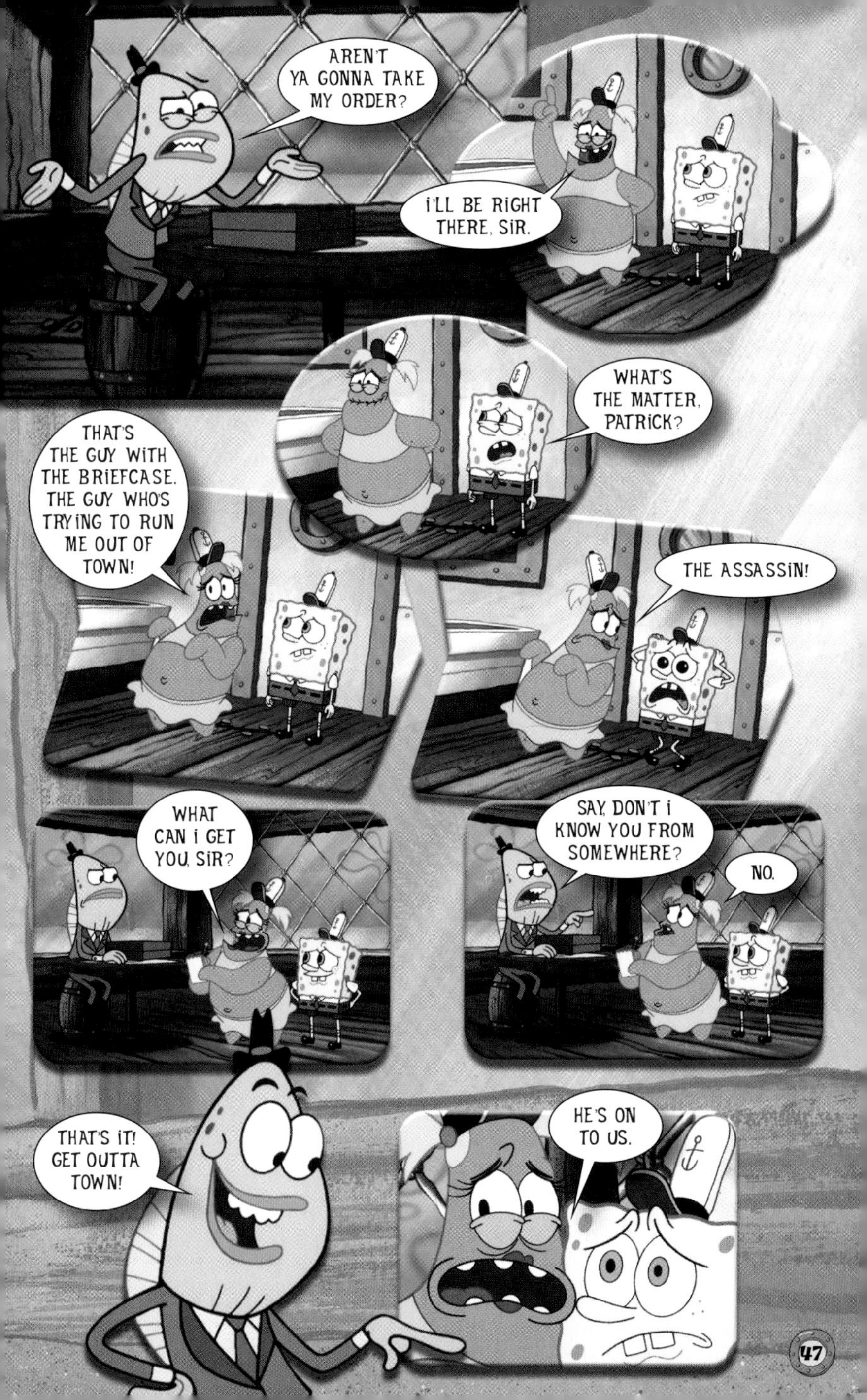

AREN'T YA GONNA TAKE MY ORDER?
I'LL BE RIGHT THERE, SIR.
WHAT'S THE MATTER, PATRICK?
THAT'S THE GUY WITH THE BRIEFCASE. THE GUY WHO'S TRYING TO RUN ME OUT OF TOWN!
THE ASSASSIN!
WHAT CAN I GET YOU, SIR?
SAY, DON'T I KNOW YOU FROM SOMEWHERE?
NO.
THAT'S IT! GET OUTTA TOWN!
HE'S ON TO US.

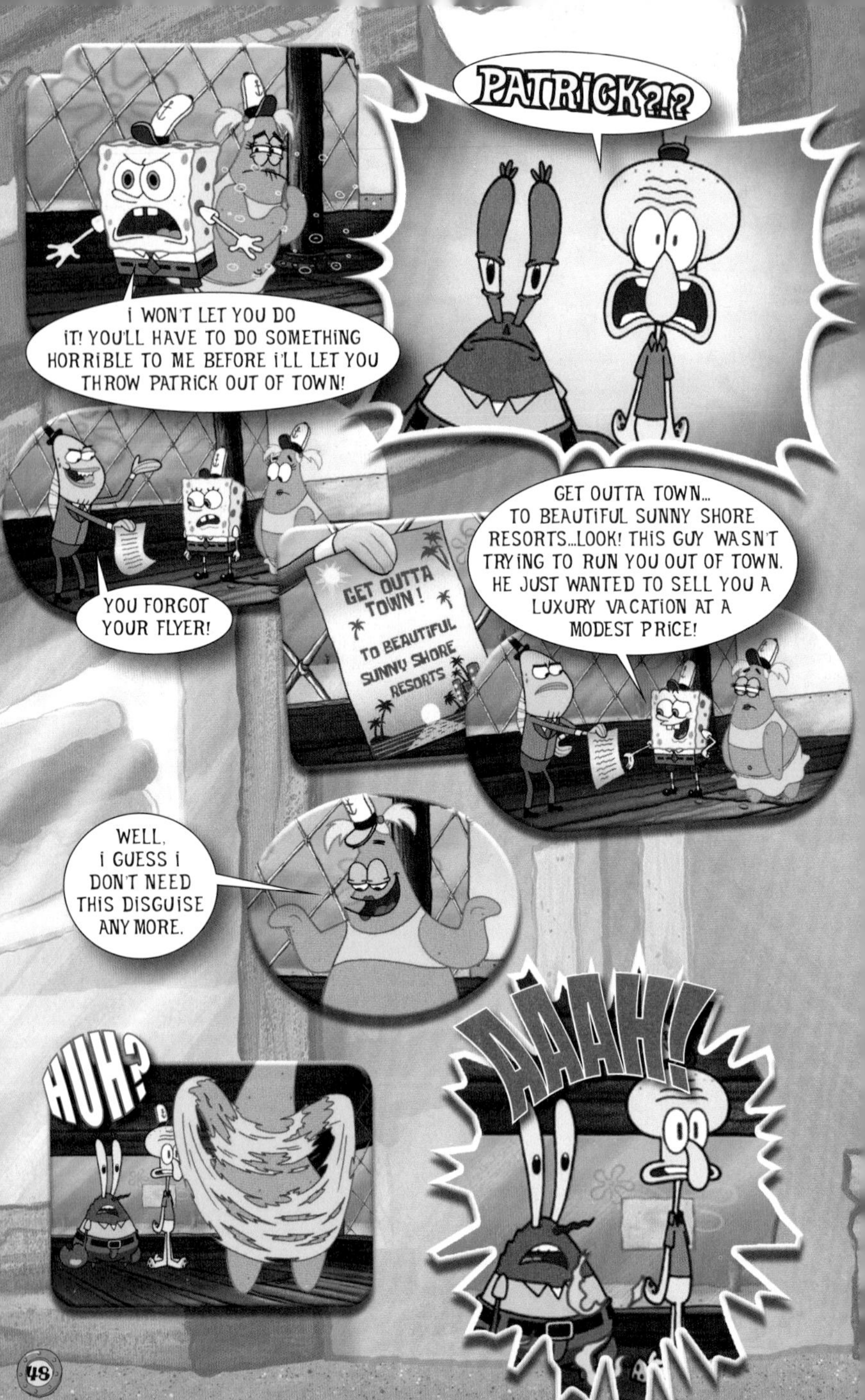
PATRICK?!?
I WON'T LET YOU DO IT! YOU'LL HAVE TO DO SOMETHING HORRIBLE TO ME BEFORE I'LL LET YOU THROW PATRICK OUT OF TOWN!
YOU FORGOT YOUR FLYER!
GET OUTTA TOWN! TO BEAUTIFUL SUNNY SHORE RESORTS
GET OUTTA TOWN... TO BEAUTIFUL SUNNY SHORE RESORTS...LOOK! THIS GUY WASN'T TRYING TO RUN YOU OUT OF TOWN. HE JUST WANTED TO SELL YOU A LUXURY VACATION AT A MODEST PRICE!
WELL, I GUESS I DON'T NEED THIS DISGUISE ANY MORE.
HUH?
AAAH!

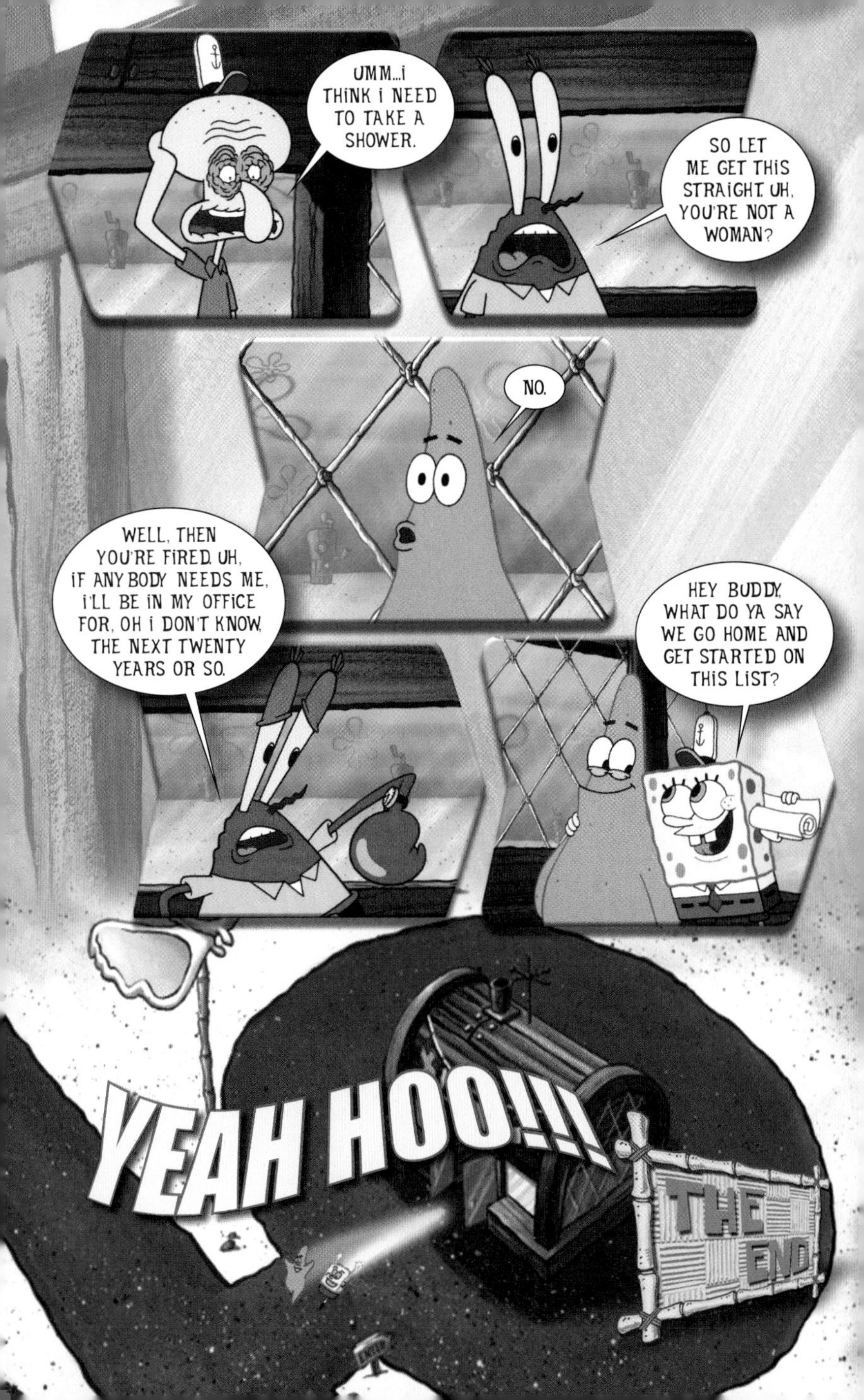
UMM...I THINK I NEED TO TAKE A SHOWER.
SO LET ME GET THIS STRAIGHT. UH, YOU'RE NOT A WOMAN?
NO.
WELL, THEN YOU'RE FIRED. UH, IF ANYBODY NEEDS ME, I'LL BE IN MY OFFICE FOR, OH I DON'T KNOW, THE NEXT TWENTY YEARS OR SO.
HEY BUDDY, WHAT DO YA SAY WE GO HOME AND GET STARTED ON THIS LIST?
YEAH HOO!!!
THE END

NICKELODEON

SpongeBob SquarePants

The Thing

By Paul Tibbitt, Kent Osborne and Joe Liss

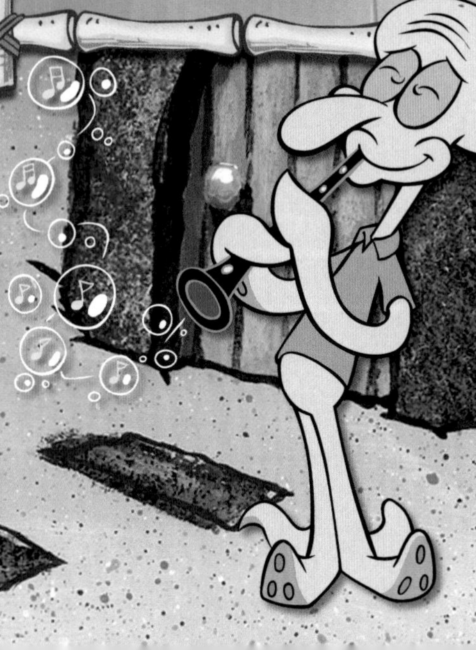

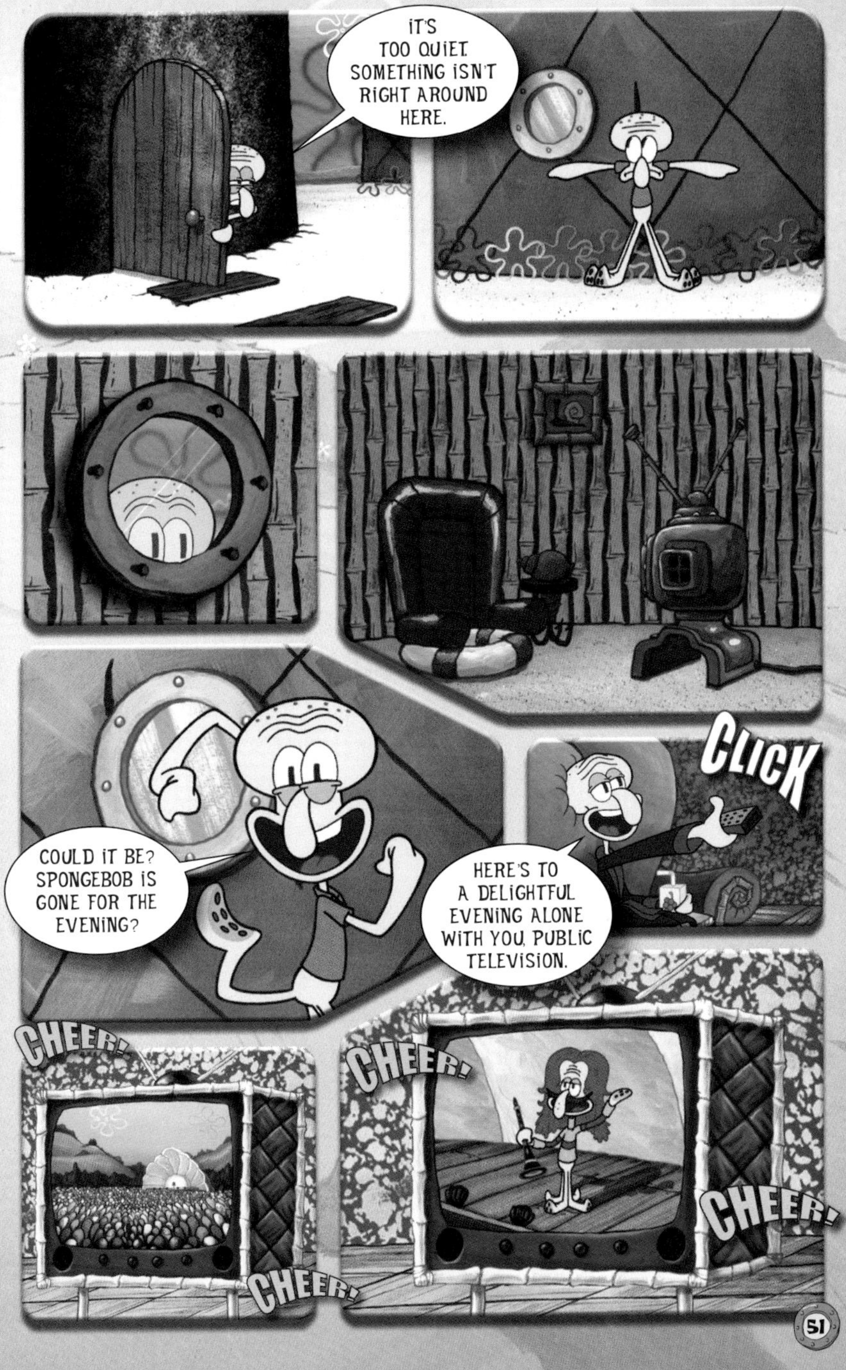
IT'S TOO QUIET. SOMETHING ISN'T RIGHT AROUND HERE.
COULD IT BE? SPONGEBOB IS GONE FOR THE EVENING?
CLICK
HERE'S TO A DELIGHTFUL EVENING ALONE WITH YOU, PUBLIC TELEVISION.
CHEER!
CHEER!
CHEER!
CHEER!

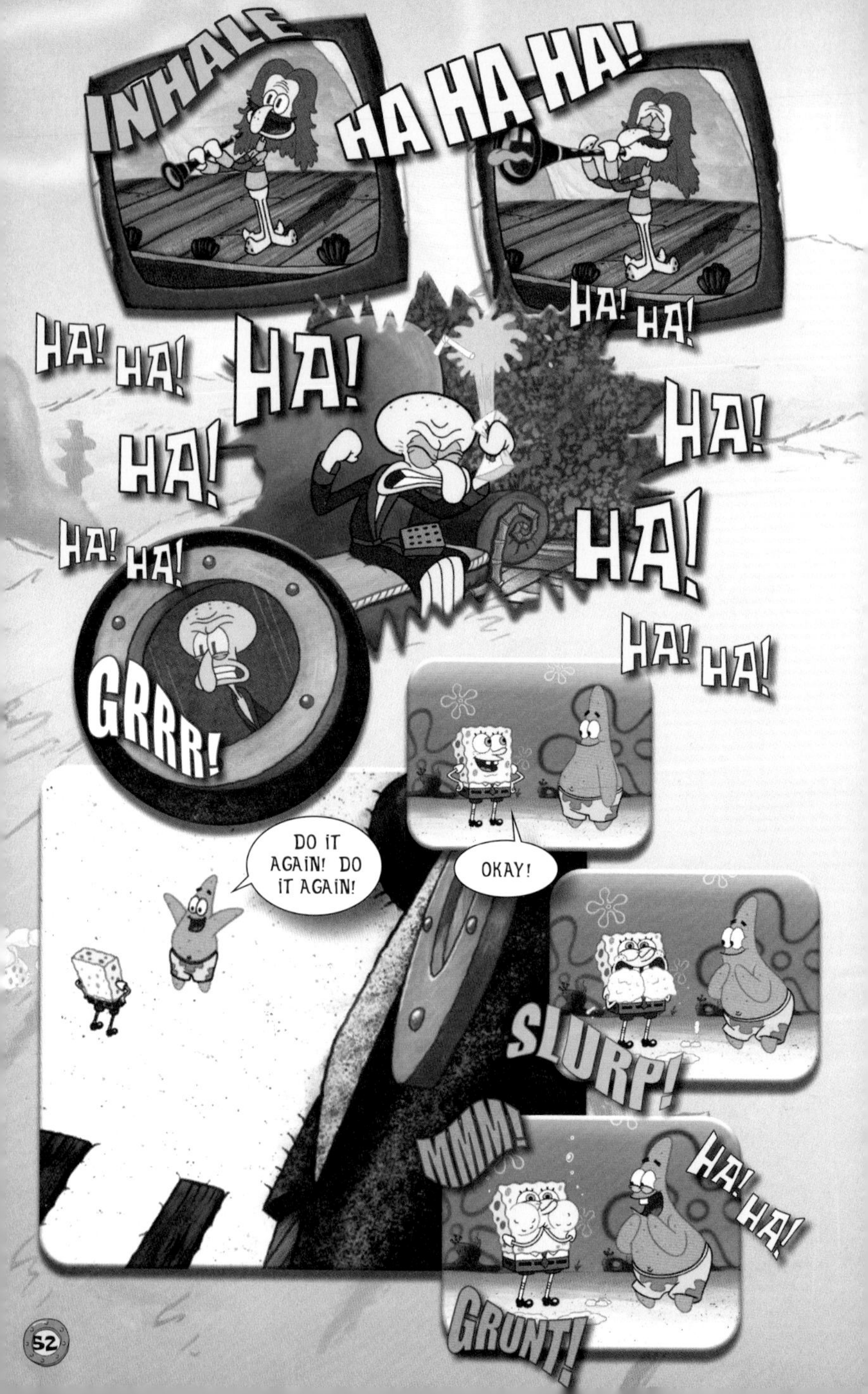
INHALE
HA HA HA HA!
HA! HA!
HA! HA!
HA!
HA!
HA! HA!
HA!
HA!
HA! HA!
GRRRR!
DO IT AGAIN! DO IT AGAIN!
OKAY!
SLURP!
MMM!
HA! HA!
GRUNT!

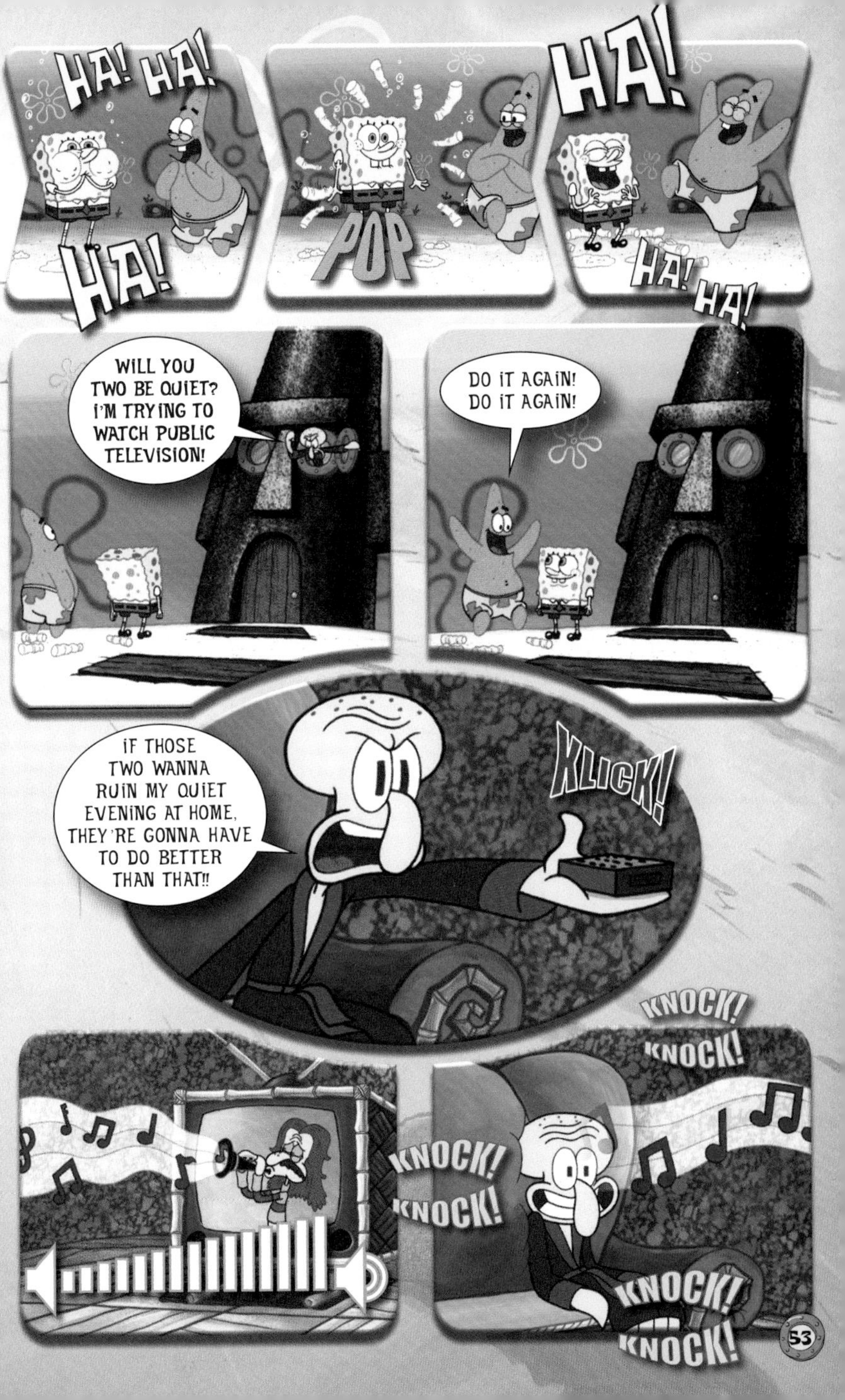
HA! HA!
HA!
POP
HA!
HA! HA!
WILL YOU TWO BE QUIET? I'M TRYING TO WATCH PUBLIC TELEVISION!
DO IT AGAIN! DO IT AGAIN!
IF THOSE TWO WANNA RUIN MY QUIET EVENING AT HOME, THEY'RE GONNA HAVE TO DO BETTER THAN THAT!!
KLICK!
KNOCK! KNOCK!
KNOCK! KNOCK!
KNOCK! KNOCK!

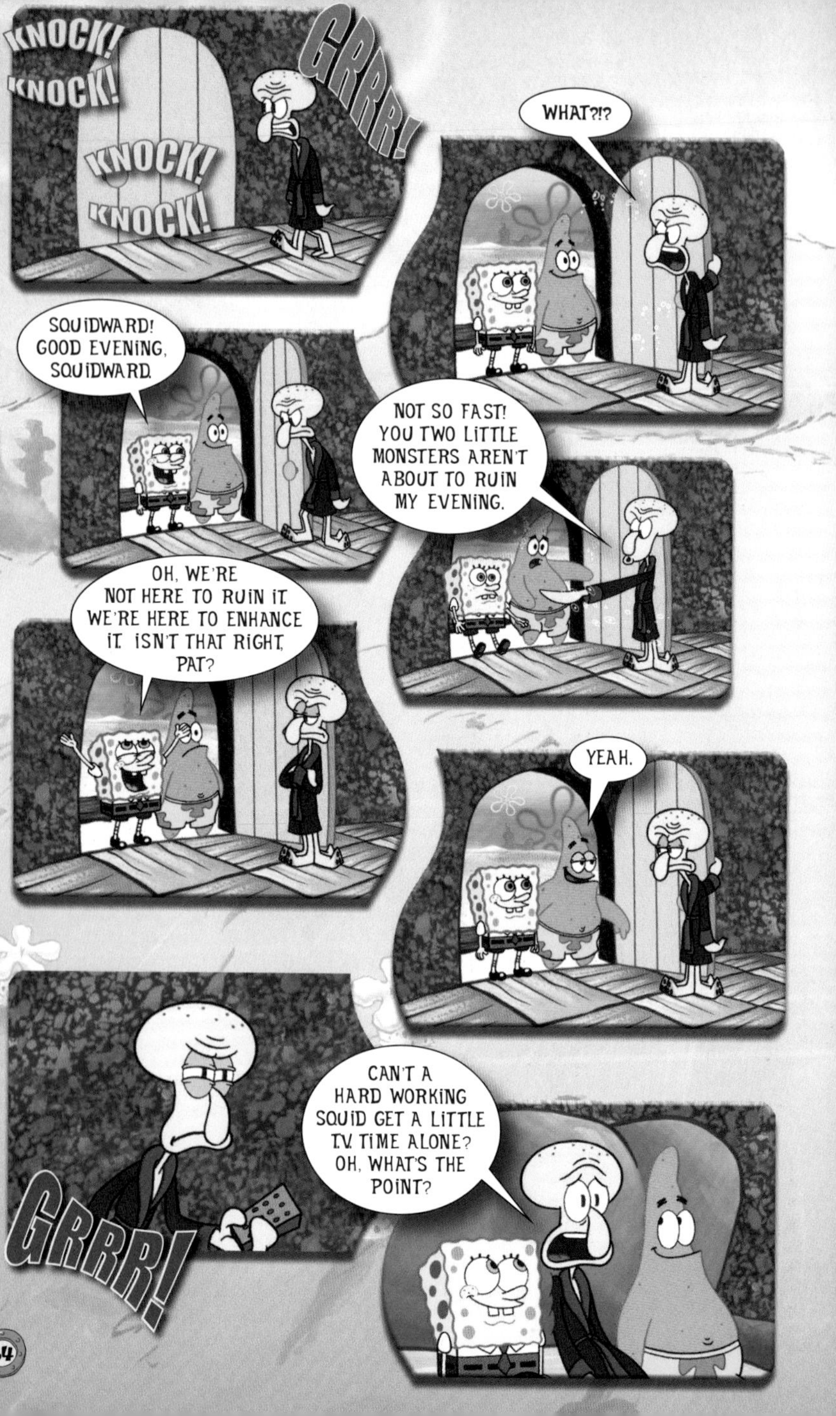
KNOCK!
KNOCK!
KNOCK!
KNOCK!
GRRR!
WHAT?!?
SQUIDWARD! GOOD EVENING, SQUIDWARD.
NOT SO FAST! YOU TWO LITTLE MONSTERS AREN'T ABOUT TO RUIN MY EVENING.
OH, WE'RE NOT HERE TO RUIN IT. WE'RE HERE TO ENHANCE IT. ISN'T THAT RIGHT, PAT?
YEAH.
GRRR!
CAN'T A HARD WORKING SQUID GET A LITTLE T.V. TIME ALONE? OH, WHAT'S THE POINT?

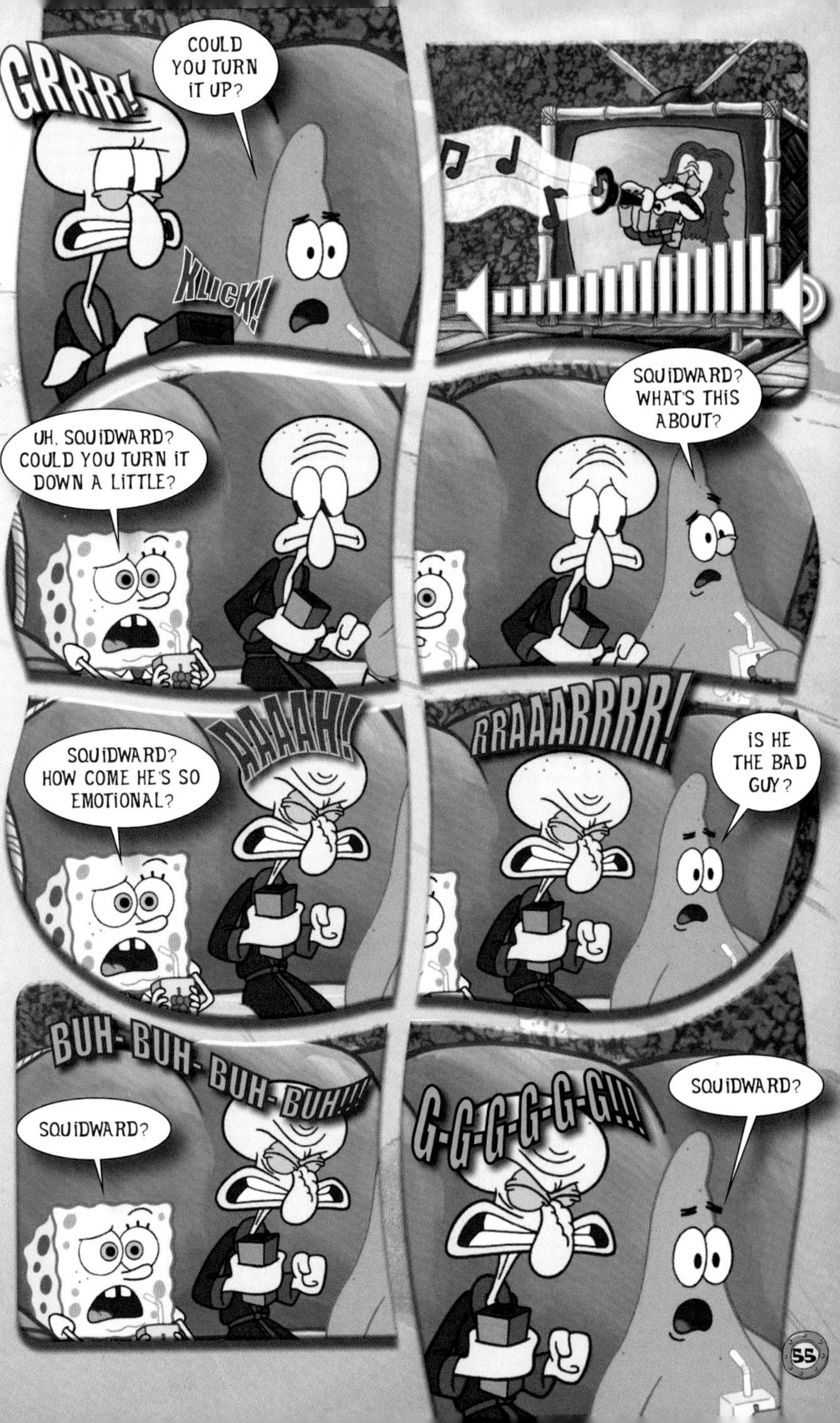
GRRR!
COULD YOU TURN IT UP?
KLICK!
UH, SQUIDWARD? COULD YOU TURN IT DOWN A LITTLE?
SQUIDWARD? WHAT'S THIS ABOUT?
AAAAH!
SQUIDWARD? HOW COME HE'S SO EMOTIONAL?
RRAAARRRR!
IS HE THE BAD GUY?
BUH-BUH-BUH-BUH!!!
SQUIDWARD?
G-G-G-G-G-G!!!
SQUIDWARD?

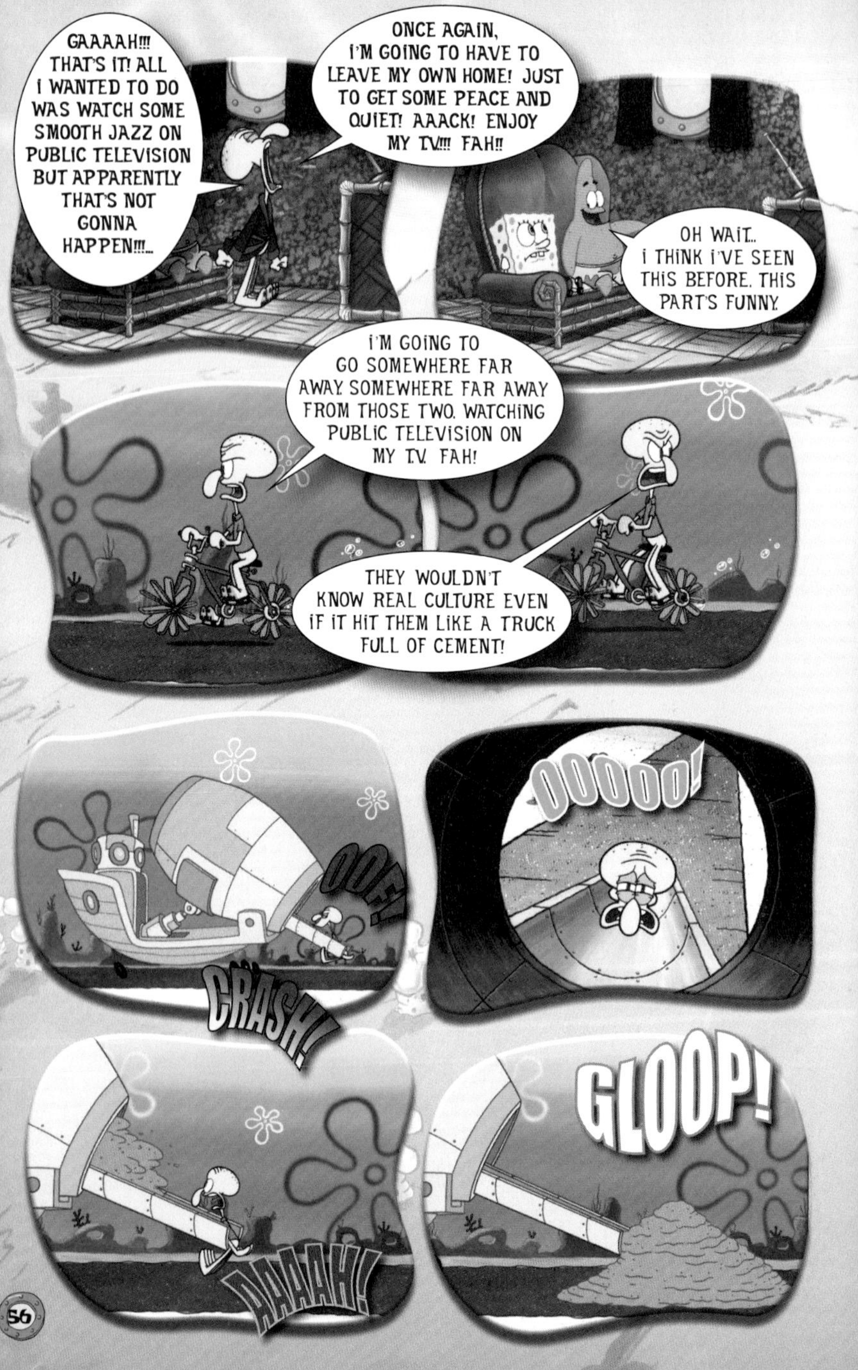
GAAAAH!!! THAT'S IT! ALL I WANTED TO DO WAS WATCH SOME SMOOTH JAZZ ON PUBLIC TELEVISION BUT APPARENTLY THAT'S NOT GONNA HAPPEN!!!...
ONCE AGAIN, I'M GOING TO HAVE TO LEAVE MY OWN HOME! JUST TO GET SOME PEACE AND QUIET! AAACK! ENJOY MY T.V.!!! FAH!!
OH WAIT... I THINK I'VE SEEN THIS BEFORE. THIS PART'S FUNNY.
I'M GOING TO GO SOMEWHERE FAR AWAY. SOMEWHERE FAR AWAY FROM THOSE TWO. WATCHING PUBLIC TELEVISION ON MY T.V. FAH!
THEY WOULDN'T KNOW REAL CULTURE EVEN IF IT HIT THEM LIKE A TRUCK FULL OF CEMENT!
OOF!
CRASH!
OOOOO!
AAAAH!
GLOOP!

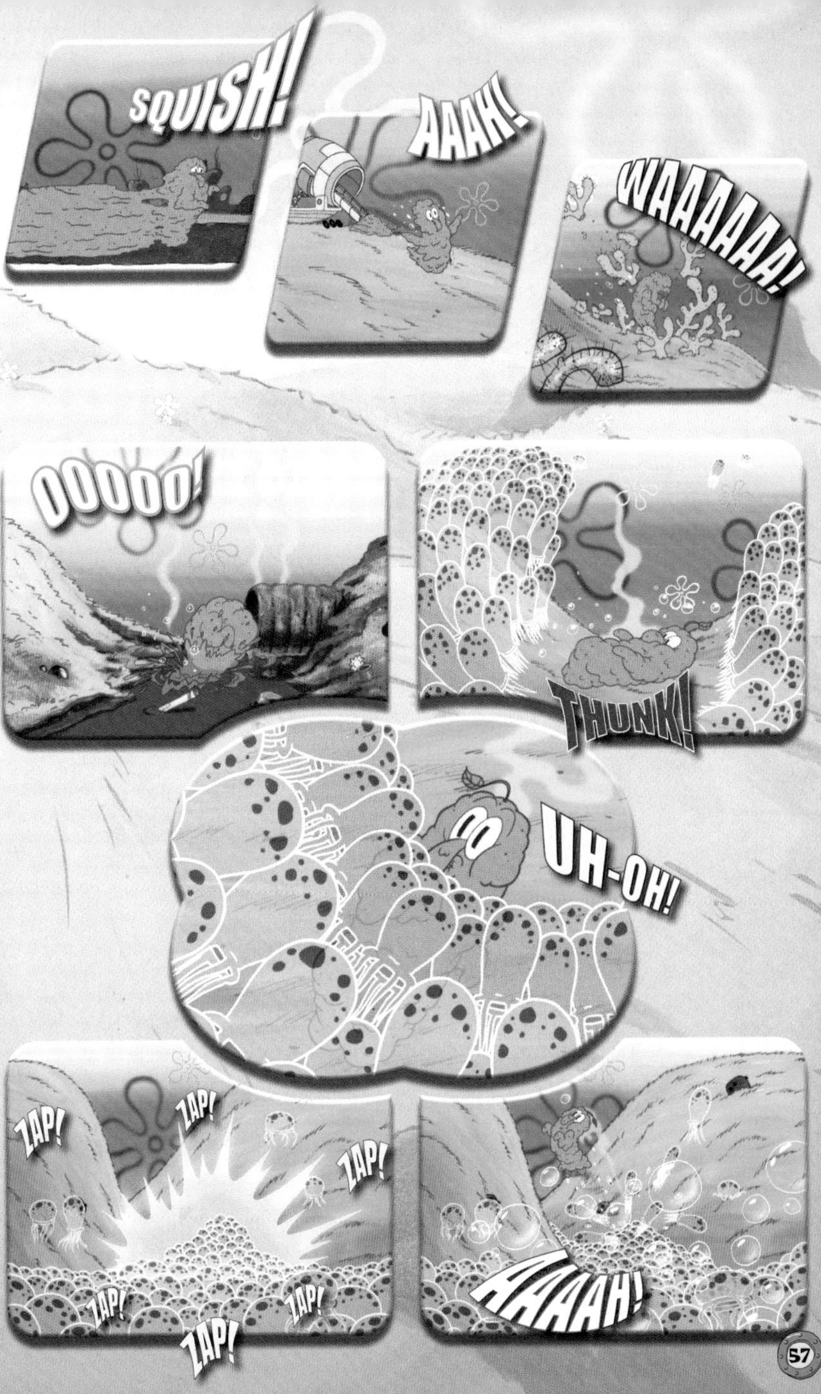
SQUISH!
AAAH!
WAAAAAA!
OOOOO!
THUNK!
UH-OH!
ZAP!
ZAP!
ZAP!
ZAP!
ZAP!
ZAP!
AAAAH!

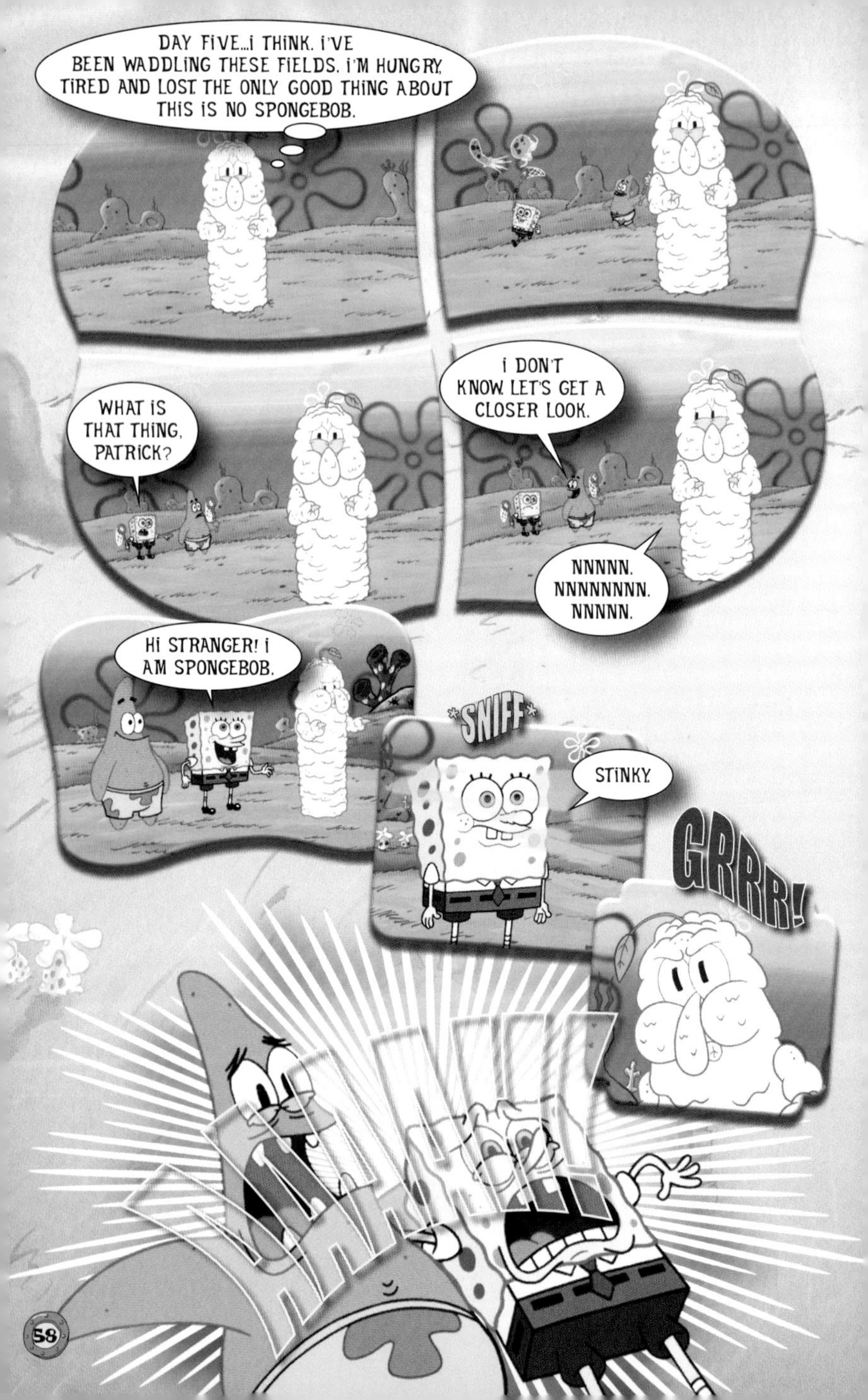
DAY FIVE...I THINK. I'VE BEEN WADDLING THESE FIELDS. I'M HUNGRY, TIRED AND LOST. THE ONLY GOOD THING ABOUT THIS IS NO SPONGEBOB.
WHAT IS THAT THING, PATRICK?
I DON'T KNOW. LET'S GET A CLOSER LOOK.
NNNNN. NNNNNNNN. NNNNN.
HI STRANGER! I AM SPONGEBOB.
SNIFF
STINKY.
GRRR!

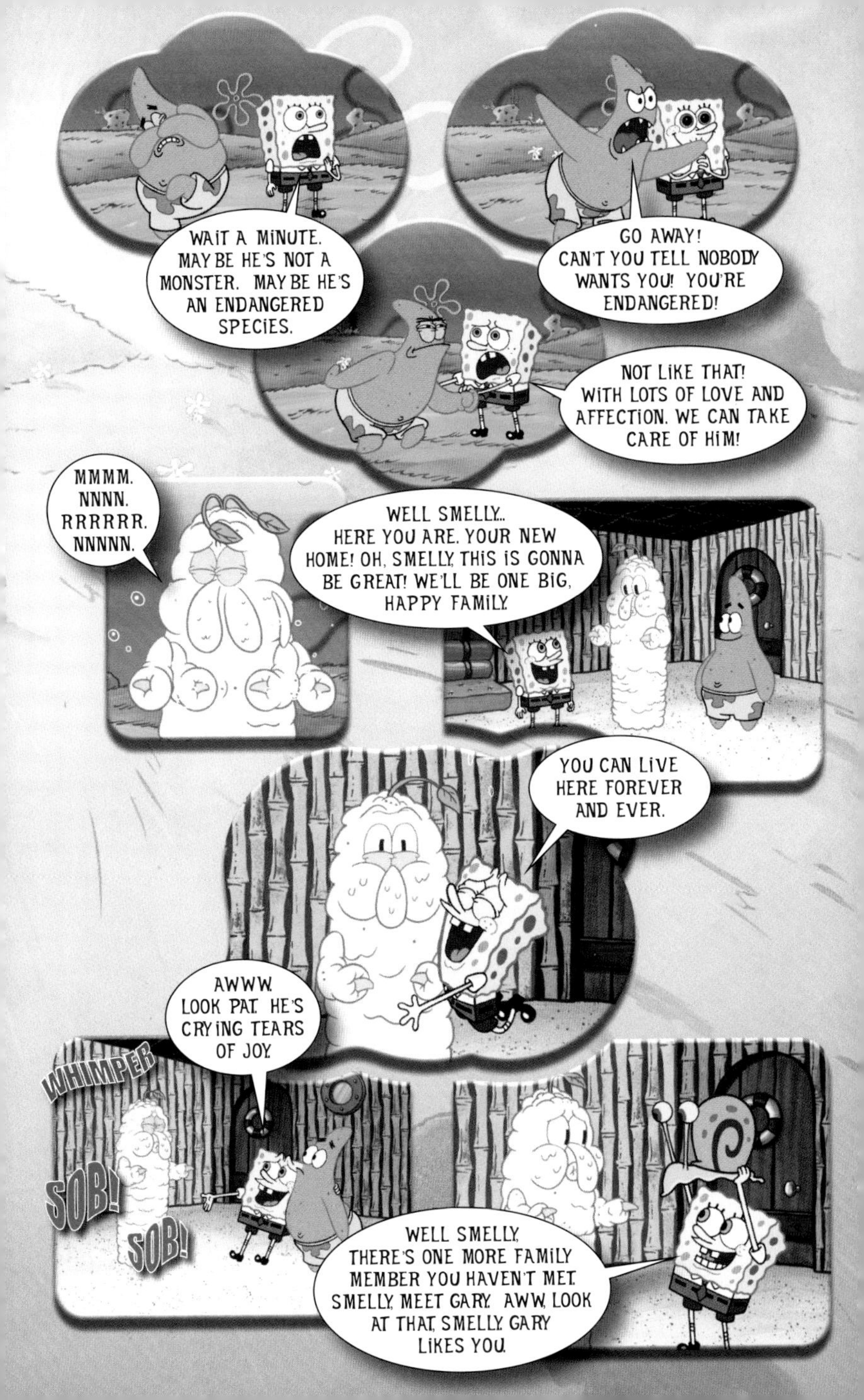
WAIT A MINUTE. MAYBE HE'S NOT A MONSTER. MAYBE HE'S AN ENDANGERED SPECIES.
GO AWAY! CAN'T YOU TELL NOBODY WANTS YOU! YOU'RE ENDANGERED!
NOT LIKE THAT! WITH LOTS OF LOVE AND AFFECTION. WE CAN TAKE CARE OF HIM!
MMMM. NNNN. RRRRRR. NNNNN.
WELL SMELLY... HERE YOU ARE. YOUR NEW HOME! OH, SMELLY, THIS IS GONNA BE GREAT! WE'LL BE ONE BIG, HAPPY FAMILY.
YOU CAN LIVE HERE FOREVER AND EVER.
AWWW. LOOK PAT. HE'S CRYING TEARS OF JOY.
WHIMPER
SOB!
SOB!
WELL SMELLY, THERE'S ONE MORE FAMILY MEMBER YOU HAVEN'T MET. SMELLY, MEET GARY. AWW, LOOK AT THAT, SMELLY. GARY LIKES YOU.

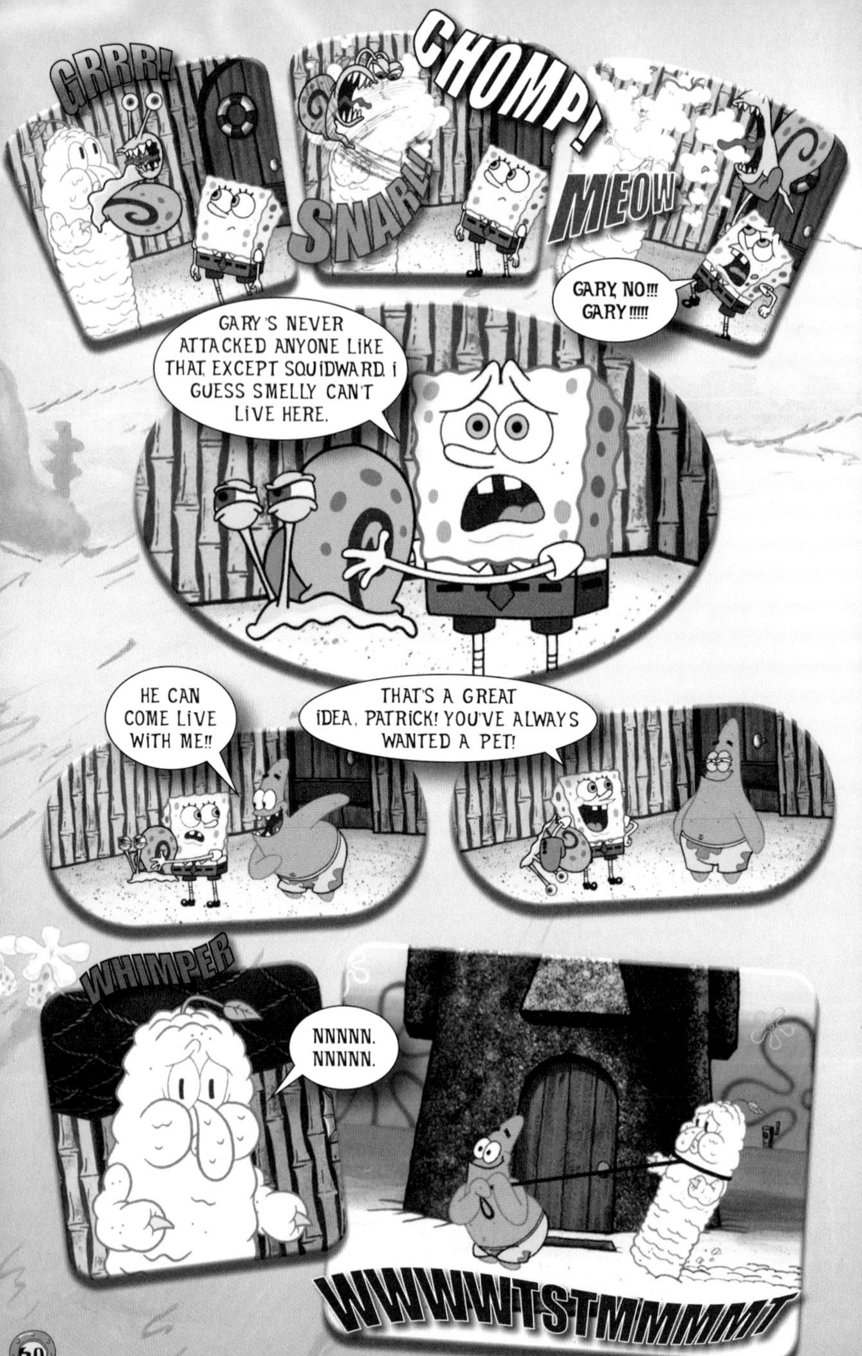
GRRR!
CHOMP!
SNARL!
MEOW
GARY, NO!!! GARY!!!!!
GARY'S NEVER ATTACKED ANYONE LIKE THAT, EXCEPT SQUIDWARD. I GUESS SMELLY CAN'T LIVE HERE.
HE CAN COME LIVE WITH ME!!
THAT'S A GREAT IDEA, PATRICK! YOU'VE ALWAYS WANTED A PET!
WHIMPER
NNNNN. NNNNN.
WWWWWTSTMMMMMT

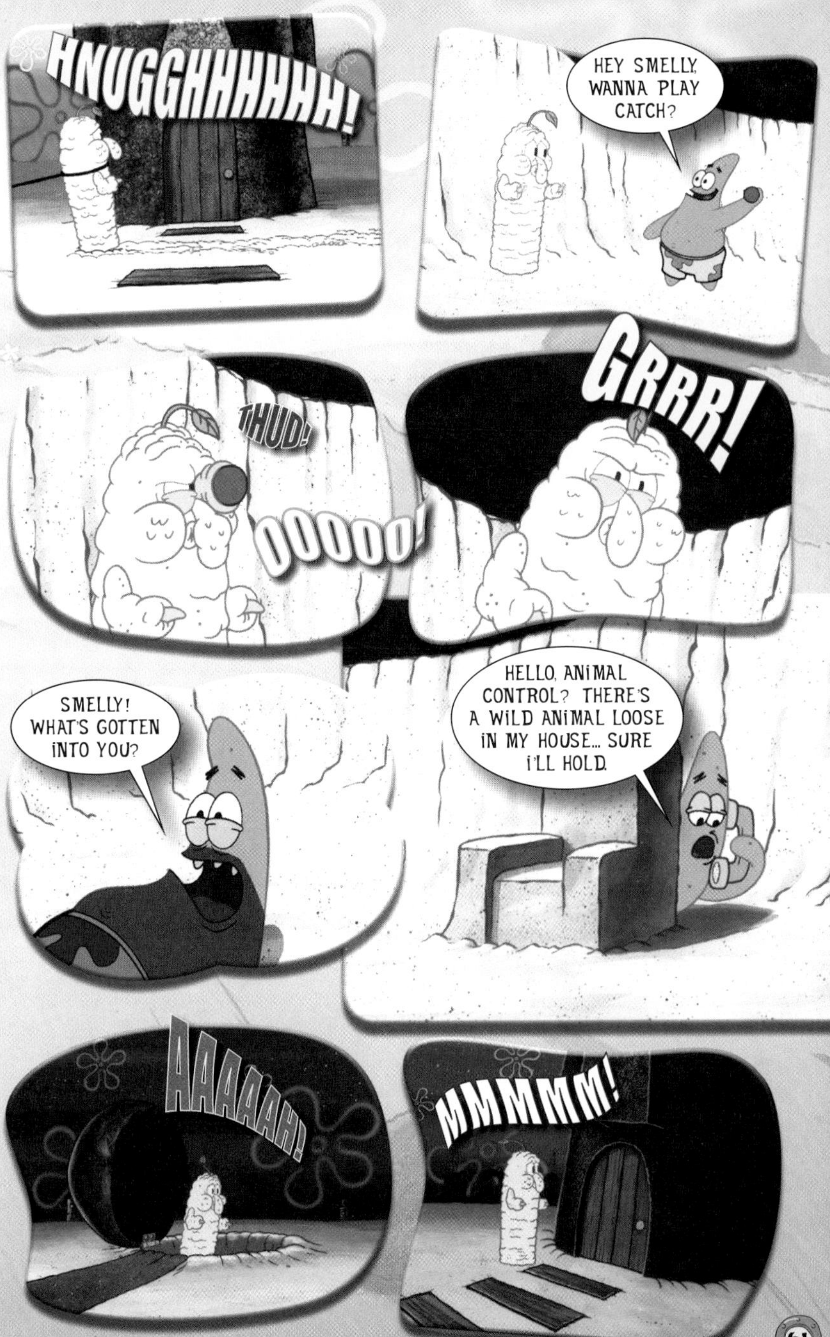
HNUGGHHHHHH!
HEY SMELLY, WANNA PLAY CATCH?
THUD!
OOOOOO!
GRRR!
SMELLY! WHAT'S GOTTEN INTO YOU?
HELLO, ANIMAL CONTROL? THERE'S A WILD ANIMAL LOOSE IN MY HOUSE... SURE I'LL HOLD.
AAAAAH!
MMMMMM!

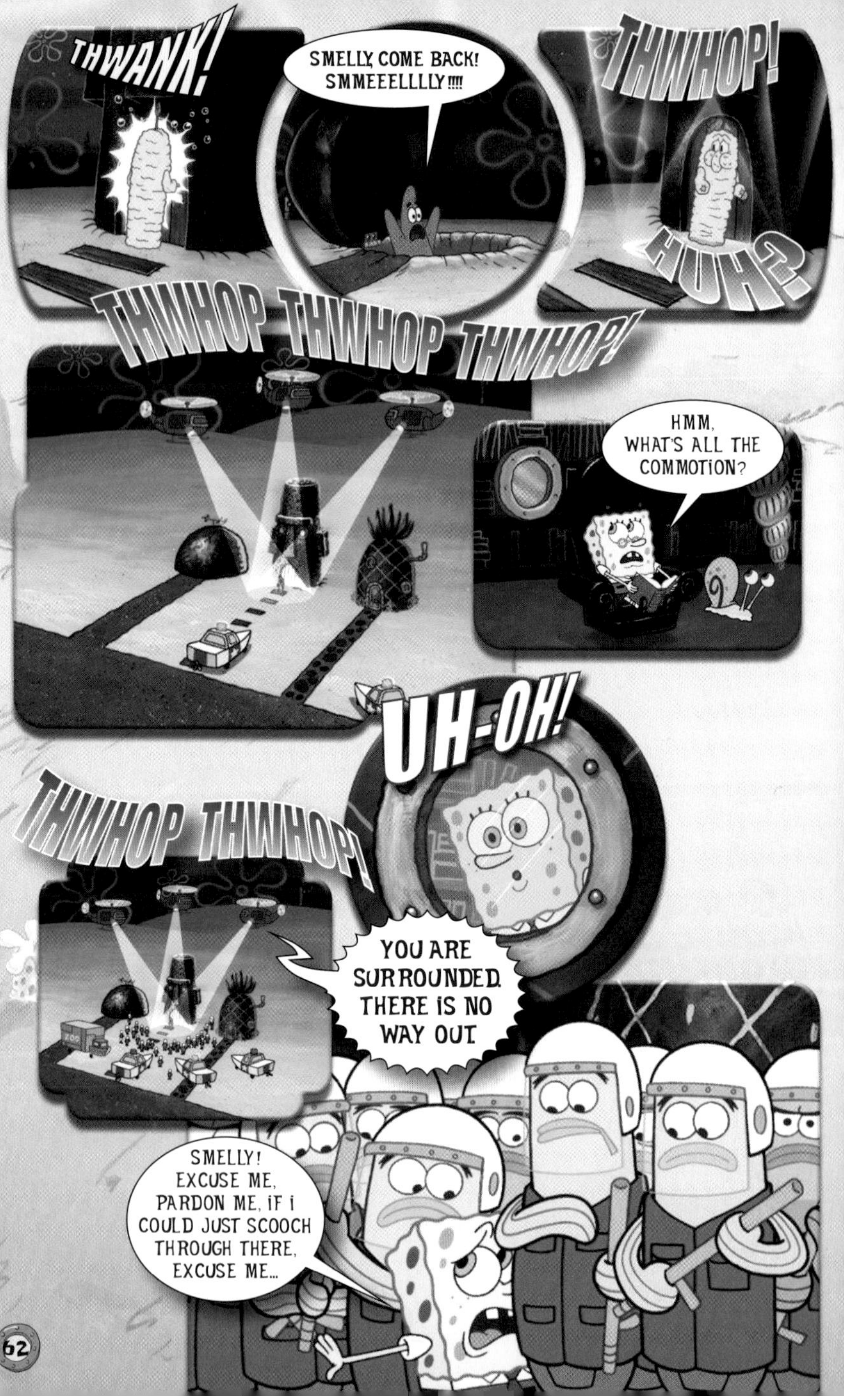
THWANK!
SMELLY, COME BACK! SMMEEELLLLY!!!!
THWHOP!
HUH?
THWHOP THWHOP THWHOP!
HMM, WHAT'S ALL THE COMMOTION?
UH-OH!
THWHOP THWHOP!
YOU ARE SURROUNDED. THERE IS NO WAY OUT.
SMELLY! EXCUSE ME, PARDON ME, IF I COULD JUST SCOOCH THROUGH THERE, EXCUSE ME...

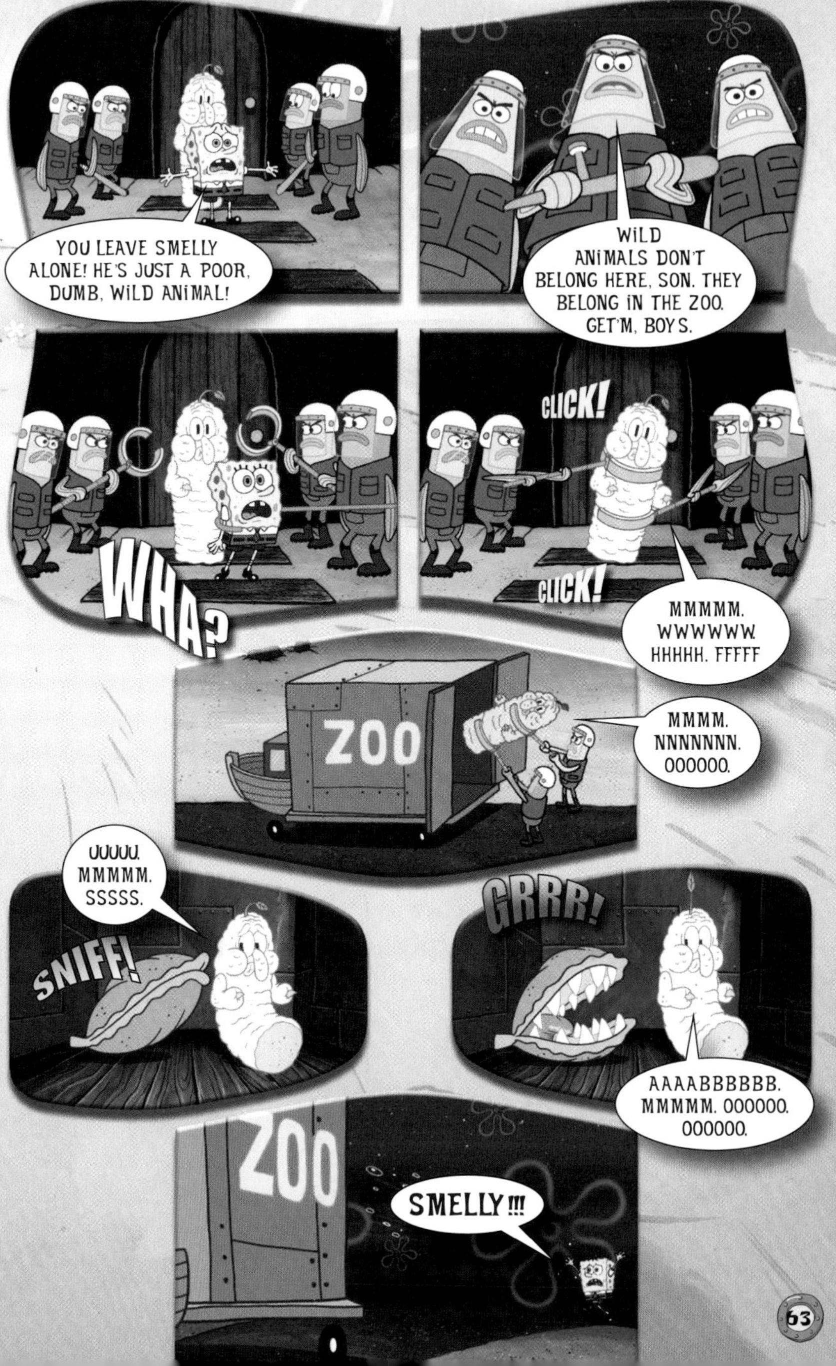

YOU LEAVE SMELLY ALONE! HE'S JUST A POOR, DUMB, WILD ANIMAL!
WILD ANIMALS DON'T BELONG HERE, SON. THEY BELONG IN THE ZOO. GET'M, BOYS.
WHA?
CLICK!
CLICK!
MMMMM. WWWWWW. HHHHH. FFFFF
ZOO
MMMM. NNNNNNN. OOOOOO.
UUUUU. MMMMM. SSSSS.
SNIFF!
GRRR!
AAAABBBBBB. MMMMM. OOOOOO. OOOOOO.
ZOO
SMELLY!!!

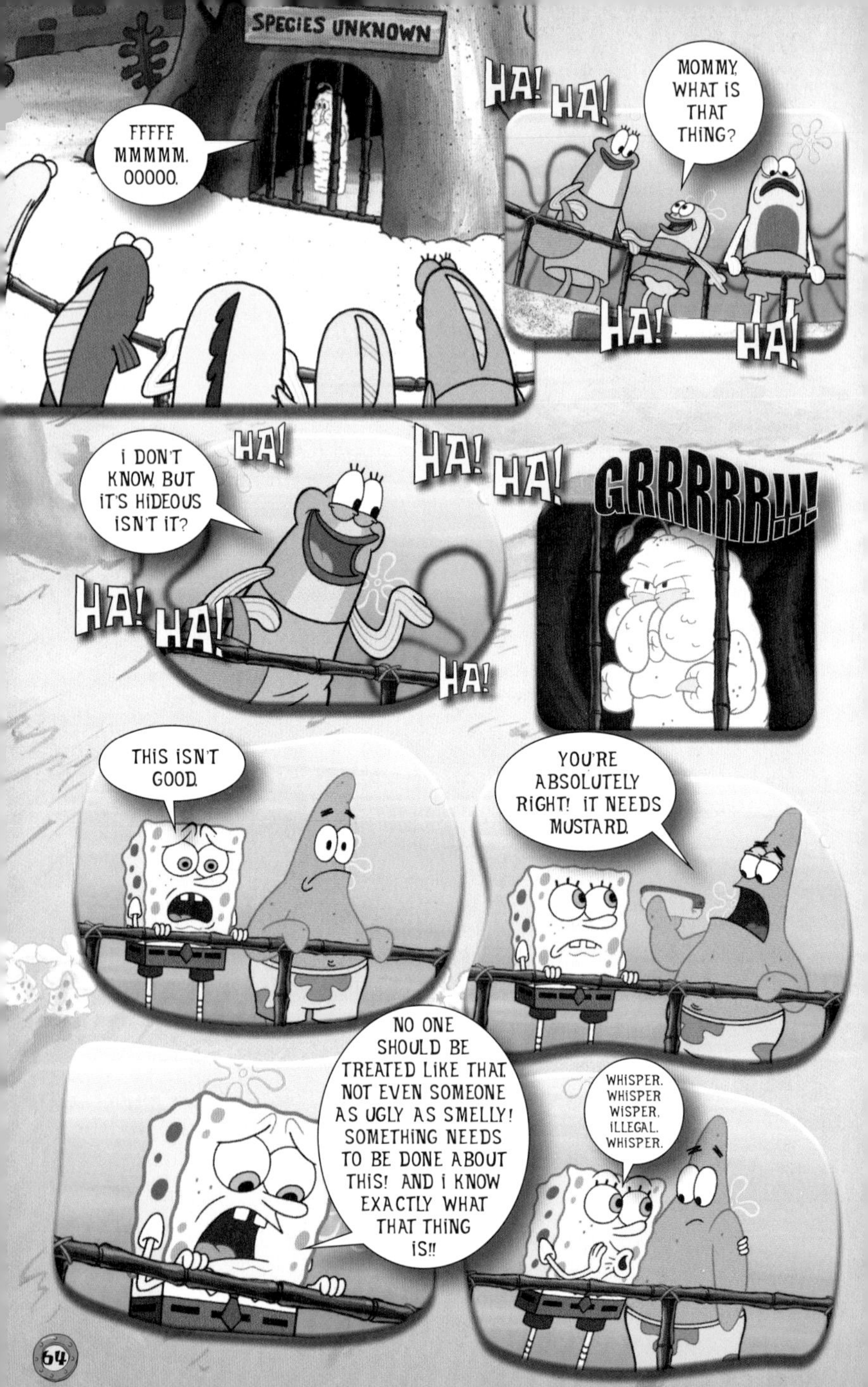
SPECIES UNKNOWN
FFFFF. MMMMM. OOOOO.
HA! HA!
MOMMY, WHAT IS THAT THING?
HA! HA!
HA!
I DON'T KNOW, BUT IT'S HIDEOUS ISN'T IT?
HA! HA!
HA! HA!
HA!
GRRRRR!!!
THIS ISN'T GOOD.
YOU'RE ABSOLUTELY RIGHT! IT NEEDS MUSTARD.
NO ONE SHOULD BE TREATED LIKE THAT. NOT EVEN SOMEONE AS UGLY AS SMELLY! SOMETHING NEEDS TO BE DONE ABOUT THIS! AND I KNOW EXACTLY WHAT THAT THING IS!!
WHISPER. WHISPER WISPER. ILLEGAL. WHISPER.

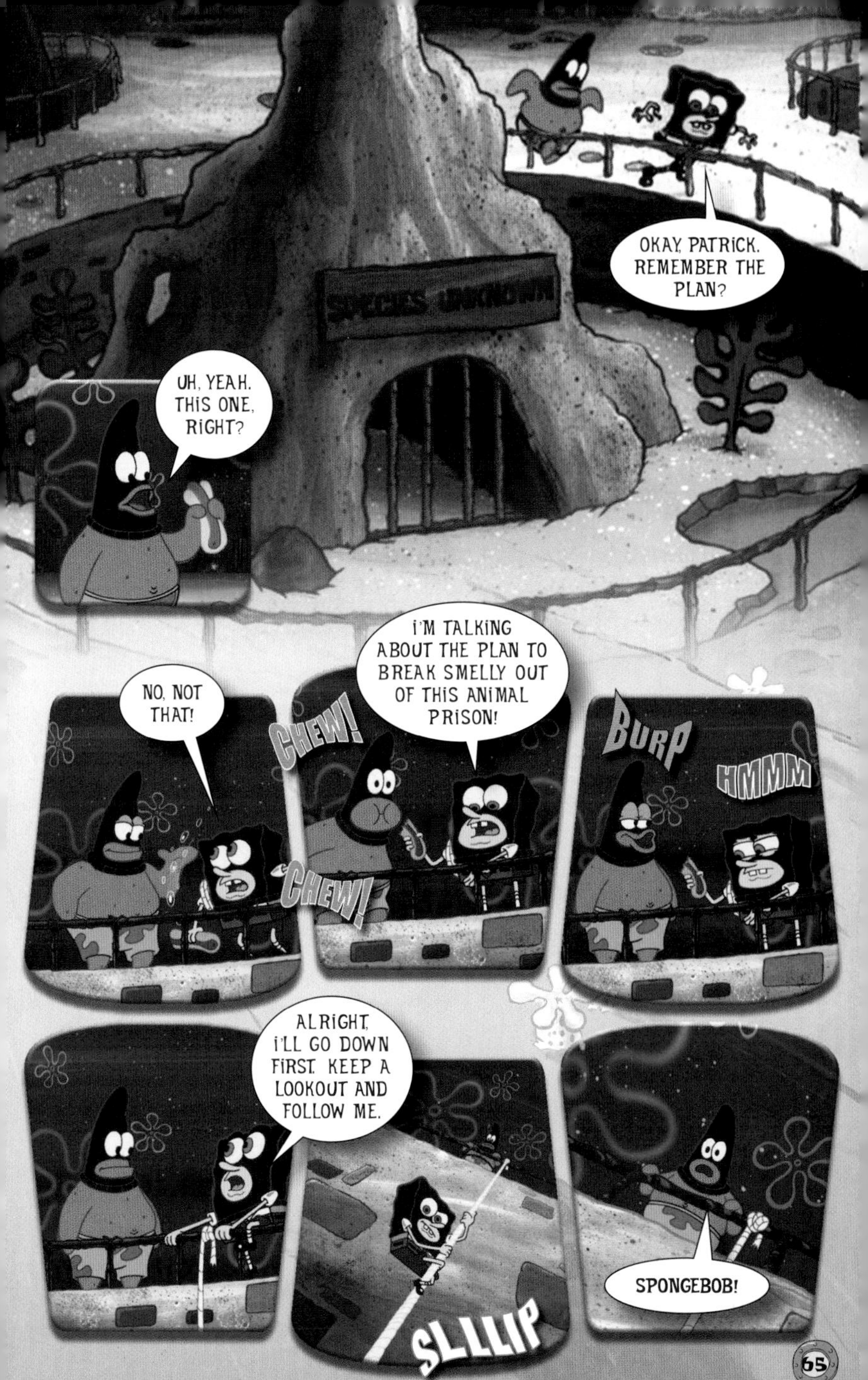

SPECIES UNKNOWN
OKAY, PATRICK. REMEMBER THE PLAN?
UH, YEAH. THIS ONE, RIGHT?
NO, NOT THAT!
CHEW!
I'M TALKING ABOUT THE PLAN TO BREAK SMELLY OUT OF THIS ANIMAL PRISON!
CHEW!
BURP
HMMM
ALRIGHT, I'LL GO DOWN FIRST. KEEP A LOOKOUT AND FOLLOW ME.
SLLLIP
SPONGEBOB!

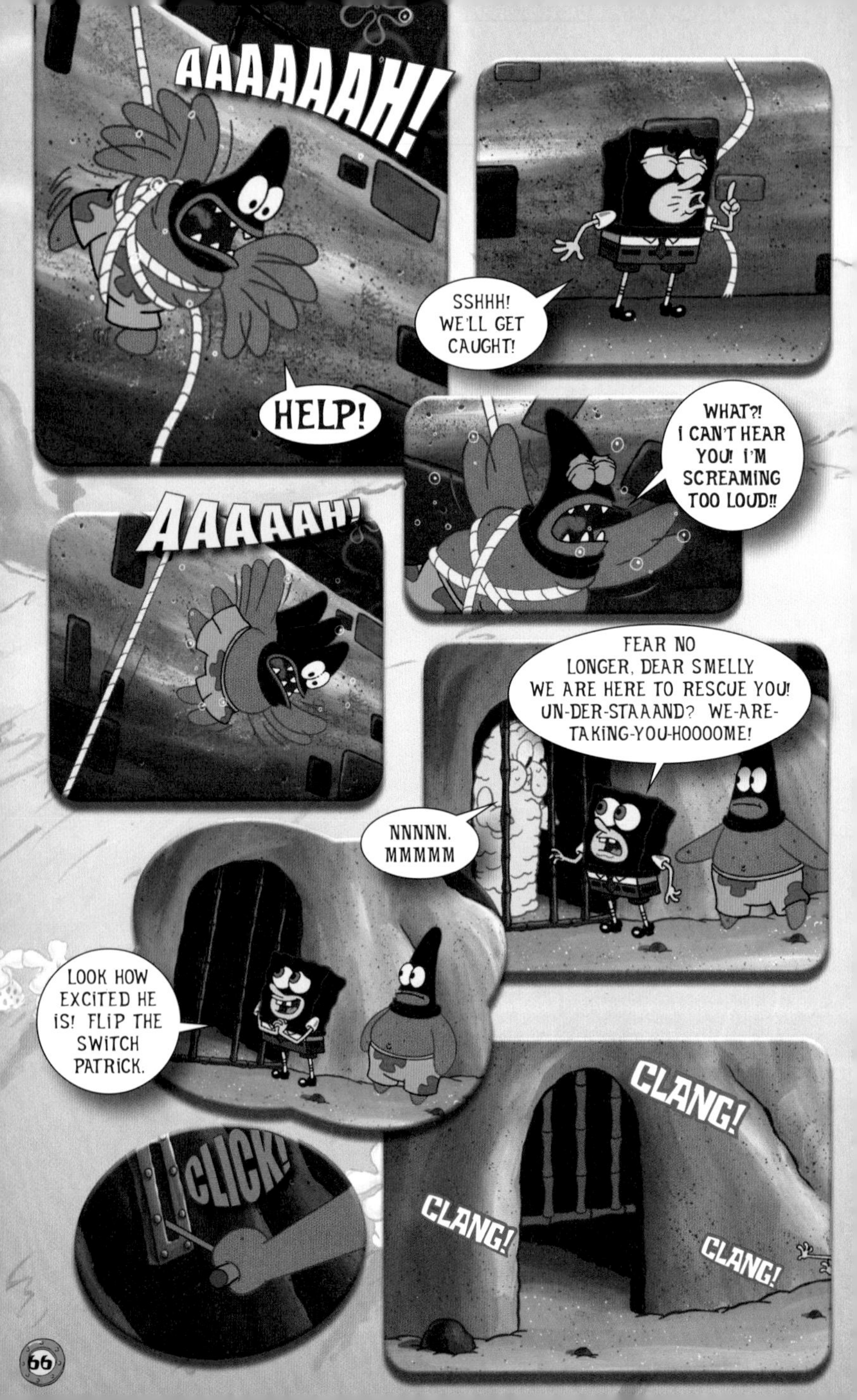
AAAAAAH!
HELP!
SSHHH! WE'LL GET CAUGHT!
WHAT?! I CAN'T HEAR YOU! I'M SCREAMING TOO LOUD!!
AAAAAH!
FEAR NO LONGER, DEAR SMELLY. WE ARE HERE TO RESCUE YOU! UN-DER-STAAAND? WE-ARE-TAKING-YOU-HOOOOME!
NNNNN. MMMMM
LOOK HOW EXCITED HE IS! FLIP THE SWITCH PATRICK.
CLICK!
CLANG!
CLANG!
CLANG!

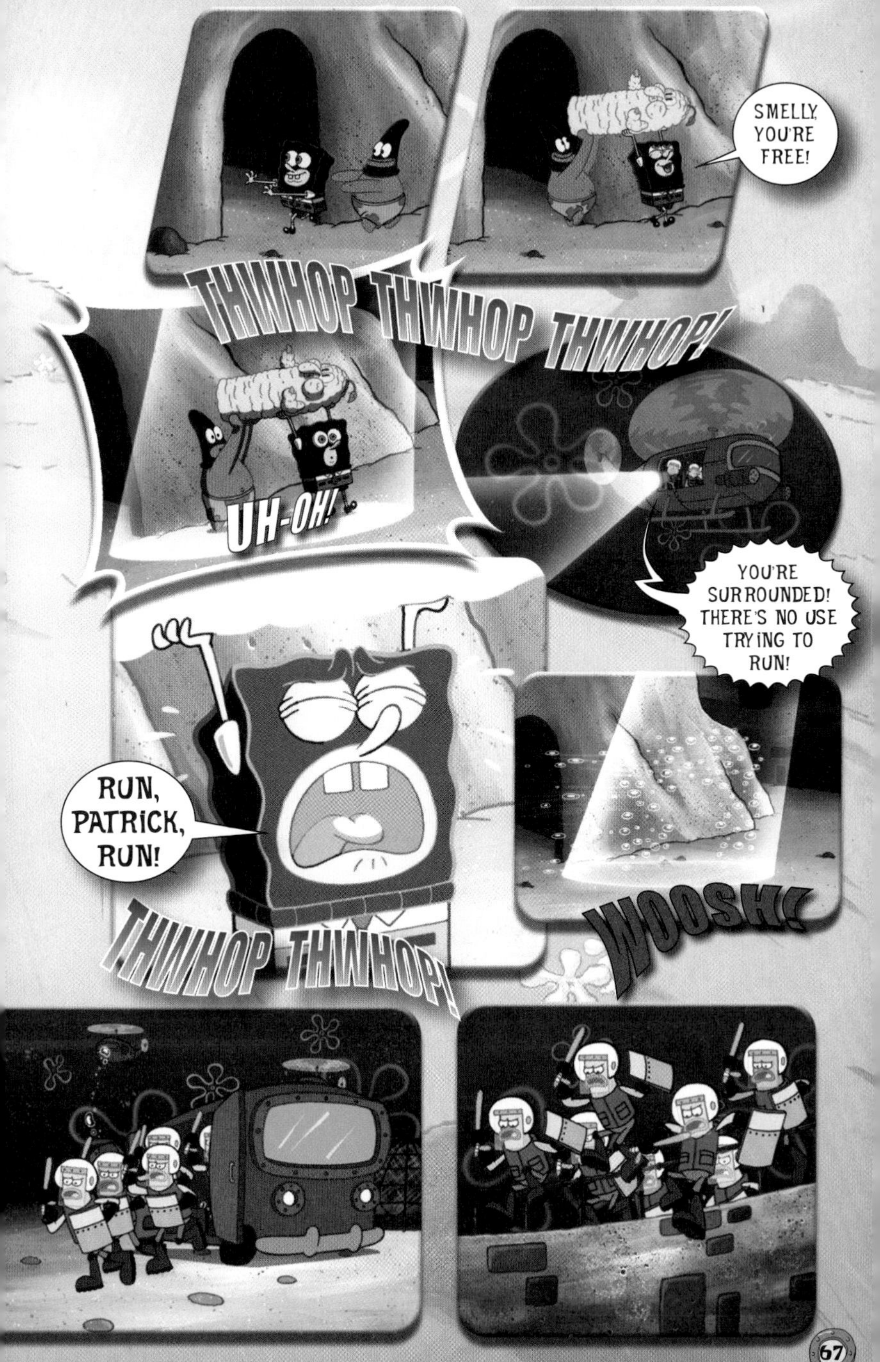

SMELLY, YOU'RE FREE!
THWHOP THWHOP THWHOP!
UH-OH!
YOU'RE SURROUNDED! THERE'S NO USE TRYING TO RUN!
RUN, PATRICK, RUN!
THWHOP THWHOP!
WOOSH!

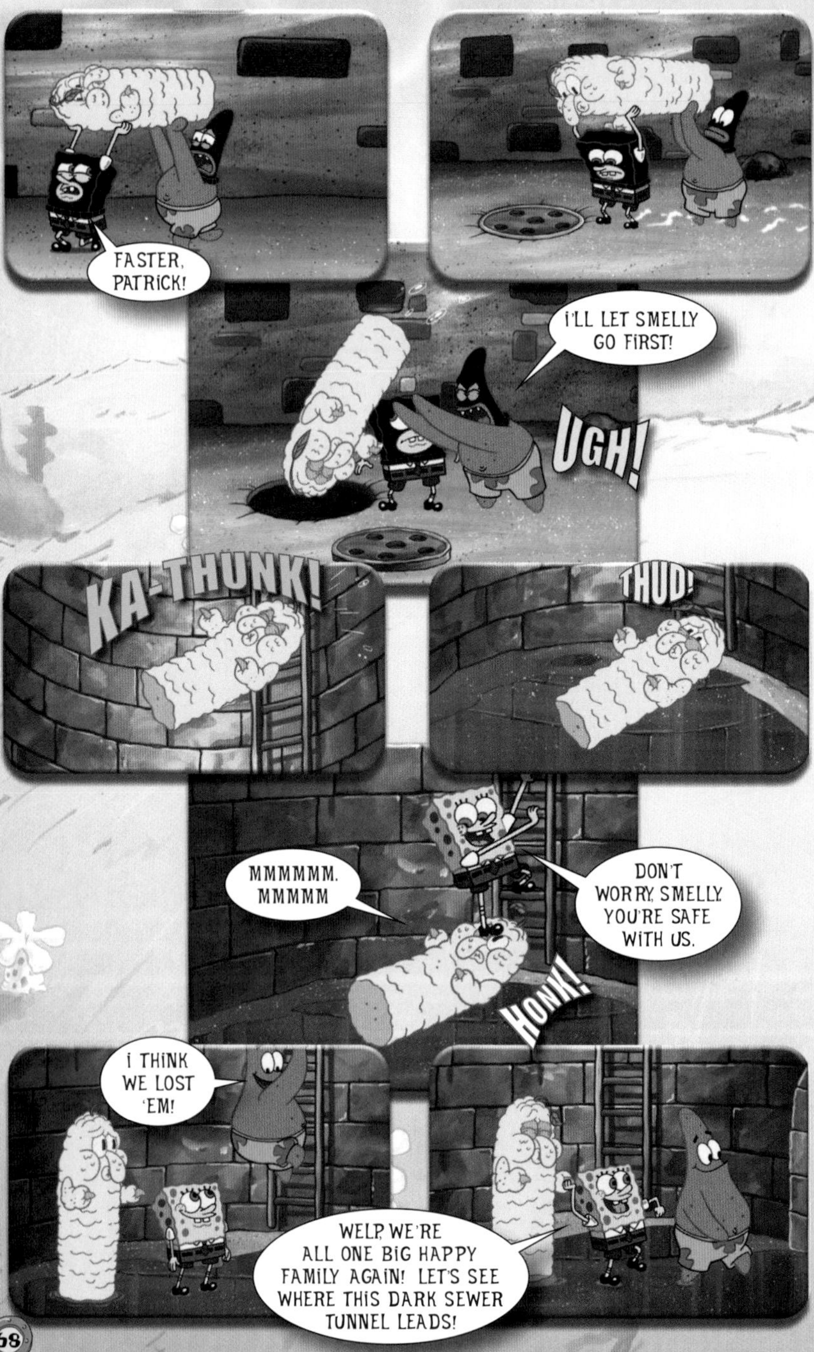
FASTER, PATRICK!
I'LL LET SMELLY GO FIRST!
UGH!
KA-THUNK!
THUD!
MMMMMM. MMMMM
DON'T WORRY, SMELLY. YOU'RE SAFE WITH US.
HONK!
I THINK WE LOST 'EM!
WELP, WE'RE ALL ONE BIG HAPPY FAMILY AGAIN! LET'S SEE WHERE THIS DARK SEWER TUNNEL LEADS!

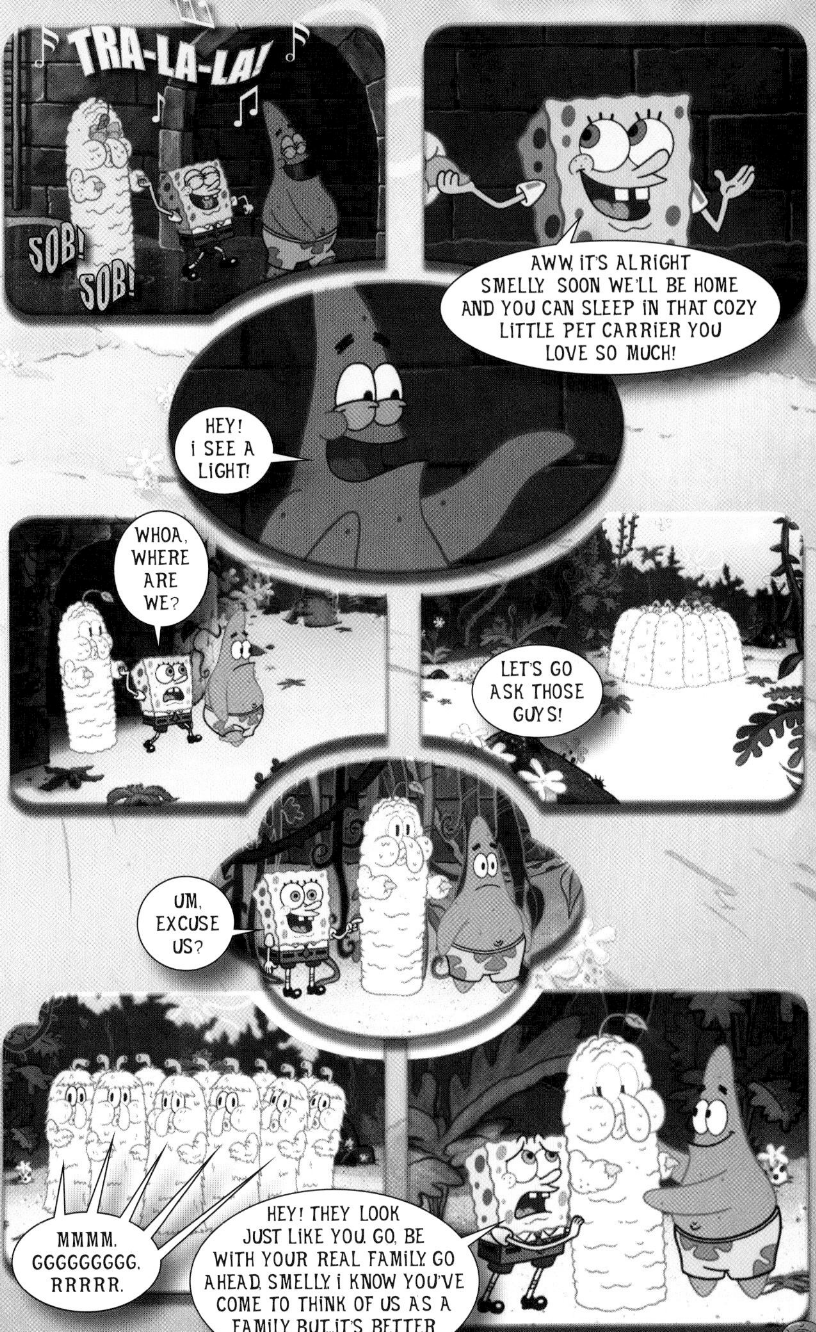
TRA-LA-LA!
SOB! SOB!
AWW, IT'S ALRIGHT SMELLY. SOON WE'LL BE HOME AND YOU CAN SLEEP IN THAT COZY LITTLE PET CARRIER YOU LOVE SO MUCH!
HEY! I SEE A LIGHT!
WHOA, WHERE ARE WE?
LET'S GO ASK THOSE GUYS!
UM, EXCUSE US?
MMMM. GGGGGGGGG. RRRRR.
HEY! THEY LOOK JUST LIKE YOU. GO, BE WITH YOUR REAL FAMILY. GO AHEAD, SMELLY. I KNOW YOU'VE COME TO THINK OF US AS A FAMILY, BUT...IT'S BETTER THIS WAY.

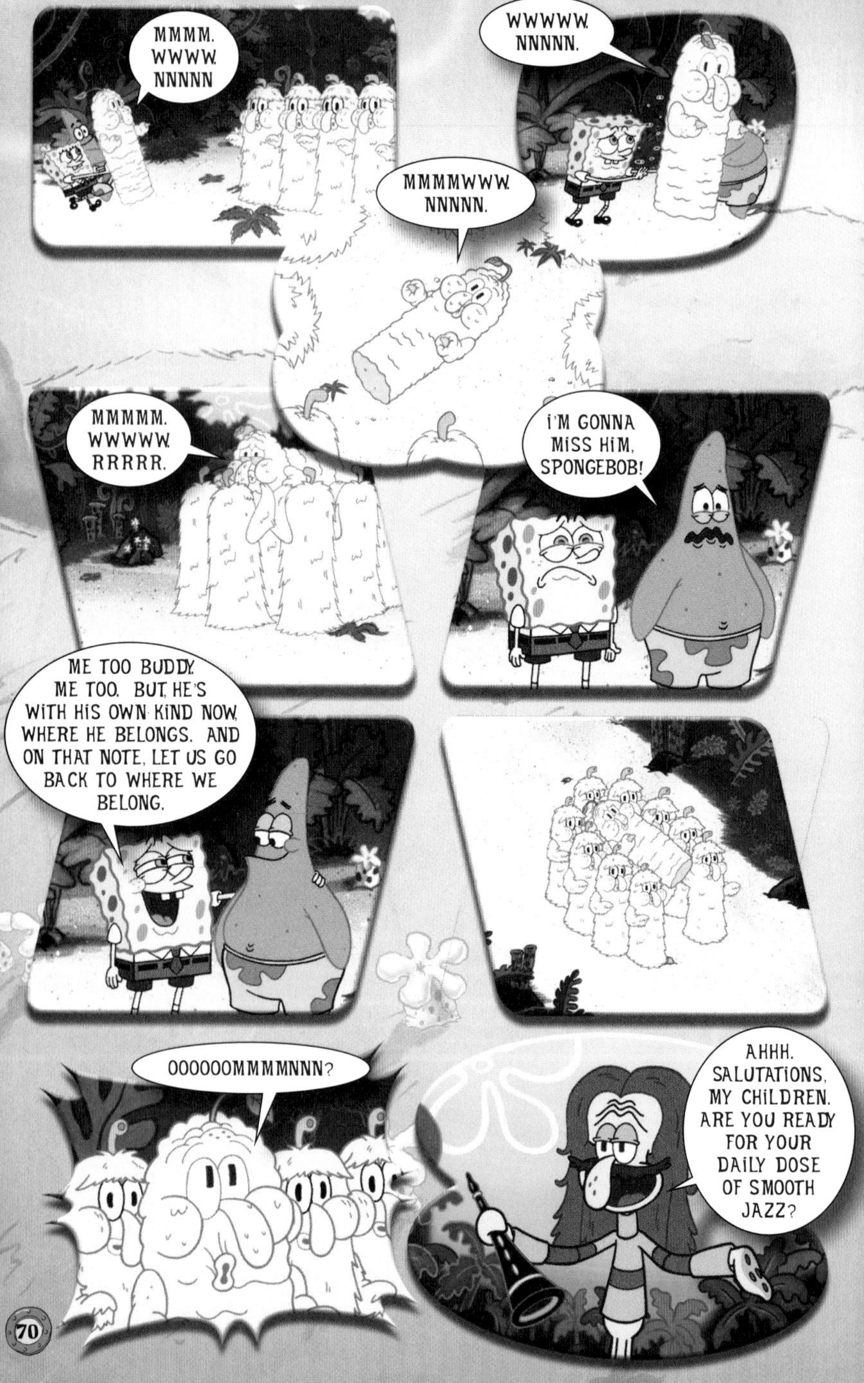
MMMM. WWWW. NNNNN
WWWWW. NNNNN.
MMMMWWW. NNNNN.
MMMMM. WWWWW. RRRRR.
I'M GONNA MISS HIM, SPONGEBOB!
ME TOO BUDDY. ME TOO. BUT, HE'S WITH HIS OWN KIND NOW, WHERE HE BELONGS. AND ON THAT NOTE, LET US GO BACK TO WHERE WE BELONG.
OOOOOOMMMNNN?
AHHH. SALUTATIONS, MY CHILDREN. ARE YOU READY FOR YOUR DAILY DOSE OF SMOOTH JAZZ?

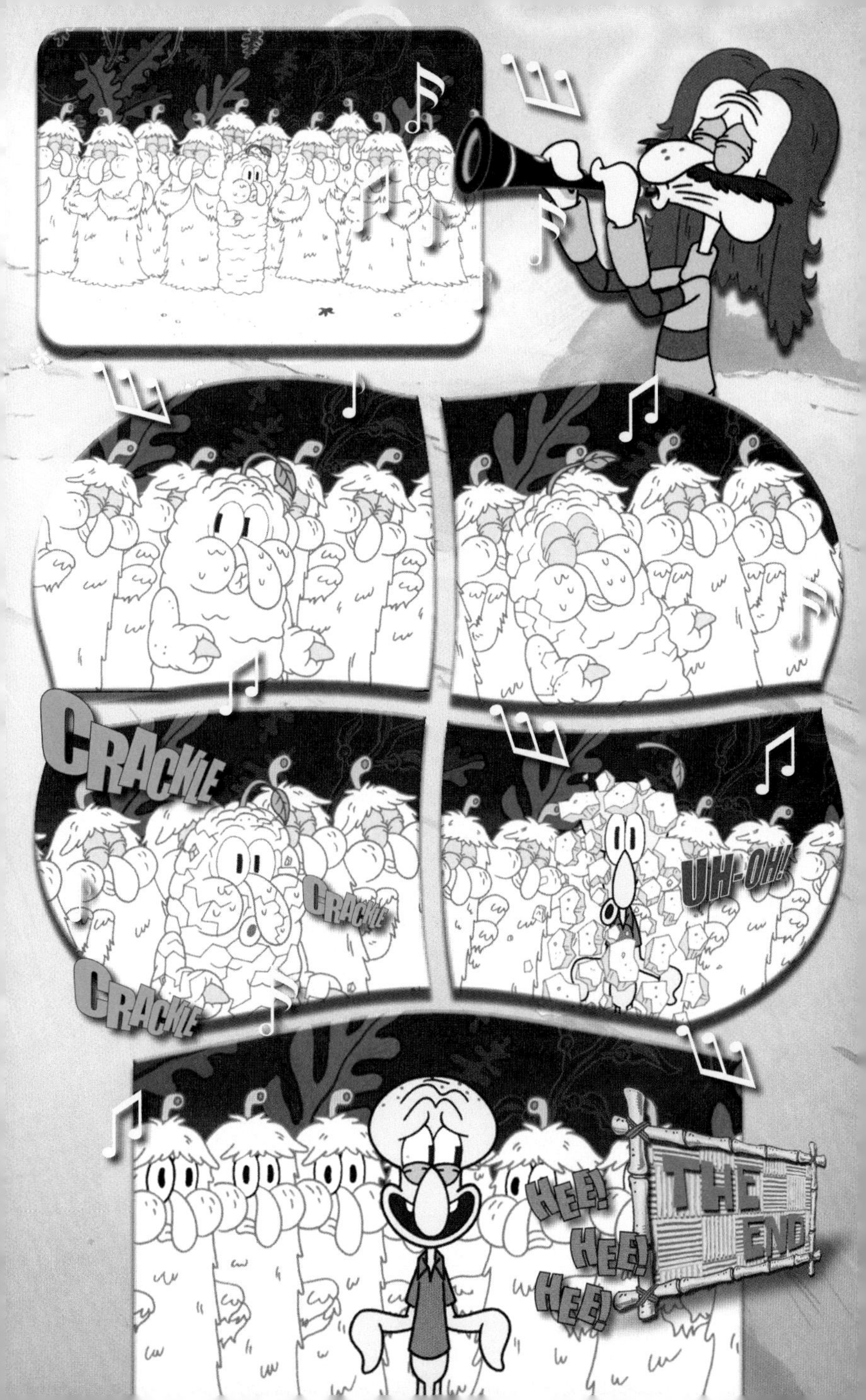
CRACKLE
CRACKLE
CRACKLE
UH-OH!
HEE!
HEE!
HEE!
THE END

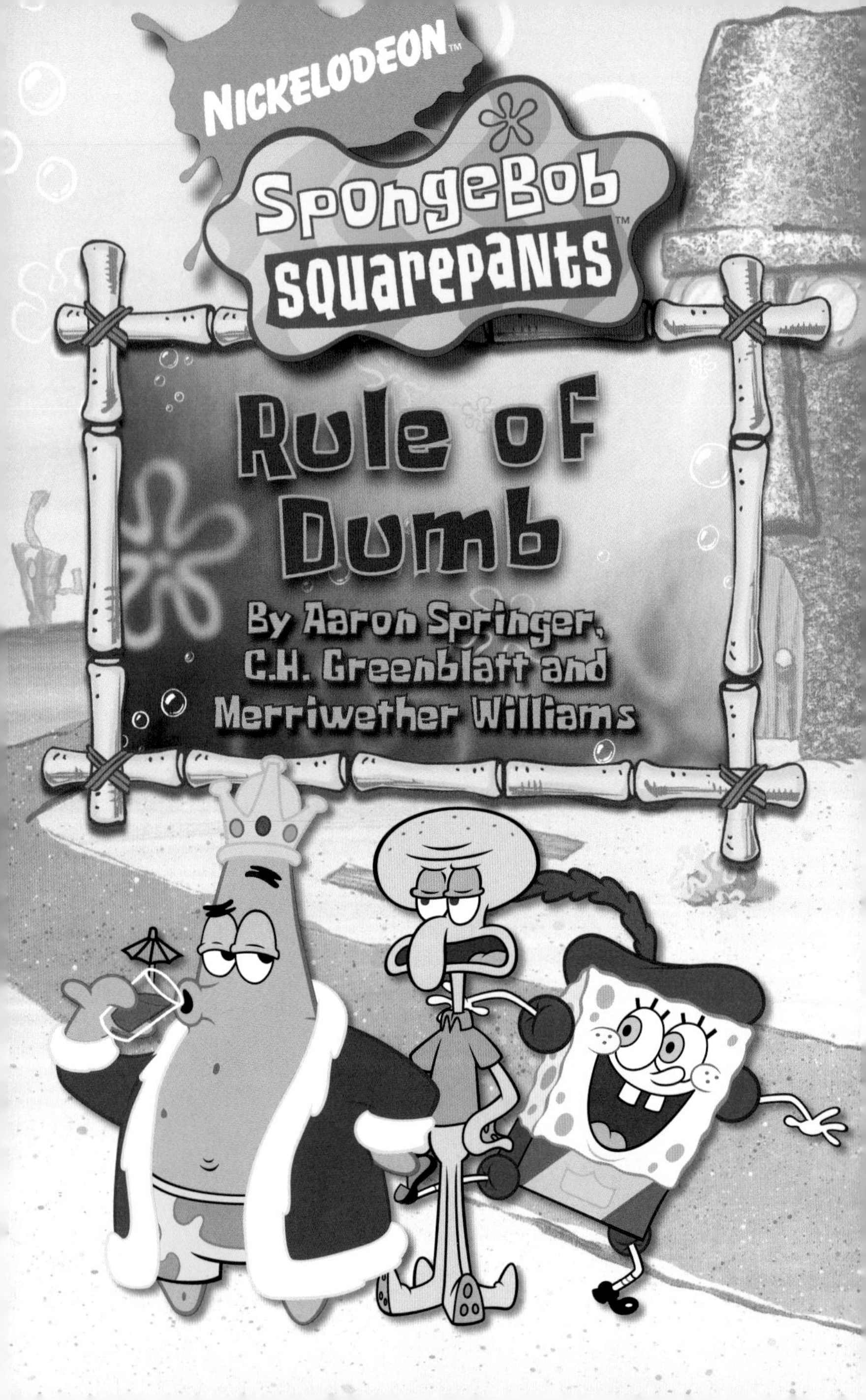
NICKELODEON™
SpongeBob SquarePants™
Rule of Dumb
By Aaron Springer, C.H. Greenblatt and Merriwether Williams

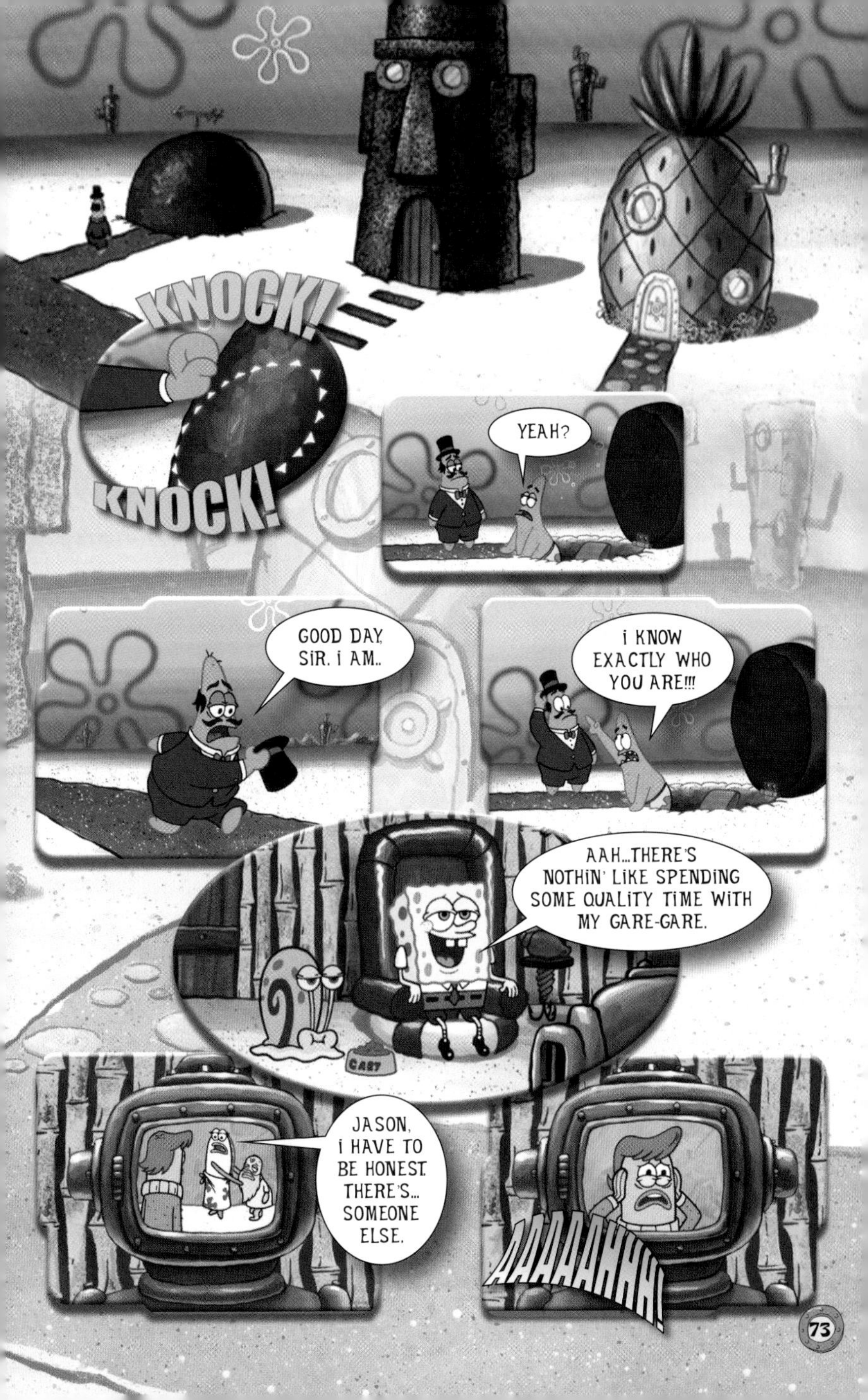
KNOCK!
KNOCK!
YEAH?
GOOD DAY, SIR. I AM..
I KNOW EXACTLY WHO YOU ARE!!!
AAH...THERE'S NOTHIN' LIKE SPENDING SOME QUALITY TIME WITH MY GARE-GARE.
JASON, I HAVE TO BE HONEST. THERE'S... SOMEONE ELSE.
AAAAAHHH!

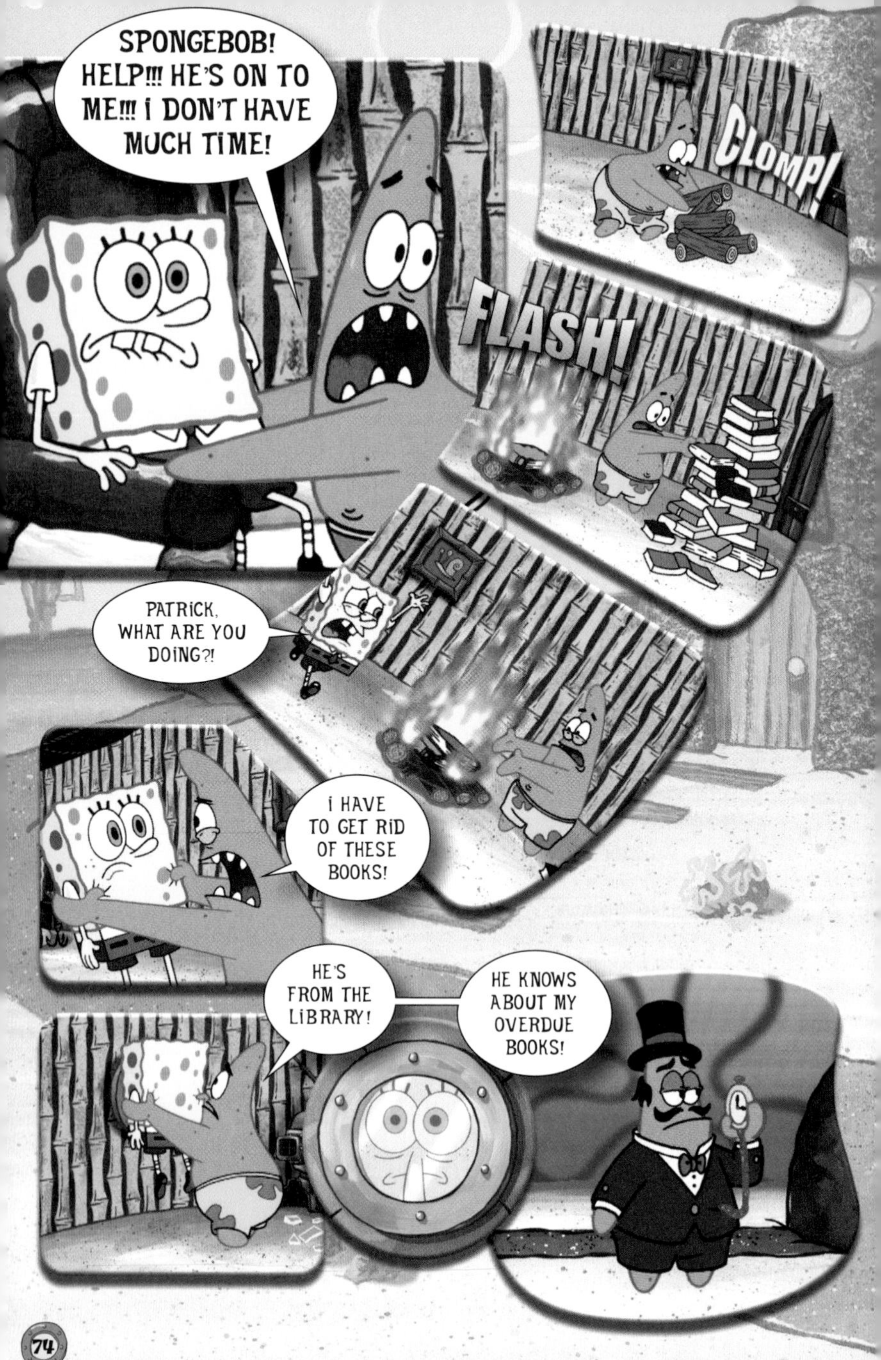
SPONGEBOB! HELP!!! HE'S ON TO ME!!! I DON'T HAVE MUCH TIME!
CLOMP!
FLASH!
PATRICK, WHAT ARE YOU DOING?!
I HAVE TO GET RID OF THESE BOOKS!
HE'S FROM THE LIBRARY!
HE KNOWS ABOUT MY OVERDUE BOOKS!

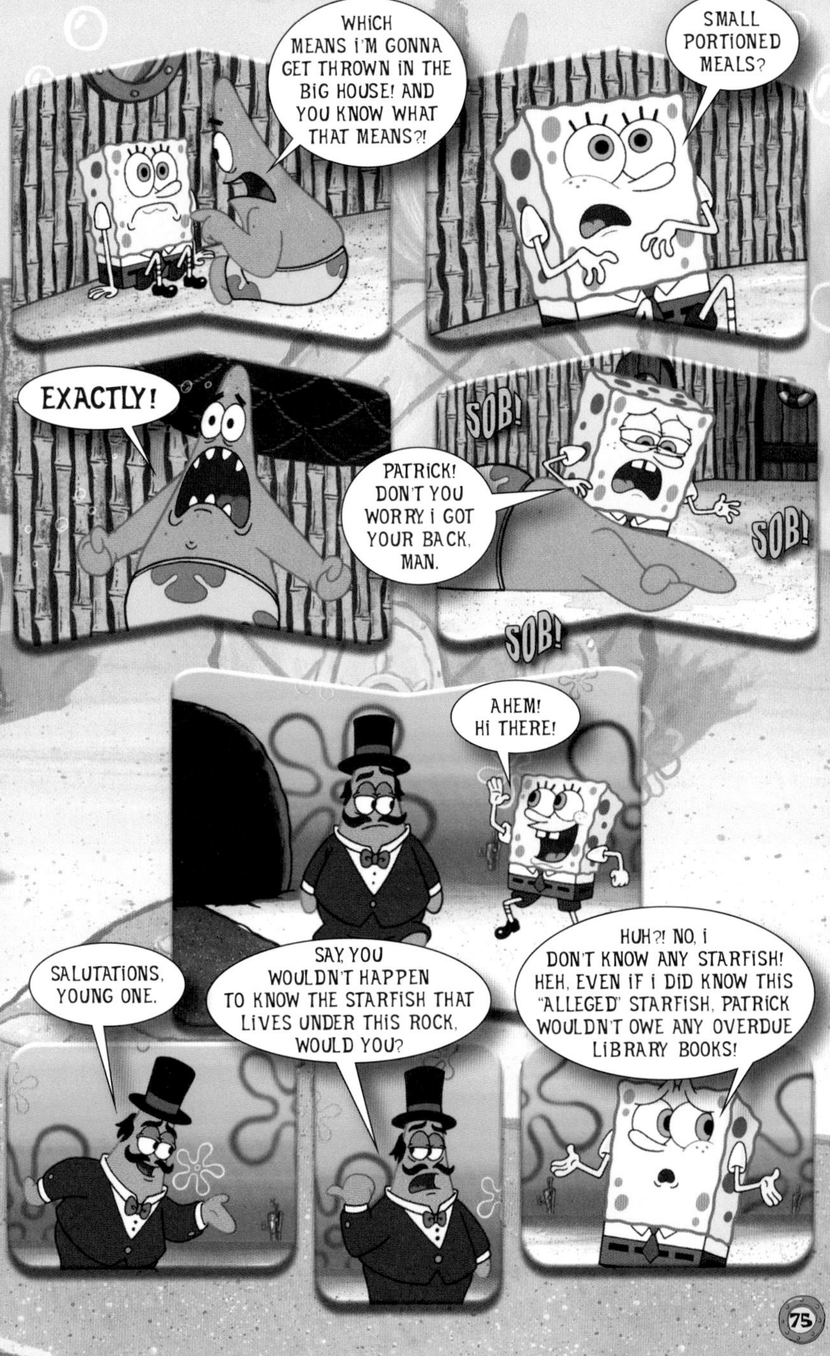
WHICH MEANS I'M GONNA GET THROWN IN THE BIG HOUSE! AND YOU KNOW WHAT THAT MEANS?!
SMALL PORTIONED MEALS?
EXACTLY!
SOB!
PATRICK! DON'T YOU WORRY. I GOT YOUR BACK, MAN.
SOB!
SOB!
AHEM! HI THERE!
SALUTATIONS, YOUNG ONE.
SAY, YOU WOULDN'T HAPPEN TO KNOW THE STARFISH THAT LIVES UNDER THIS ROCK, WOULD YOU?
HUH?! NO, I DON'T KNOW ANY STARFISH! HEH, EVEN IF I DID KNOW THIS "ALLEGED" STARFISH, PATRICK WOULDN'T OWE ANY OVERDUE LIBRARY BOOKS!

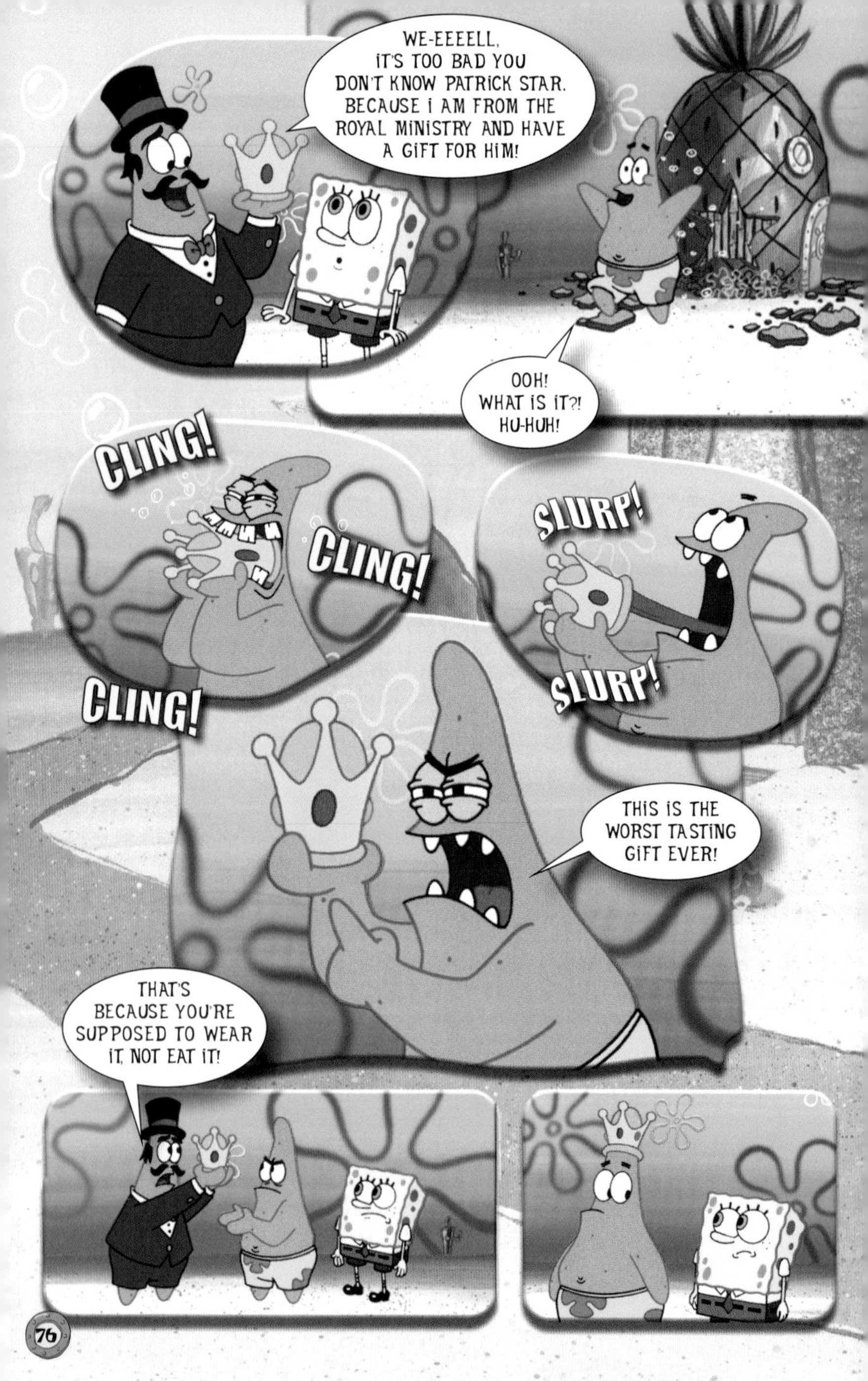
WE-EEEELL, IT'S TOO BAD YOU DON'T KNOW PATRICK STAR. BECAUSE I AM FROM THE ROYAL MINISTRY AND HAVE A GIFT FOR HIM!
OOH! WHAT IS IT?! HU-HUH!
CLING!
CLING!
SLURP!
SLURP!
CLING!
THIS IS THE WORST TASTING GIFT EVER!
THAT'S BECAUSE YOU'RE SUPPOSED TO WEAR IT, NOT EAT IT!

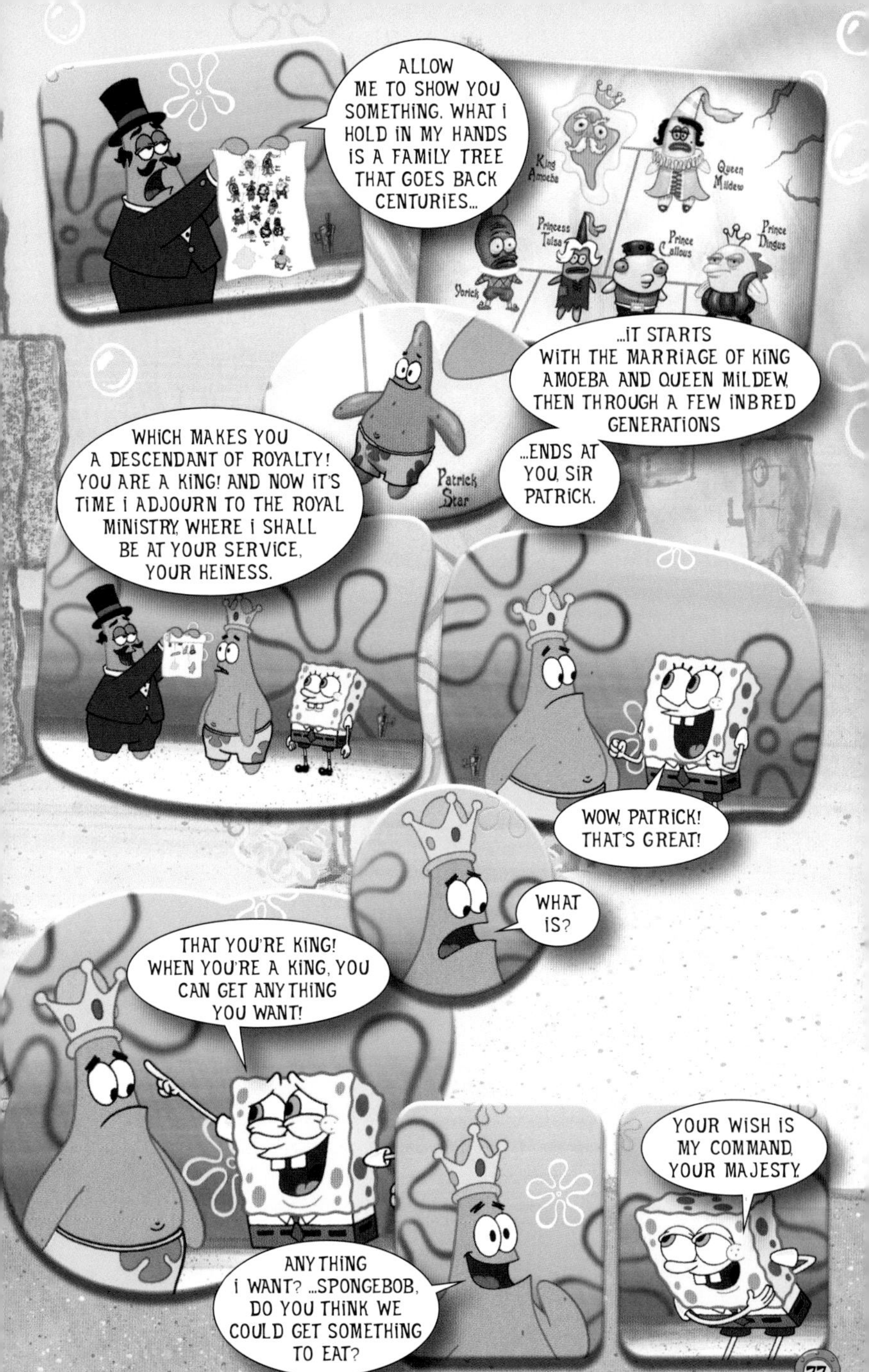
ALLOW ME TO SHOW YOU SOMETHING. WHAT I HOLD IN MY HANDS IS A FAMILY TREE THAT GOES BACK CENTURIES...
King Amoeba
Queen Mildew
Princess Tulsa
Prince Callous
Prince Dingus
Yorick
...IT STARTS WITH THE MARRIAGE OF KING AMOEBA AND QUEEN MILDEW, THEN THROUGH A FEW INBRED GENERATIONS
...ENDS AT YOU, SIR PATRICK.
Patrick Star
WHICH MAKES YOU A DESCENDANT OF ROYALTY! YOU ARE A KING! AND NOW IT'S TIME I ADJOURN TO THE ROYAL MINISTRY, WHERE I SHALL BE AT YOUR SERVICE, YOUR HEINESS.
WOW, PATRICK! THAT'S GREAT!
WHAT IS?
THAT YOU'RE KING! WHEN YOU'RE A KING, YOU CAN GET ANYTHING YOU WANT!
ANYTHING I WANT? ...SPONGEBOB, DO YOU THINK WE COULD GET SOMETHING TO EAT?
YOUR WISH IS MY COMMAND, YOUR MAJESTY.

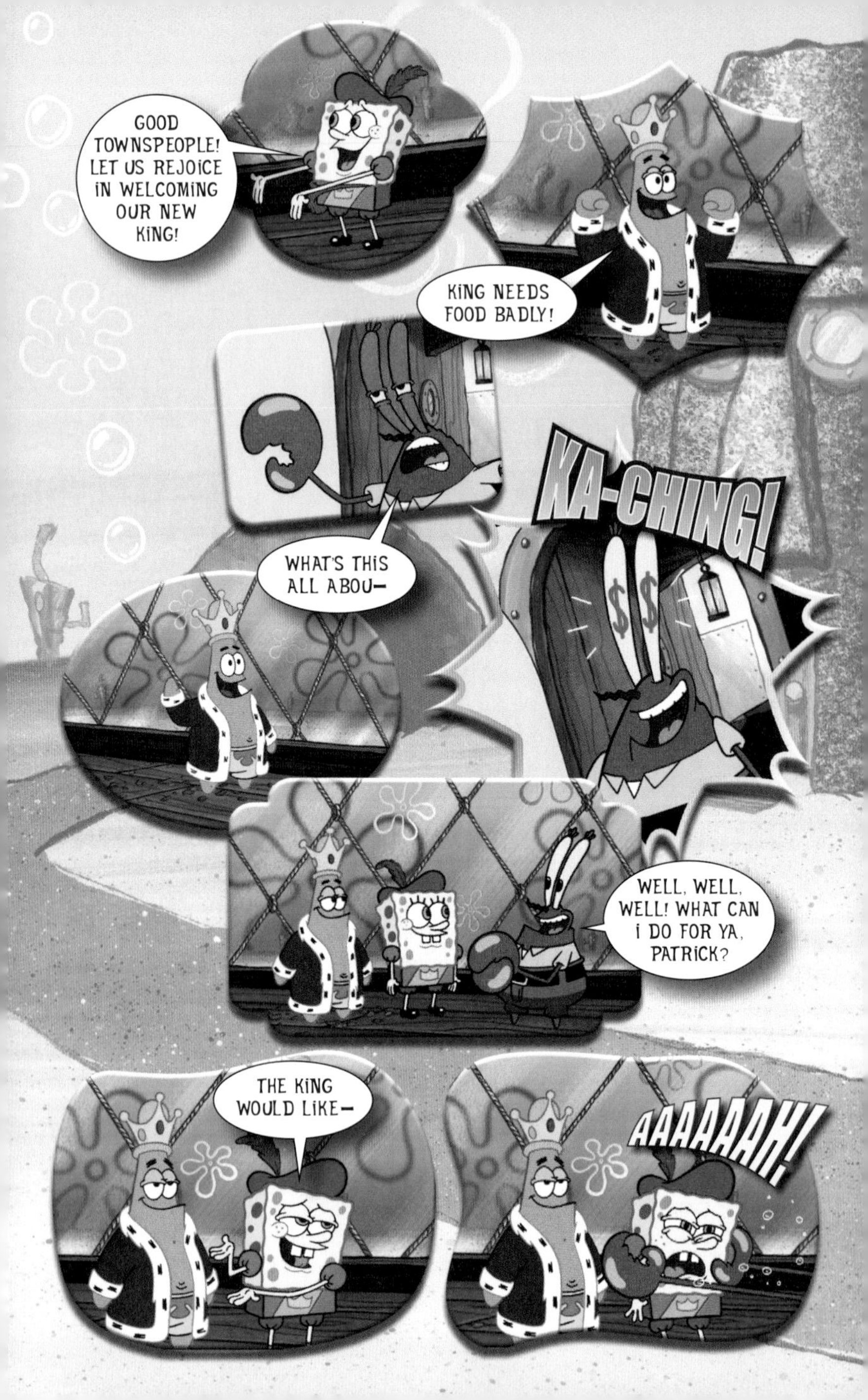
GOOD TOWNSPEOPLE! LET US REJOICE IN WELCOMING OUR NEW KING!
KING NEEDS FOOD BADLY!
WHAT'S THIS ALL ABOU—
KA-CHING!
WELL, WELL, WELL! WHAT CAN I DO FOR YA, PATRICK?
THE KING WOULD LIKE—
AAAAAAH!

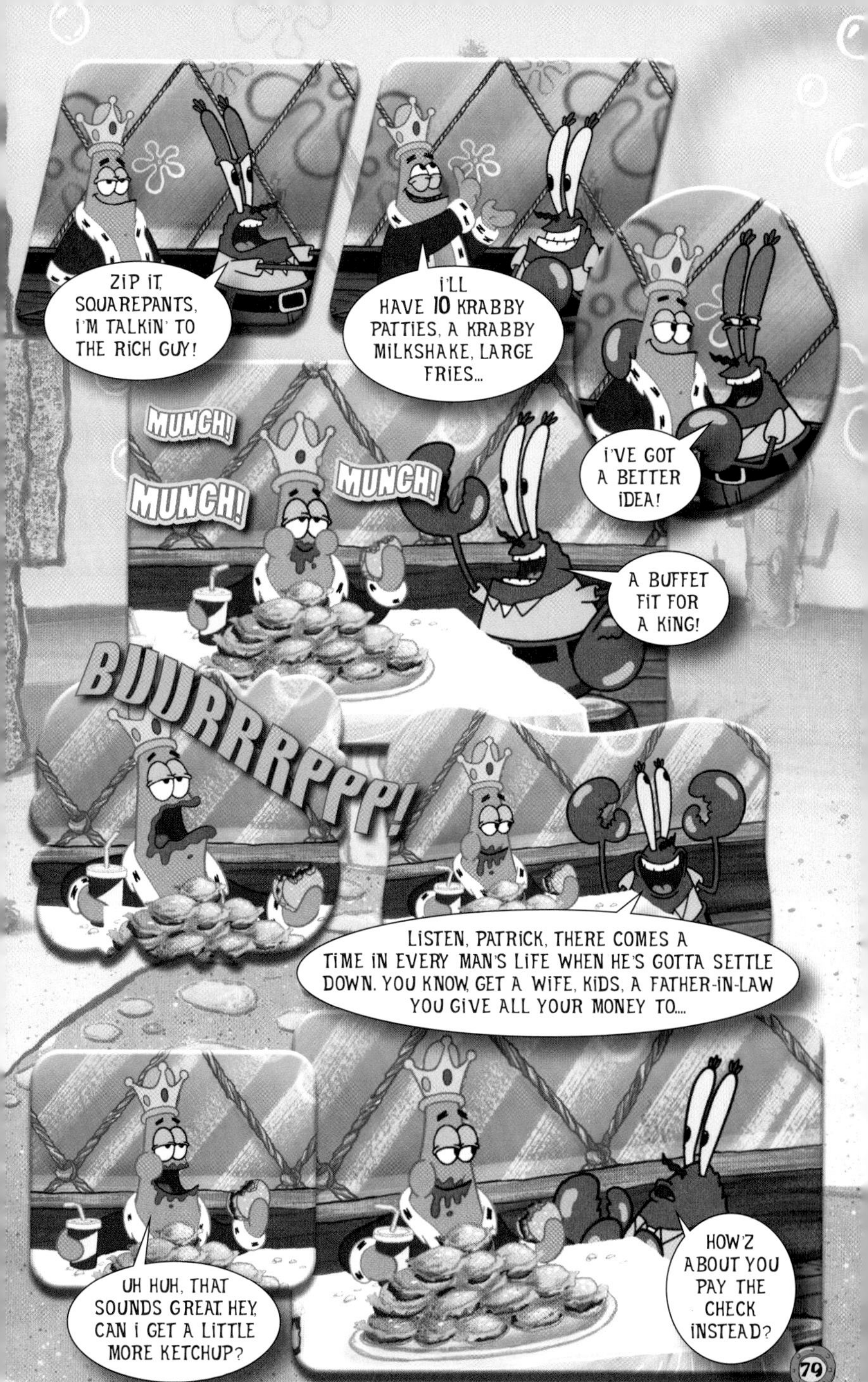

ZIP IT, SQUAREPANTS, I'M TALKIN' TO THE RICH GUY!
I'LL HAVE 10 KRABBY PATTIES, A KRABBY MILKSHAKE, LARGE FRIES...
I'VE GOT A BETTER IDEA!
MUNCH!
MUNCH!
MUNCH!
A BUFFET FIT FOR A KING!
BUURRRRPPP!
LISTEN, PATRICK, THERE COMES A TIME IN EVERY MAN'S LIFE WHEN HE'S GOTTA SETTLE DOWN. YOU KNOW, GET A WIFE, KIDS, A FATHER-IN-LAW YOU GIVE ALL YOUR MONEY TO....
UH HUH, THAT SOUNDS GREAT. HEY, CAN I GET A LITTLE MORE KETCHUP?
HOW'Z ABOUT YOU PAY THE CHECK INSTEAD?

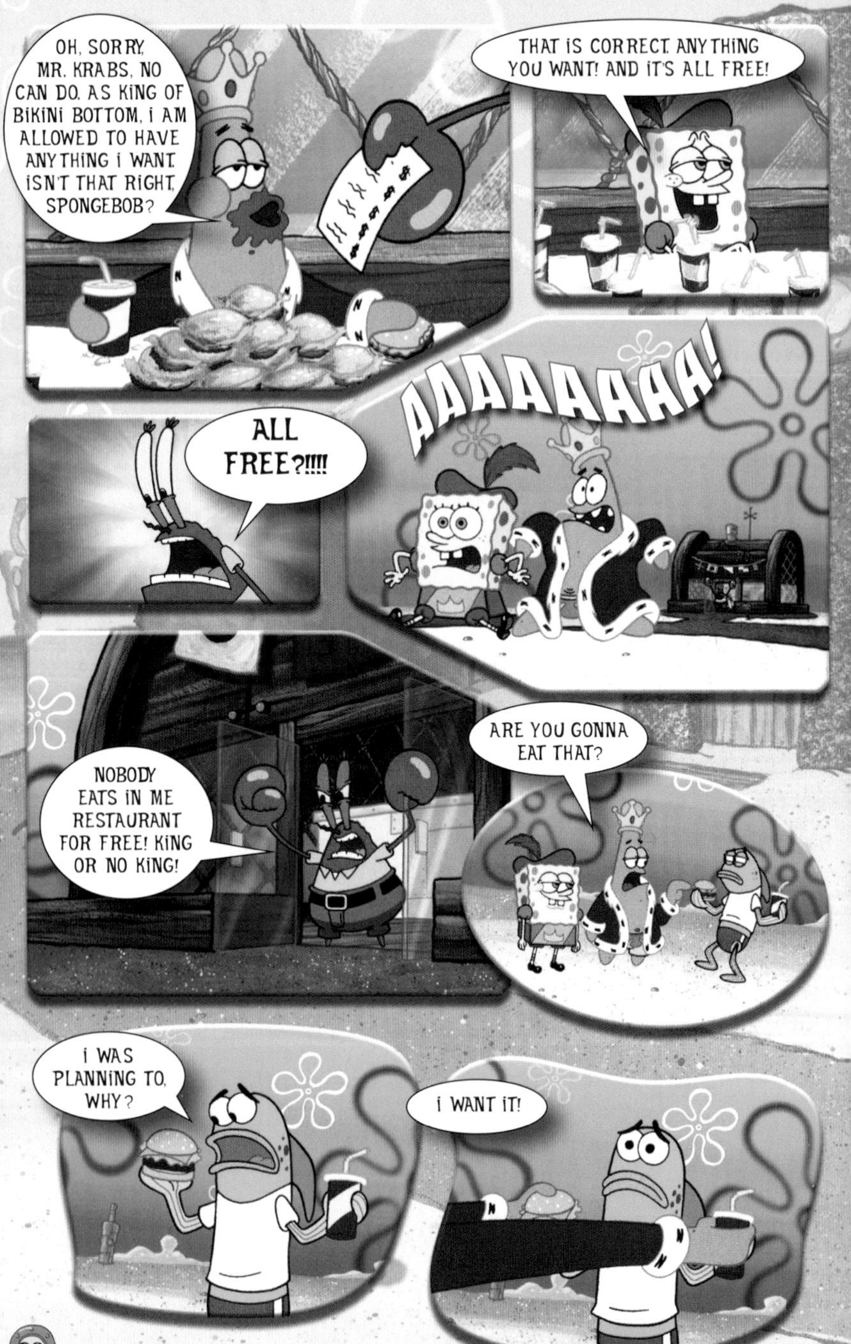

OH, SORRY, MR. KRABS, NO CAN DO. AS KING OF BIKINI BOTTOM, I AM ALLOWED TO HAVE ANYTHING I WANT. ISN'T THAT RIGHT, SPONGEBOB?
THAT IS CORRECT. ANYTHING YOU WANT! AND IT'S ALL FREE!
ALL FREE?!!!!
AAAAAAAAA!
NOBODY EATS IN ME RESTAURANT FOR FREE! KING OR NO KING!
ARE YOU GONNA EAT THAT?
I WAS PLANNING TO, WHY?
I WANT IT!

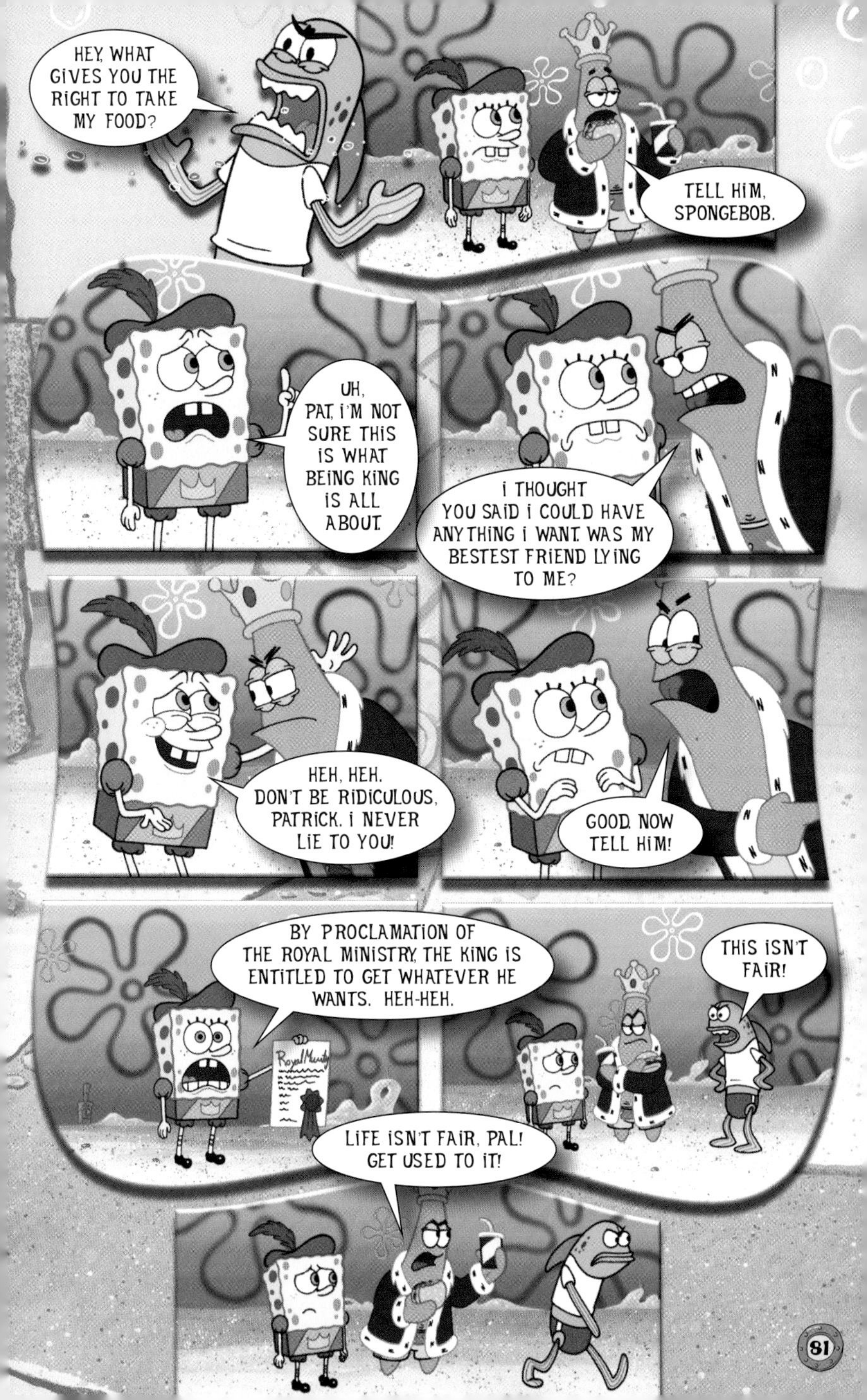
HEY, WHAT GIVES YOU THE RIGHT TO TAKE MY FOOD?
TELL HIM, SPONGEBOB.
UH, PAT, I'M NOT SURE THIS IS WHAT BEING KING IS ALL ABOUT.
I THOUGHT YOU SAID I COULD HAVE ANYTHING I WANT. WAS MY BESTEST FRIEND LYING TO ME?
HEH, HEH. DON'T BE RIDICULOUS, PATRICK. I NEVER LIE TO YOU!
GOOD. NOW TELL HIM!
BY PROCLAMATION OF THE ROYAL MINISTRY, THE KING IS ENTITLED TO GET WHATEVER HE WANTS. HEH-HEH.
THIS ISN'T FAIR!
LIFE ISN'T FAIR, PAL! GET USED TO IT!

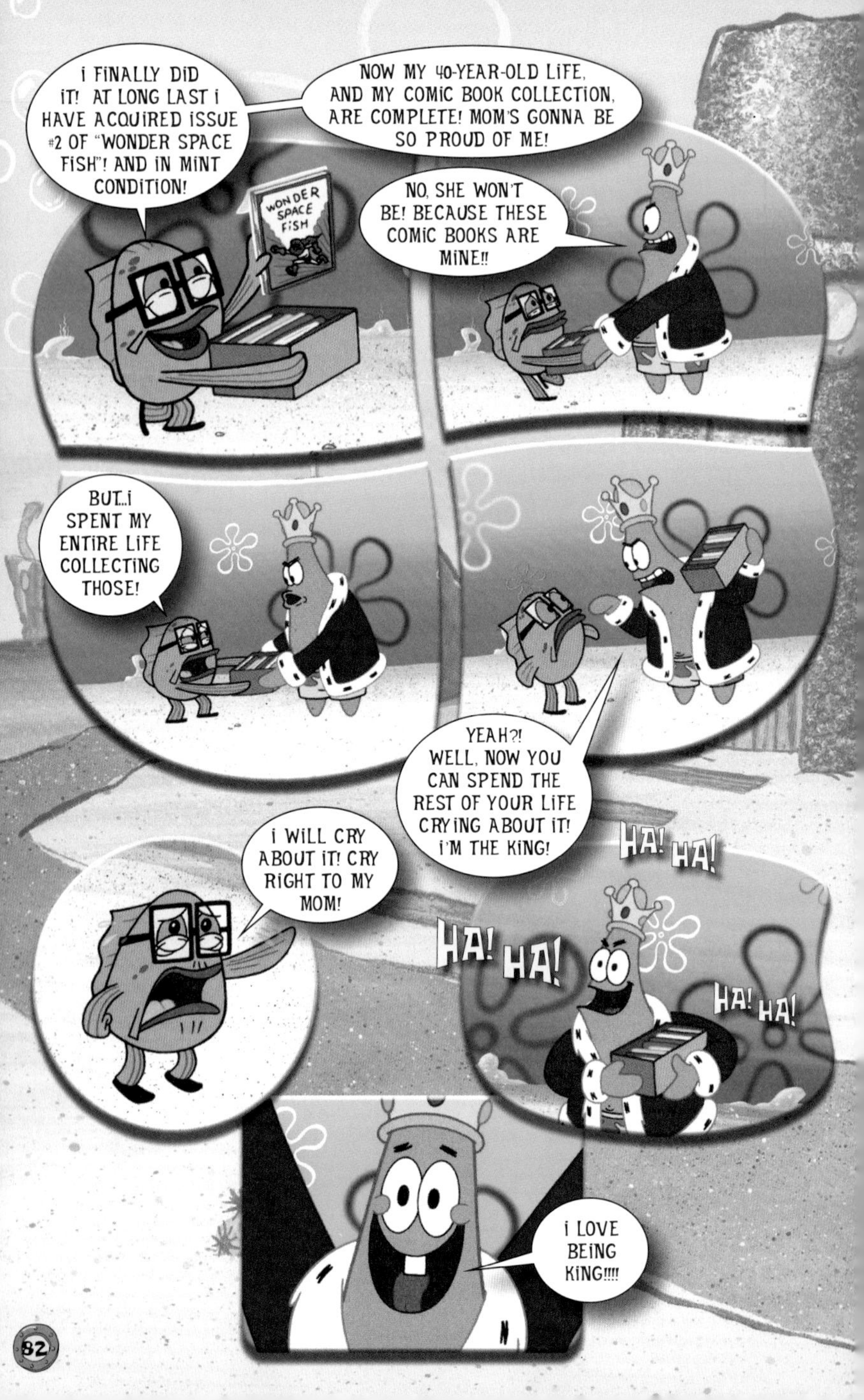

i FINALLY DiD iT! AT LONG LAST i HAVE ACQUIRED iSSUE #2 OF "WONDER SPACE FISH"! AND iN MINT CONDITION!
NOW MY 40-YEAR-OLD LiFE, AND MY COMiC BOOK COLLECTiON, ARE COMPLETE! MOM'S GONNA BE SO PROUD OF ME!
WONDER SPACE FISH
NO, SHE WON'T BE! BECAUSE THESE COMiC BOOKS ARE MiNE!!
BUT...i SPENT MY ENTiRE LiFE COLLECTiNG THOSE!
YEAH?! WELL, NOW YOU CAN SPEND THE REST OF YOUR LiFE CRYiNG ABOUT iT! i'M THE KiNG!
i WiLL CRY ABOUT iT! CRY RiGHT TO MY MOM!
HA! HA!
HA! HA!
HA! HA!
i LOVE BEiNG KiNG!!!!

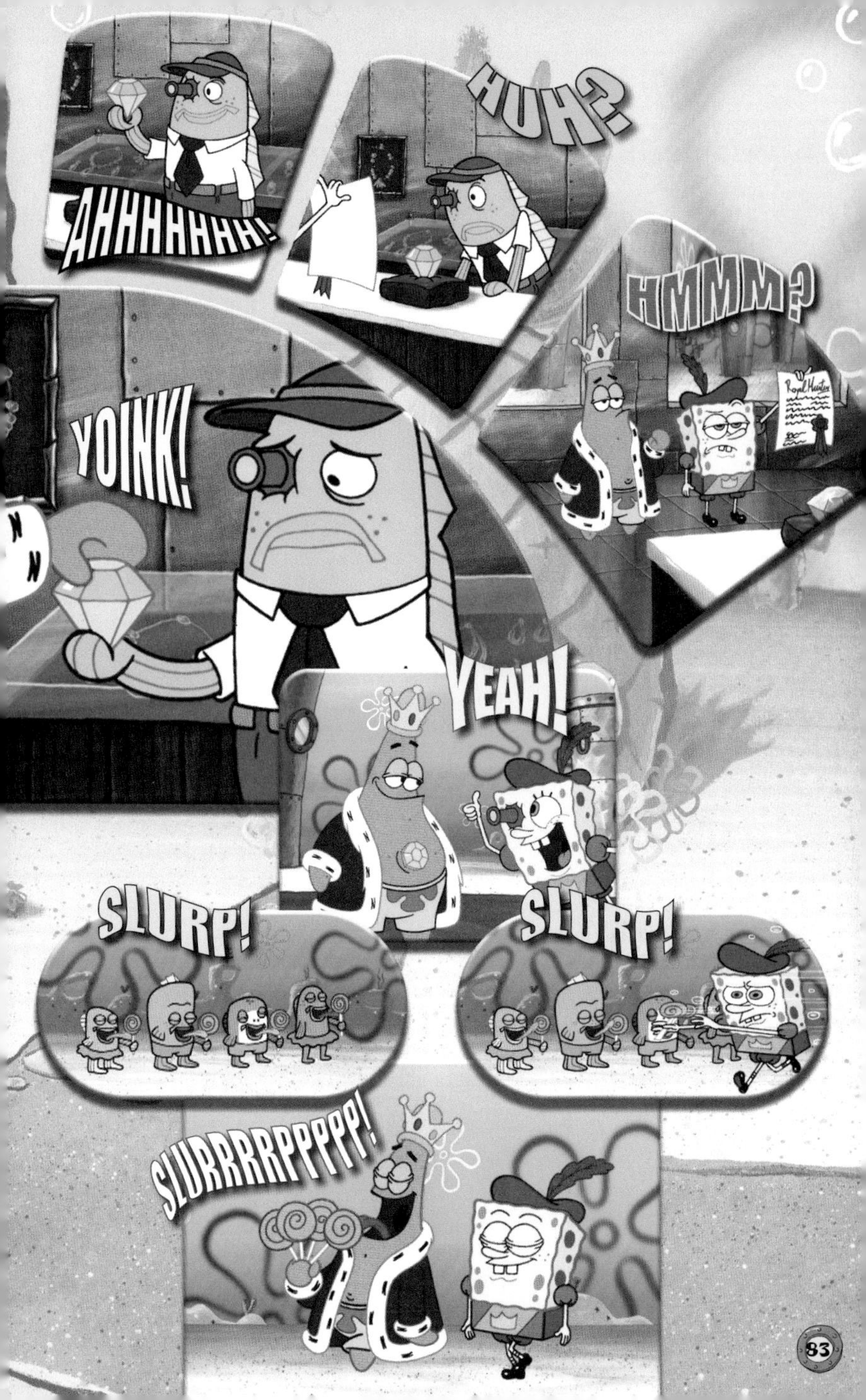
AHHHHHHH!
HUH?
YOINK!
HMMM?
YEAH!
SLURP!
SLURP!
SLURRRRPPPPP!

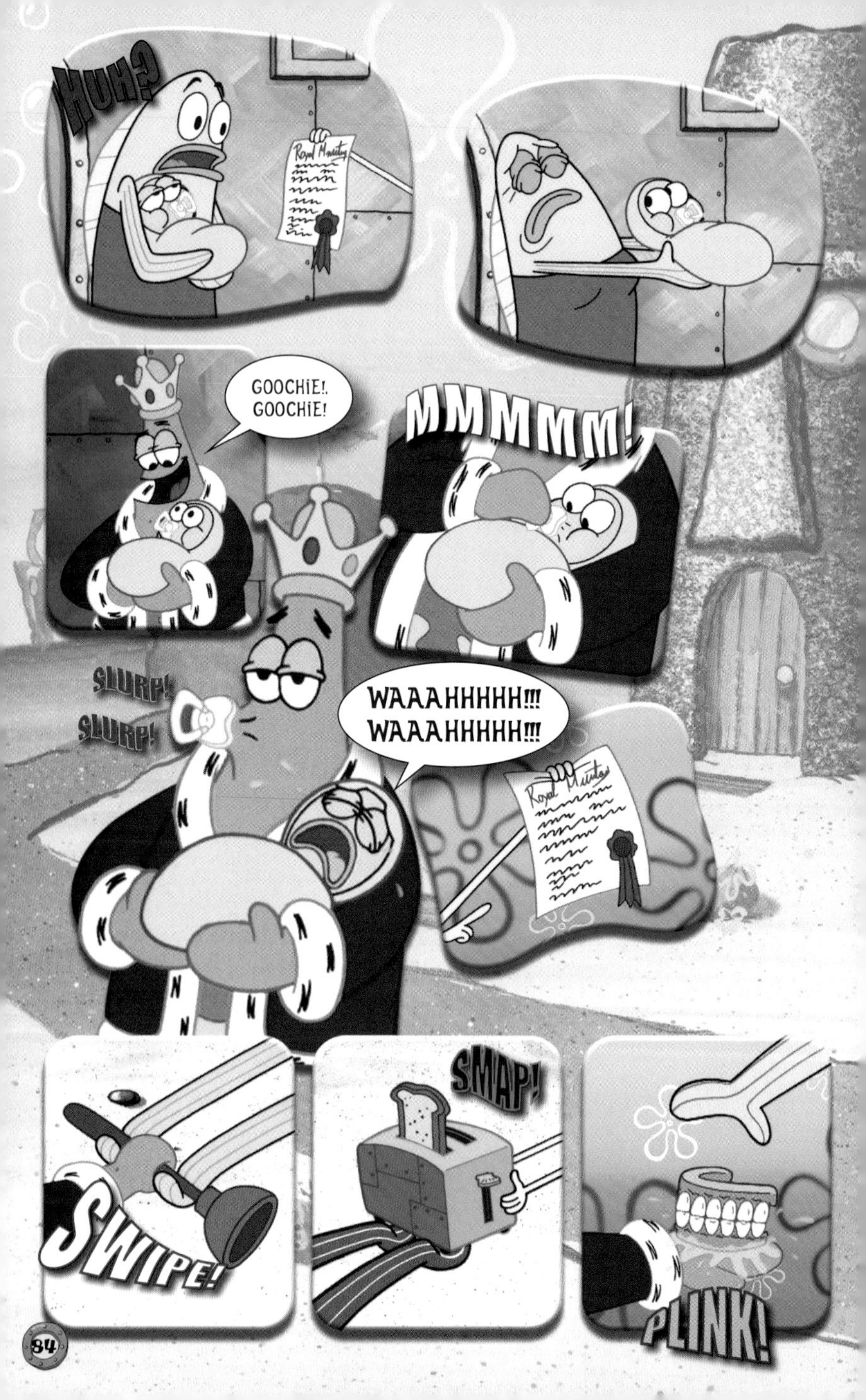
HUH?
GOOCHIE!. GOOCHIE!
MMMMMM!
SLURP!
SLURP!
WAAAHHHHH!!! WAAAHHHHH!!!
SWIPE!
SNAP!
PLINK!

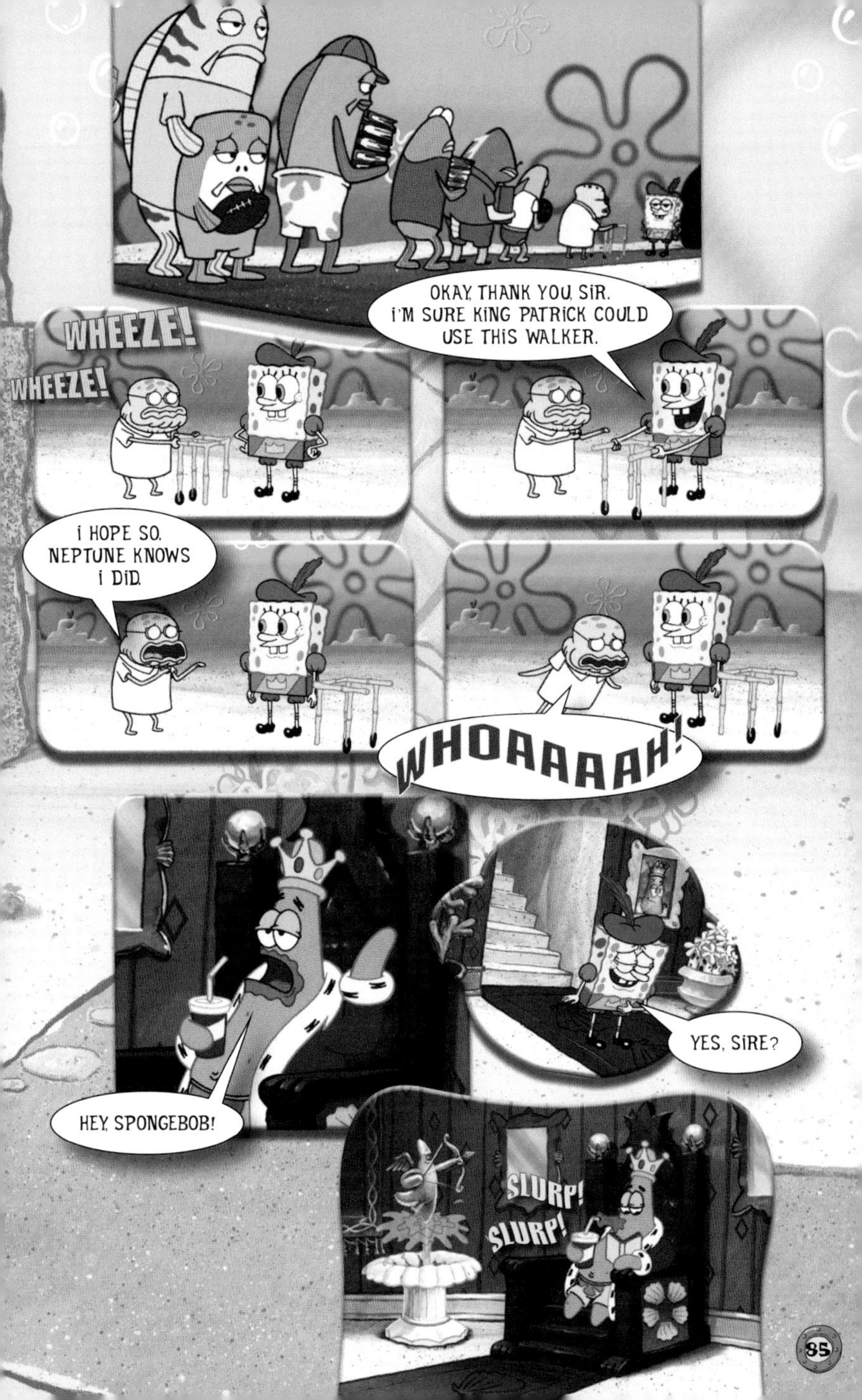
WHEEZE!
WHEEZE!
OKAY, THANK YOU, SIR. I'M SURE KING PATRICK COULD USE THIS WALKER.
I HOPE SO. NEPTUNE KNOWS I DID.
WHOAAAAH!
HEY, SPONGEBOB!
YES, SIRE?
SLURP!
SLURP!

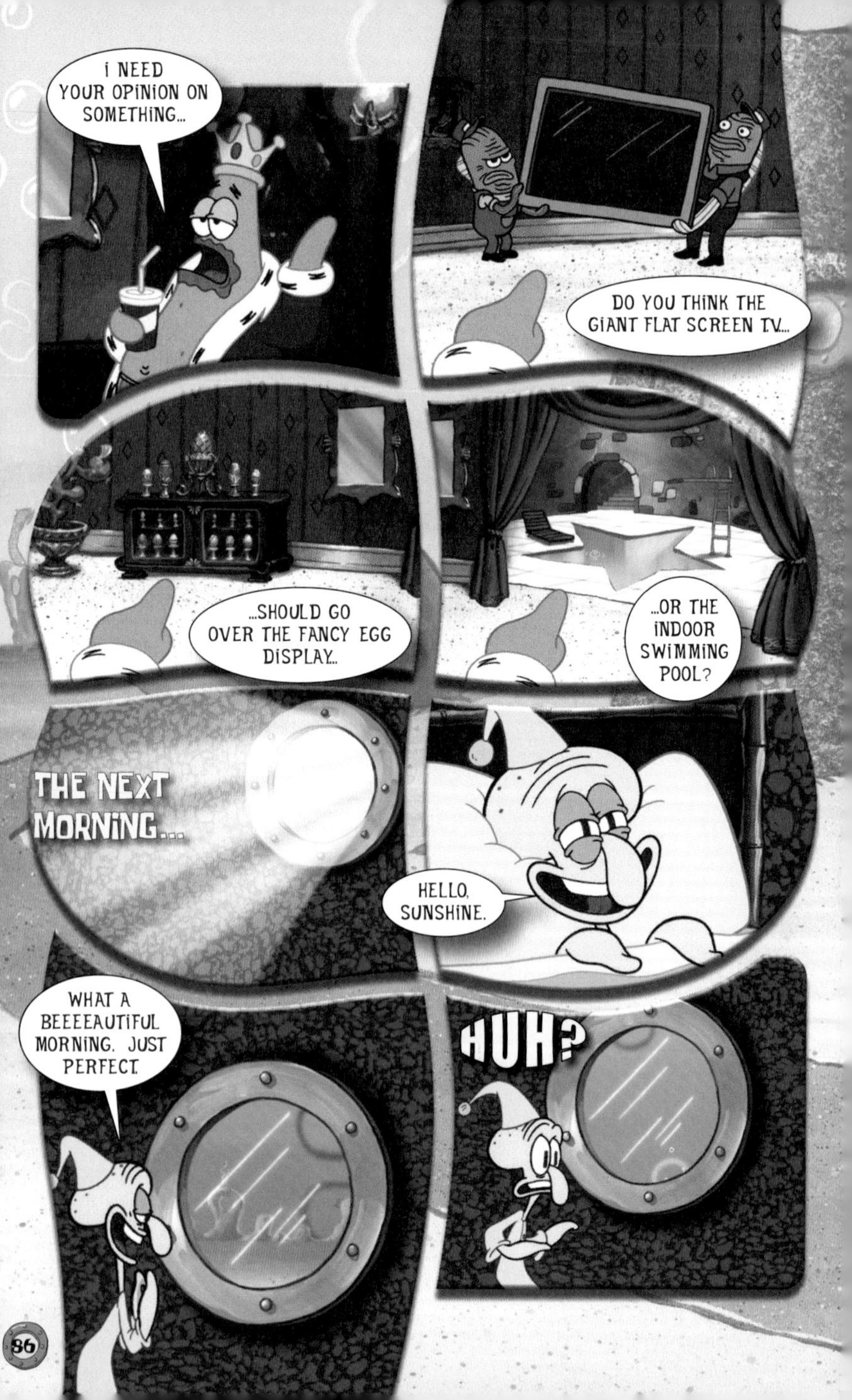
I NEED YOUR OPINION ON SOMETHING...
DO YOU THINK THE GIANT FLAT SCREEN T.V....
...SHOULD GO OVER THE FANCY EGG DISPLAY...
...OR THE INDOOR SWIMMING POOL?
THE NEXT MORNING...
HELLO, SUNSHINE.
WHAT A BEEEEAUTIFUL MORNING. JUST PERFECT.
HUH?

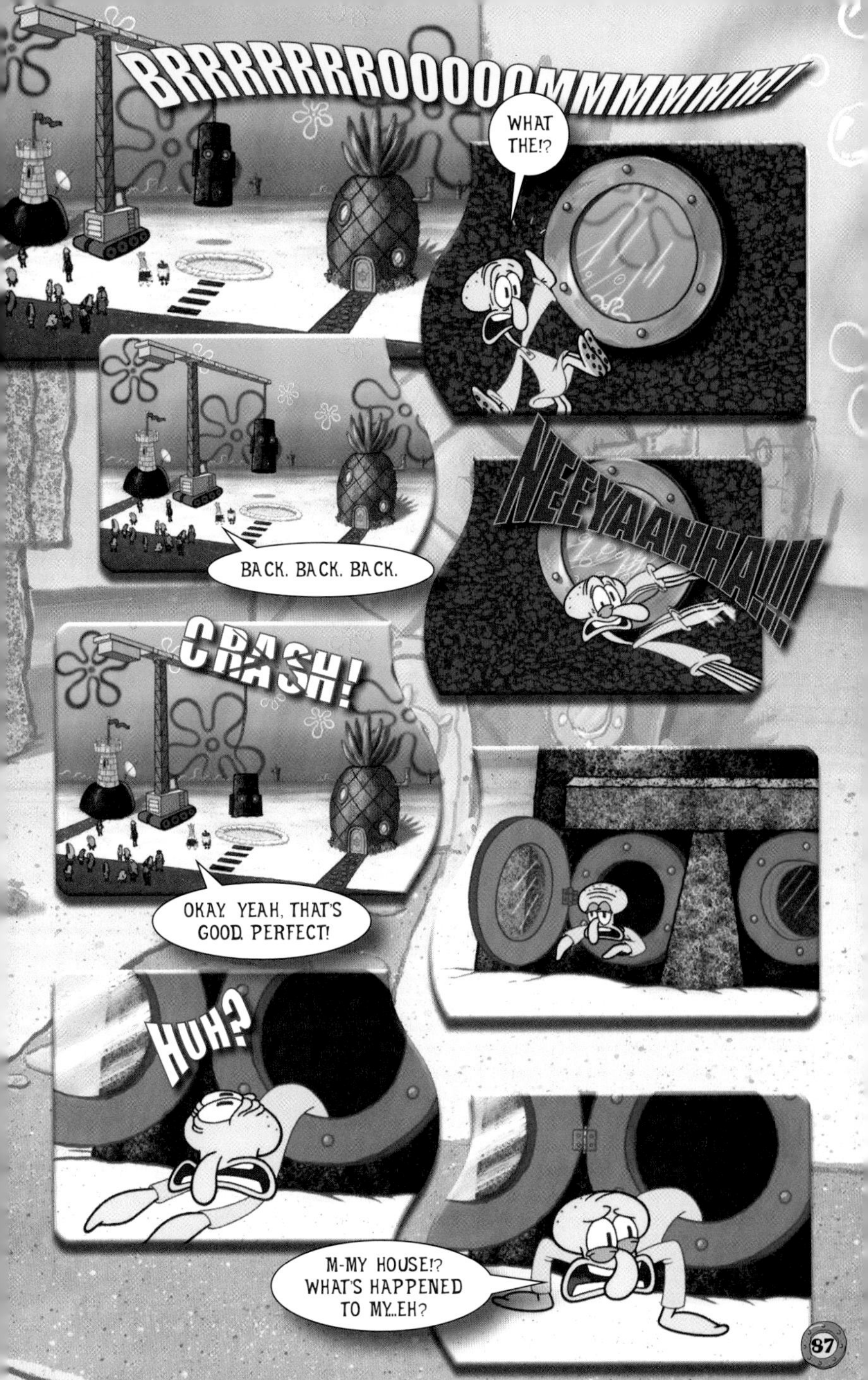
BRRRRRRROOOOOOMMMMMMM!
WHAT THE!?
BACK. BACK. BACK.
NEEYAAHHA!!!!
CRASH!
OKAY. YEAH, THAT'S GOOD. PERFECT!
HUH?
M-MY HOUSE!? WHAT'S HAPPENED TO MY...EH?

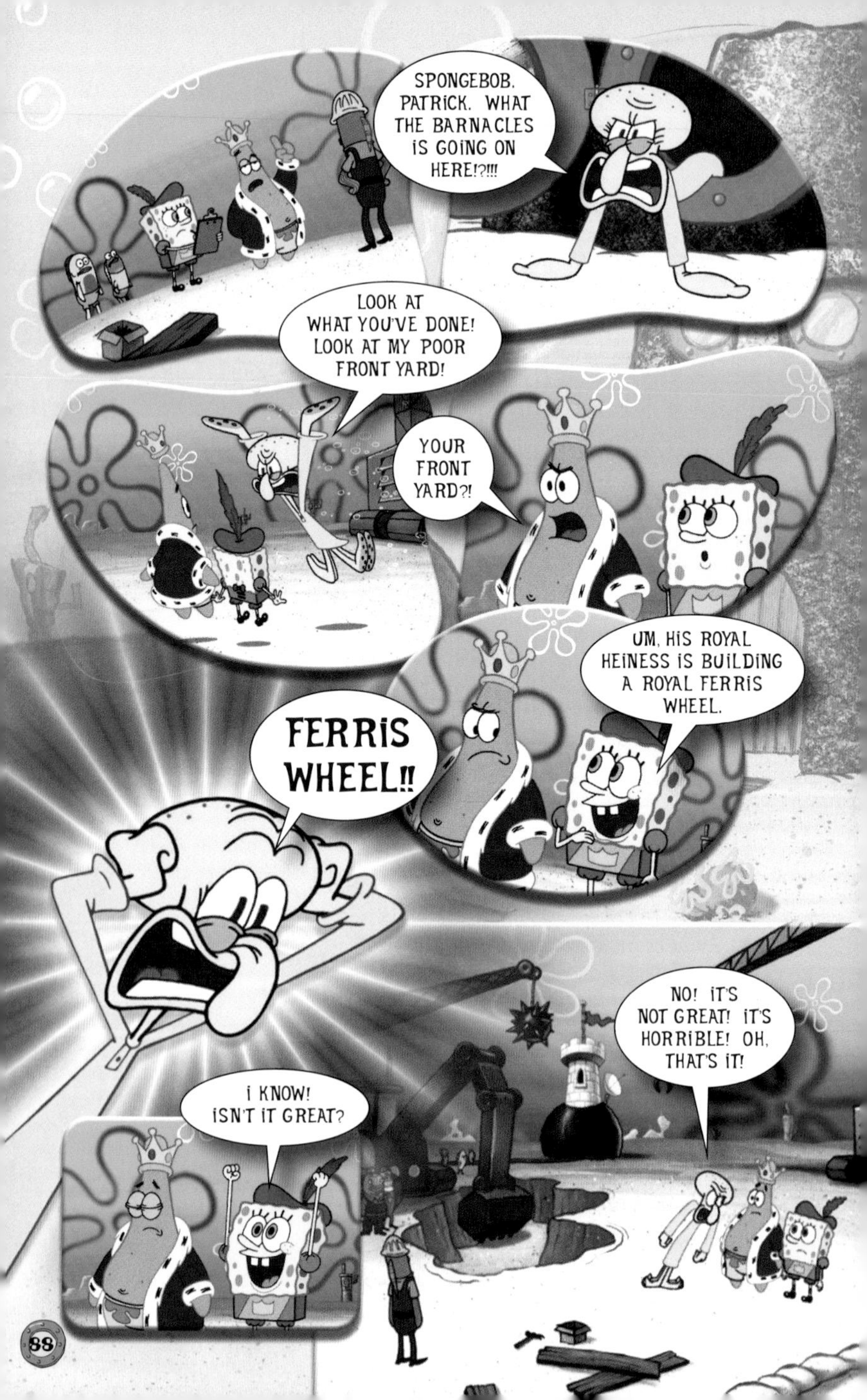
SPONGEBOB. PATRICK. WHAT THE BARNACLES IS GOING ON HERE!?!!!
LOOK AT WHAT YOU'VE DONE! LOOK AT MY POOR FRONT YARD!
YOUR FRONT YARD?!
UM, HIS ROYAL HEINESS IS BUILDING A ROYAL FERRIS WHEEL.
FERRIS WHEEL!!
I KNOW! ISN'T IT GREAT?
NO! IT'S NOT GREAT! IT'S HORRIBLE! OH, THAT'S IT!

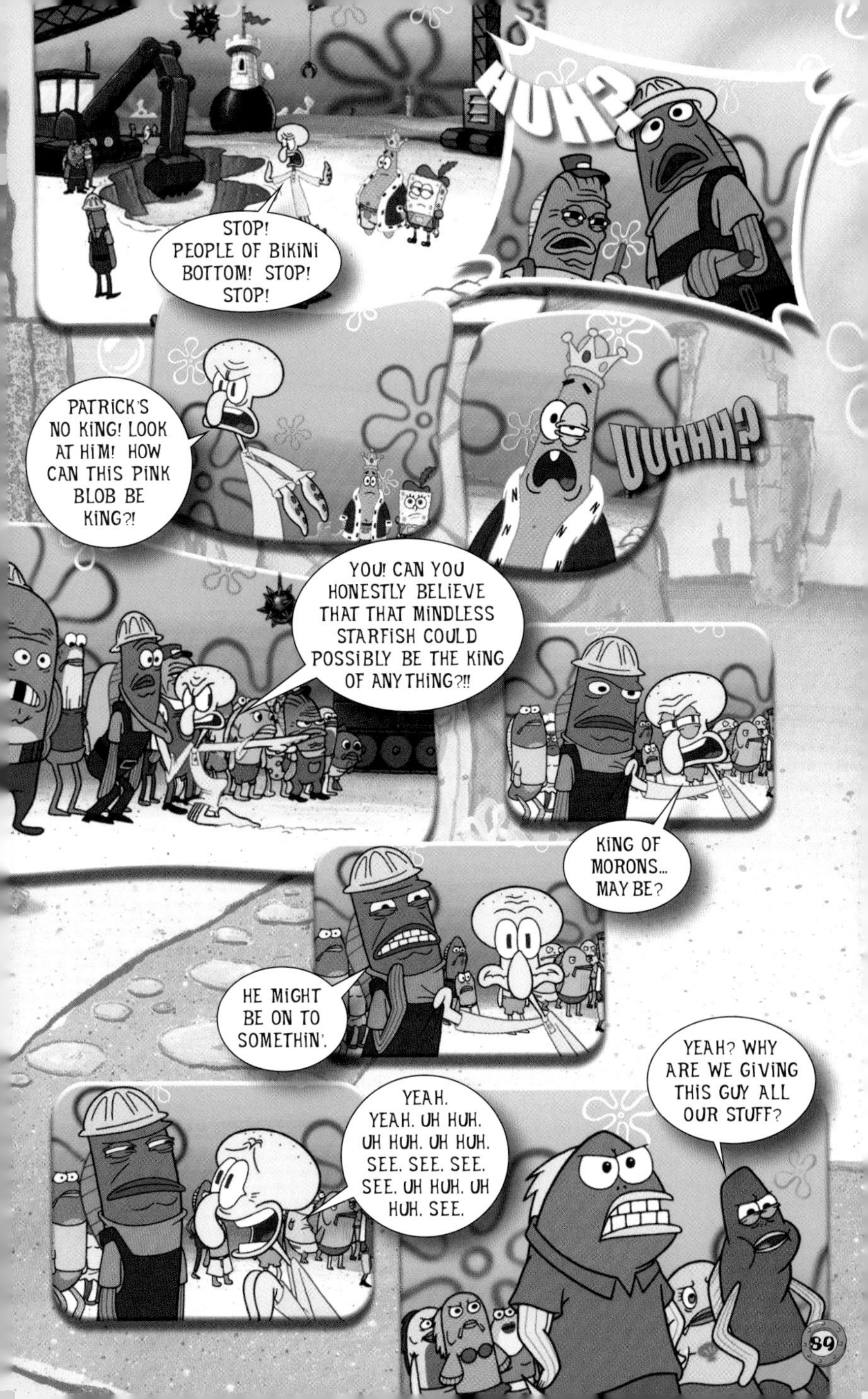
STOP! PEOPLE OF BIKINI BOTTOM! STOP! STOP!
HUH?!
PATRICK'S NO KING! LOOK AT HIM! HOW CAN THIS PINK BLOB BE KING?!
UUHHH?
YOU! CAN YOU HONESTLY BELIEVE THAT THAT MINDLESS STARFISH COULD POSSIBLY BE THE KING OF ANYTHING?!!
KING OF MORONS... MAYBE?
HE MIGHT BE ON TO SOMETHIN'.
YEAH. YEAH. UH HUH. UH HUH. UH HUH. SEE. SEE. SEE. SEE. UH HUH. UH HUH. SEE.
YEAH? WHY ARE WE GIVING THIS GUY ALL OUR STUFF?

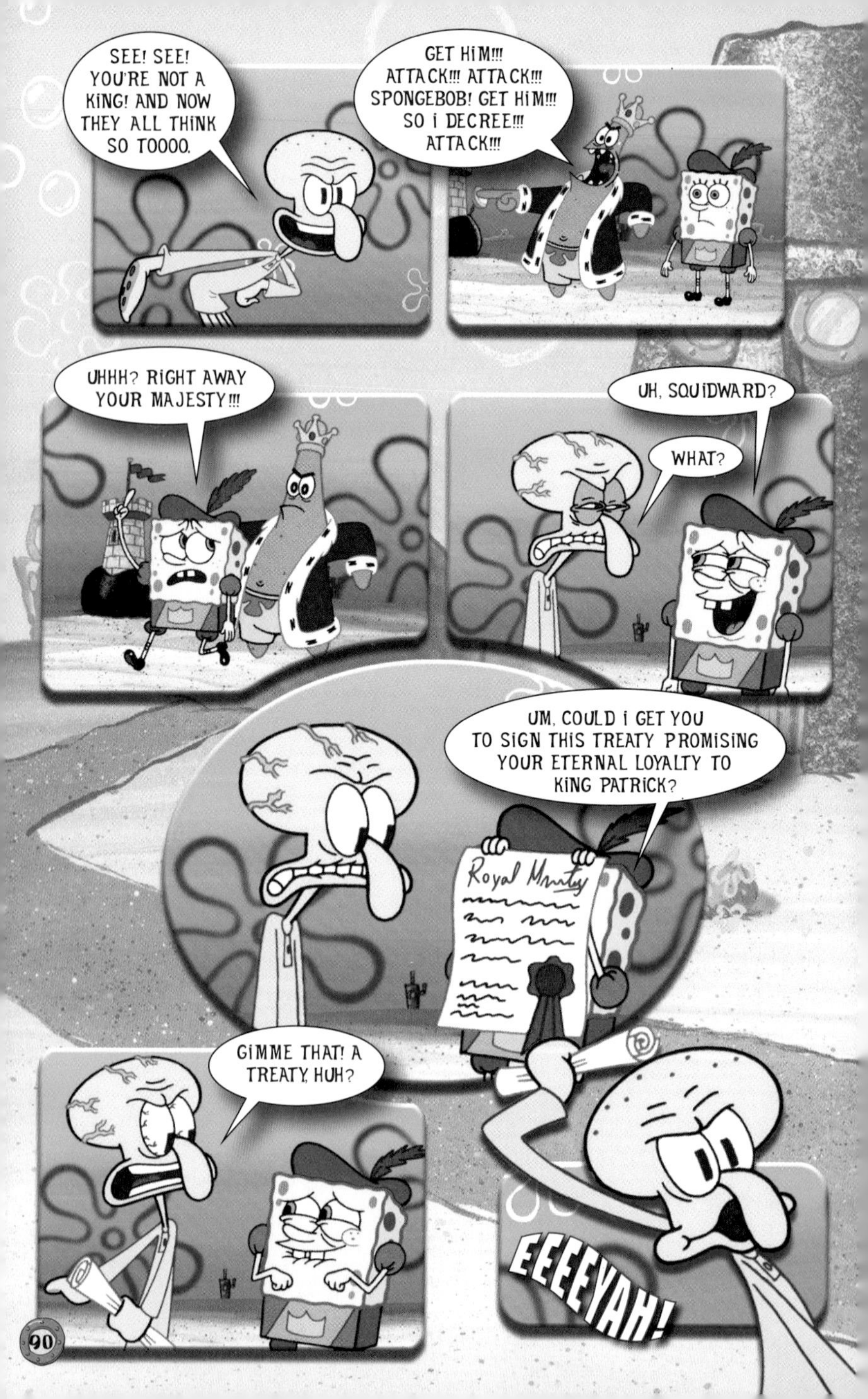

SEE! SEE! YOU'RE NOT A KING! AND NOW THEY ALL THINK SO TOOOO.
GET HIM!!! ATTACK!!! ATTACK!!! SPONGEBOB! GET HIM!!! SO I DECREE!!! ATTACK!!!
UHHH? RIGHT AWAY YOUR MAJESTY!!!
UH, SQUIDWARD?
WHAT?
UM, COULD I GET YOU TO SIGN THIS TREATY PROMISING YOUR ETERNAL LOYALTY TO KING PATRICK?
Royal Mutiny
GIMME THAT! A TREATY, HUH?
EEEEYAH!

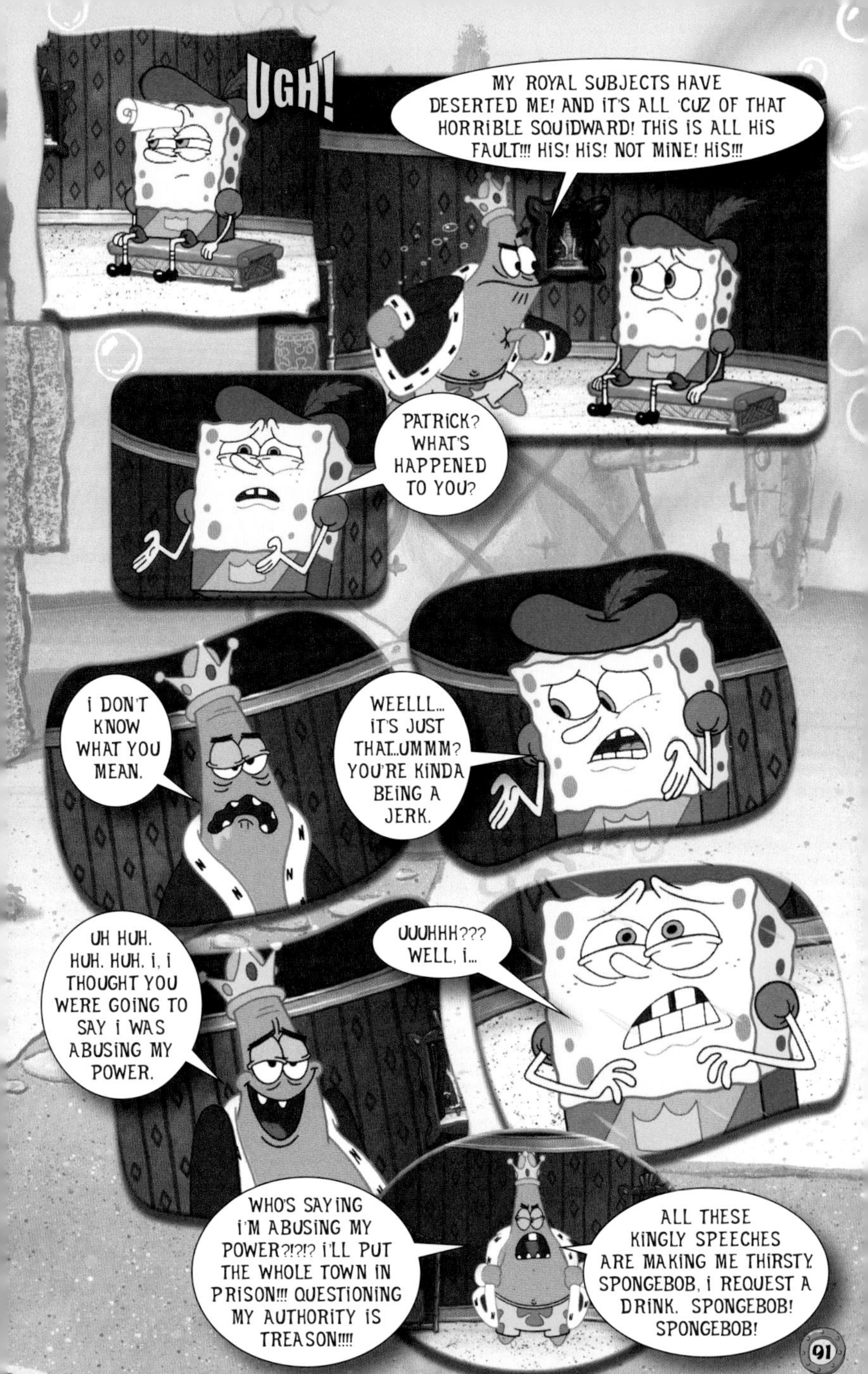
UGH!
MY ROYAL SUBJECTS HAVE DESERTED ME! AND IT'S ALL 'CUZ OF THAT HORRIBLE SQUIDWARD! THIS IS ALL HIS FAULT!!! HIS! HIS! NOT MINE! HIS!!!
PATRICK? WHAT'S HAPPENED TO YOU?
I DON'T KNOW WHAT YOU MEAN.
WEELLL... IT'S JUST THAT...UMMM? YOU'RE KINDA BEING A JERK.
UH HUH. HUH. HUH. I, I THOUGHT YOU WERE GOING TO SAY I WAS ABUSING MY POWER.
UUUHHH??? WELL, I...
WHO'S SAYING I'M ABUSING MY POWER?!?!? I'LL PUT THE WHOLE TOWN IN PRISON!!! QUESTIONING MY AUTHORITY IS TREASON!!!!
ALL THESE KINGLY SPEECHES ARE MAKING ME THIRSTY. SPONGEBOB, I REQUEST A DRINK. SPONGEBOB! SPONGEBOB!

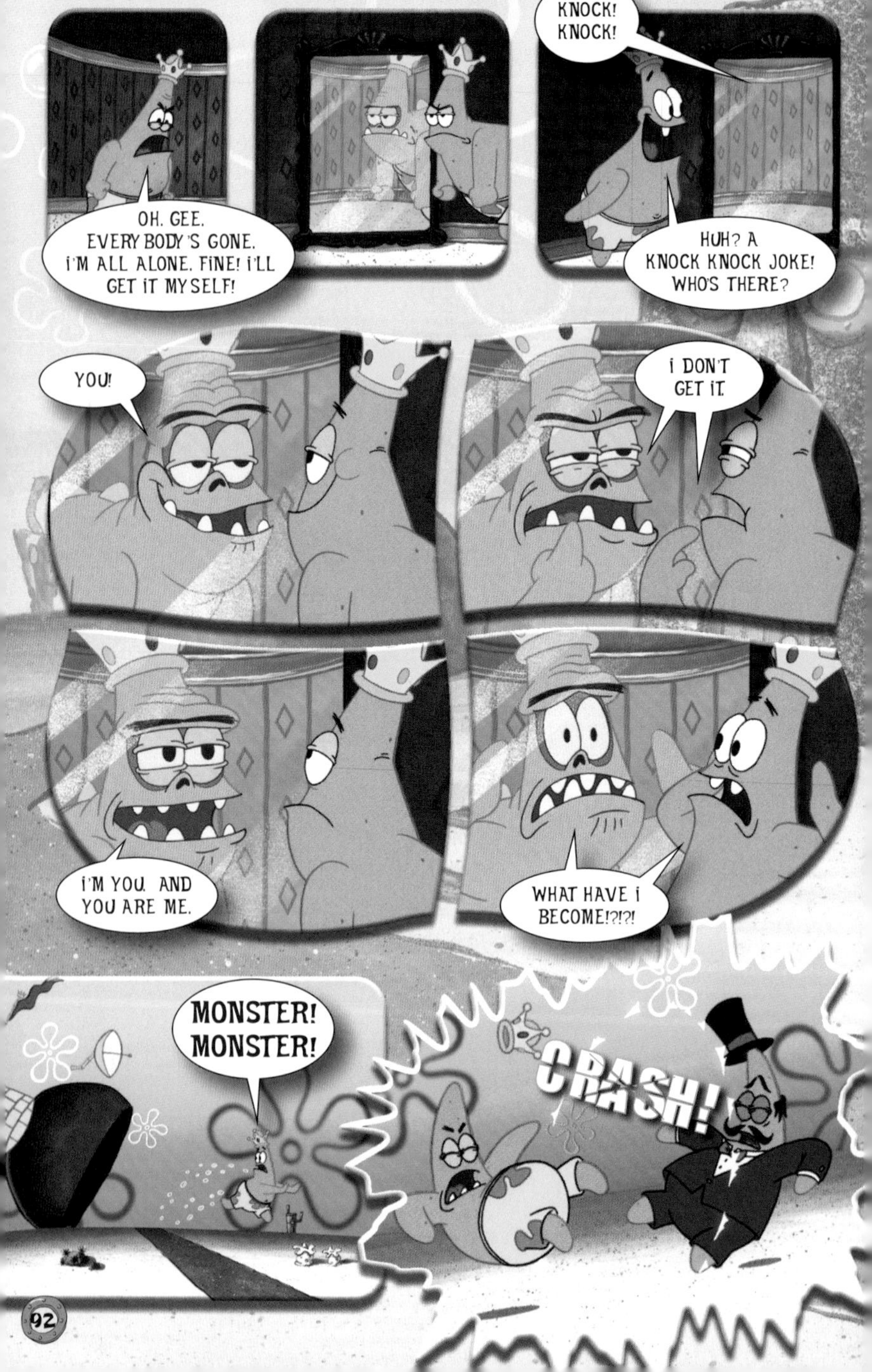
OH. GEE. EVERY BODY'S GONE. I'M ALL ALONE. FINE! I'LL GET IT MYSELF!
KNOCK! KNOCK!
HUH? A KNOCK KNOCK JOKE! WHO'S THERE?
YOU!
I DON'T GET IT.
I'M YOU. AND YOU ARE ME.
WHAT HAVE I BECOME!?!?!
MONSTER! MONSTER!
CRASH!

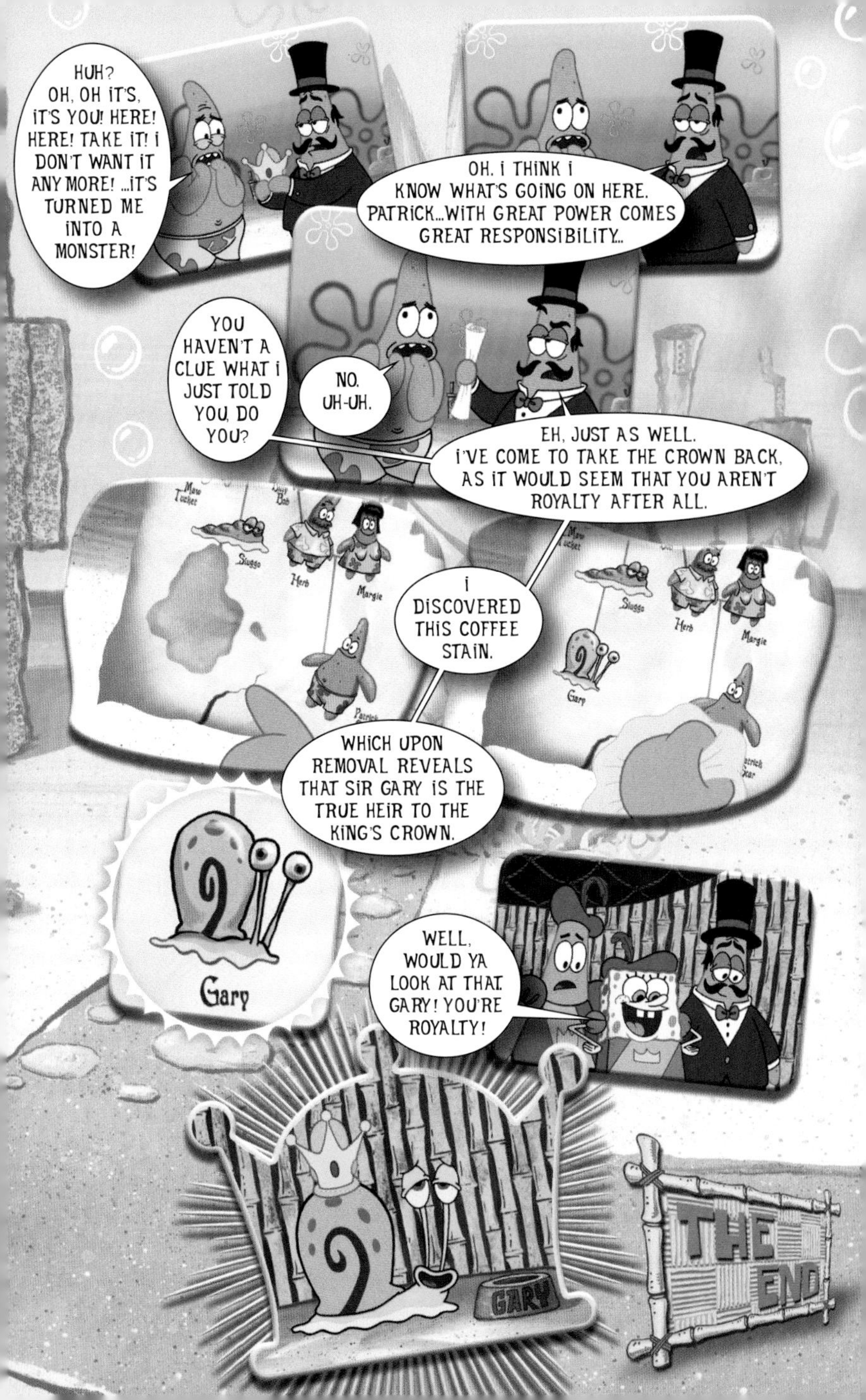
HUH? OH, OH IT'S, IT'S YOU! HERE! HERE! TAKE IT! I DON'T WANT IT ANY MORE! ...IT'S TURNED ME INTO A MONSTER!
OH. I THINK I KNOW WHAT'S GOING ON HERE. PATRICK...WITH GREAT POWER COMES GREAT RESPONSIBILITY...
YOU HAVEN'T A CLUE WHAT I JUST TOLD YOU, DO YOU?
NO. UH-UH.
EH, JUST AS WELL. I'VE COME TO TAKE THE CROWN BACK, AS IT WOULD SEEM THAT YOU AREN'T ROYALTY AFTER ALL.
Sluggo
Herb
Margie
I DISCOVERED THIS COFFEE STAIN.
Sluggo
Herb
Margie
Gary
WHICH UPON REMOVAL REVEALS THAT SIR GARY IS THE TRUE HEIR TO THE KING'S CROWN.
Gary
WELL, WOULD YA LOOK AT THAT. GARY! YOU'RE ROYALTY!
GARY
THE END

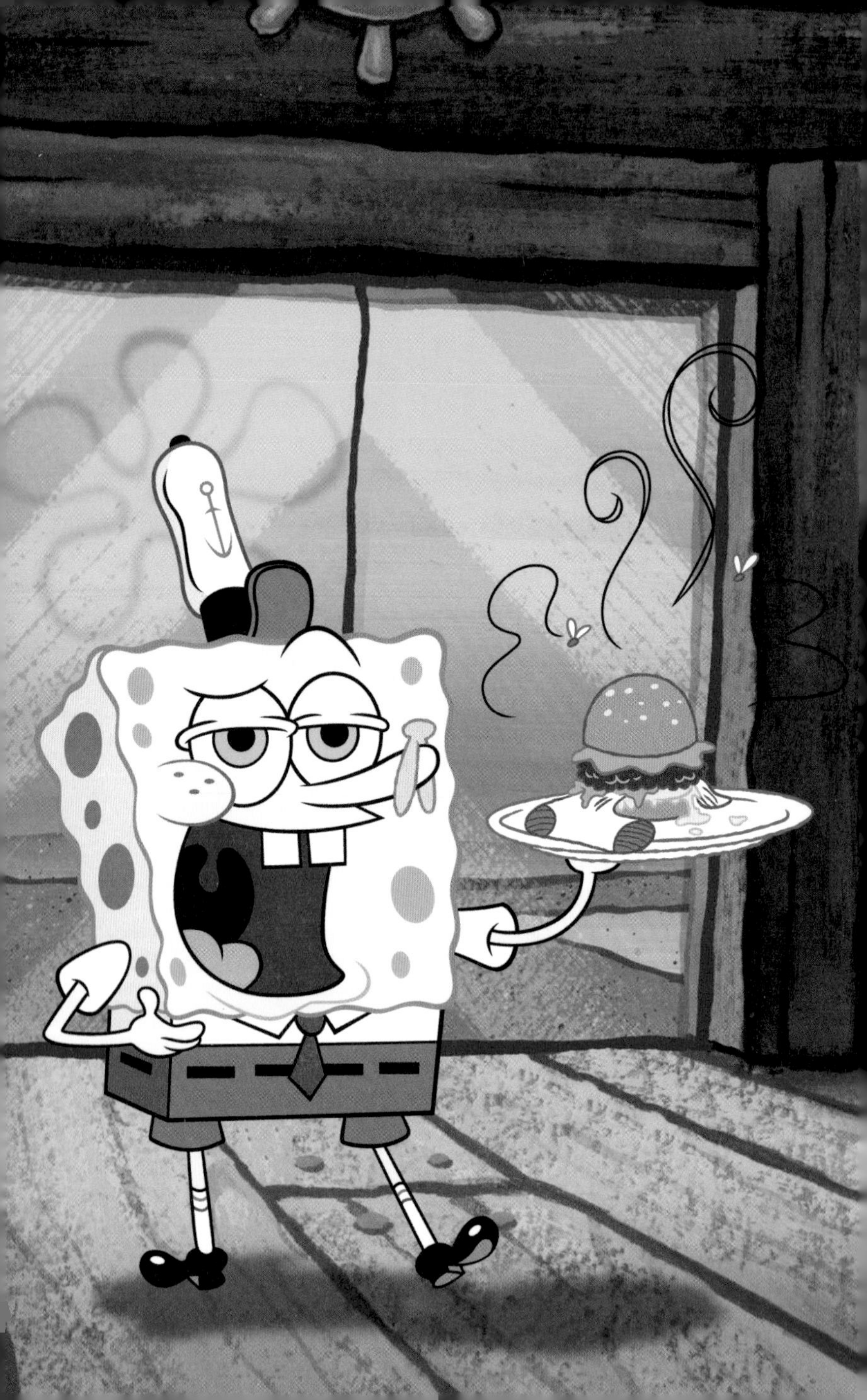

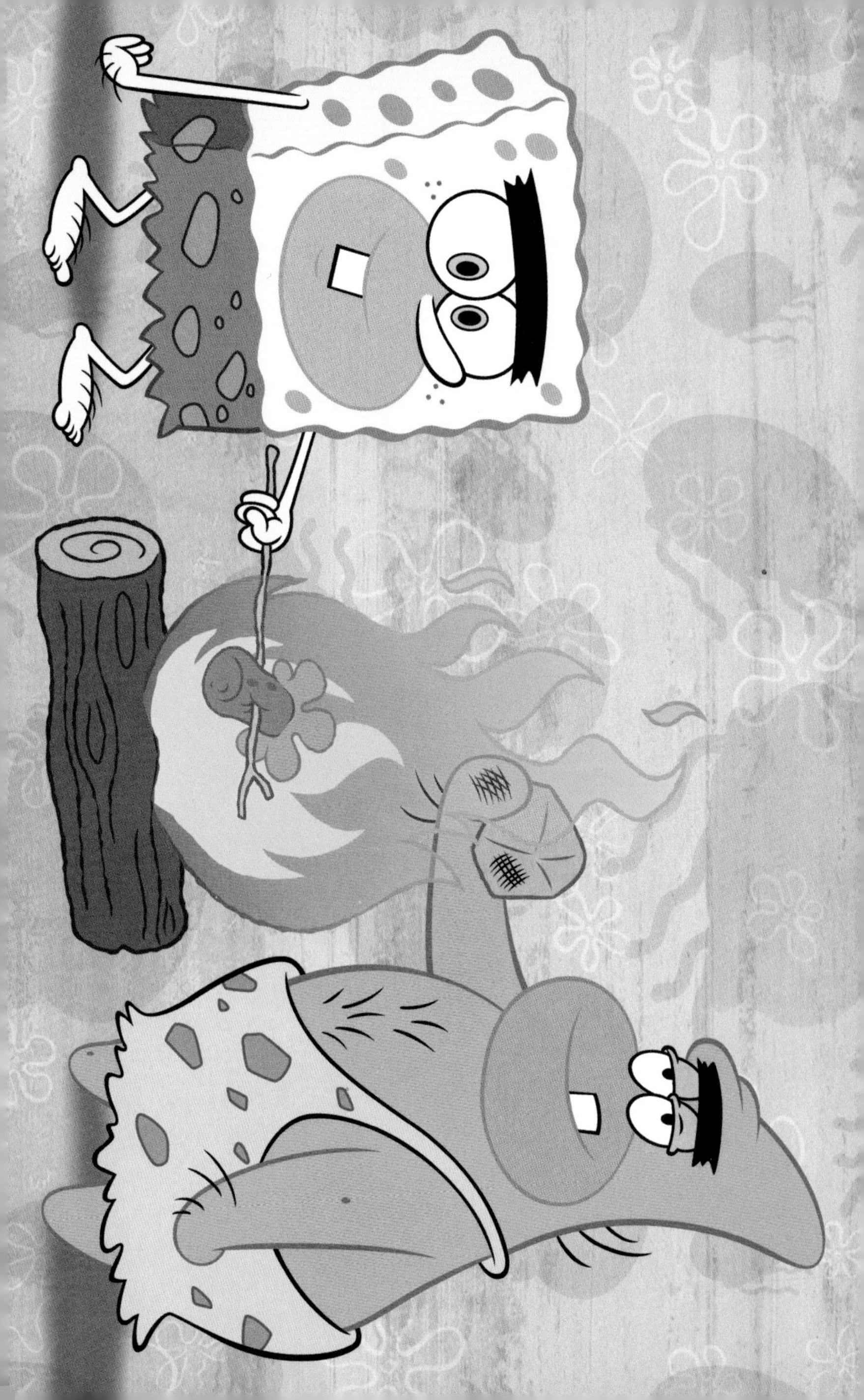

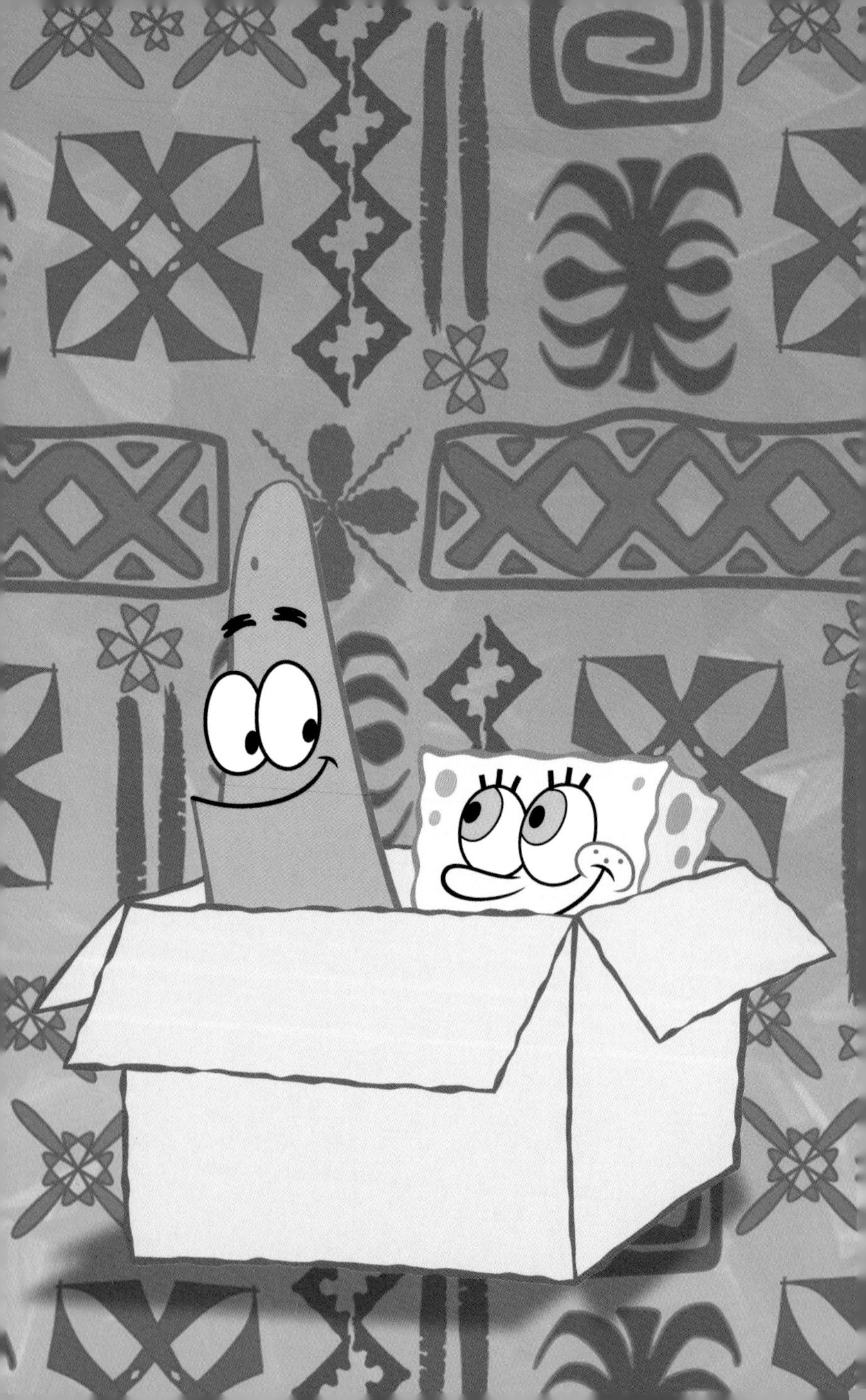